The Complete Guide to Investing in Bonds and Bond Funds:

How To Earn High Rates of Return — Safely

By Martha Maeda

The Complete Guide to Investing in Bonds and Bond Funds: How to Earn High Rates of Return — Safely

Copyright © 2009 by Atlantic Publishing Group, Inc.
1405 SW 6th Ave. • Ocala, Florida 34471 • 800-814-1132 • 352-622-1875–Fax
Web site: www.atlantic-pub.com • E-mail: sales@atlantic-pub.com
SAN Number: 268-1250

General Trademark Disclaimer
All trademarks, trade names, or logos mentioned or used are the property of their respective owners and are used only to directly describe the products being provided. Every effort has been made to properly capitalize, punctuate, identify and attribute trademarks and trade names to their respective owners, including the use of ® and ™ wherever possible and practical. Atlantic Publishing Group, Inc. is not a partner, affiliate, or licensee with the holders of said trademarks.

ISBN-13: 978-1-60138-293-1   ISBN-10: 1-60138-293-6

Library of Congress Cataloging-in-Publication Data

Maeda, Martha, 1953-
  The complete guide to investing in bonds and bond funds : how to earn high rates of return--safely / by Martha Maeda.
     p. cm.
  Includes bibliographical references and index.
  ISBN-13: 978-1-60138-293-1 (alk. paper)
  ISBN-10: 1-60138-293-6 (alk. paper)
  1. Bonds. 2. Bond funds. 3. Investments. I. Title.
  HG4651.M34 2009
  332.63'23--dc22
                             2008052662

Printed in the United States
PROJECT MANAGER: Melissa Peterson • mpeterson@atlantic-pub.com
COVER DESIGN: Jackie Miller • sullmill@charter.net
INTERIOR DESIGN: Shannon Preston

We recently lost our beloved pet "Bear," who was not only our best and dearest friend but also the "Vice President of Sunshine" here at Atlantic Publishing. He did not receive a salary but worked tirelessly 24 hours a day to please his parents. Bear was a rescue dog that turned around and showered myself, my wife Sherri, his grandparents Jean, Bob and Nancy and every person and animal he met (maybe not rabbits) with friendship and love. He made a lot of people smile every day.

We wanted you to know that a portion of the profits of this book will be donated to The Humane Society of the United States. *–Douglas & Sherri Brown*

The human-animal bond is as old as human history. We cherish our animal companions for their unconditional affection and acceptance. We feel a thrill when we glimpse wild creatures in their natural habitat or in our own backyard.

Unfortunately, the human-animal bond has at times been weakened. Humans have exploited some animal species to the point of extinction.

The Humane Society of the United States makes a difference in the lives of animals here at home and worldwide. The HSUS is dedicated to creating a world where our relationship with animals is guided by compassion. We seek a truly humane society in which animals are respected for their intrinsic value, and where the human-animal bond is strong.

Want to help animals? We have plenty of suggestions. Adopt a pet from a local shelter, join The Humane Society and be a part of our work to help companion animals and wildlife. You will be funding our educational, legislative, investigative and outreach projects in the U.S. and across the globe.

Or perhaps you'd like to make a memorial donation in honor of a pet, friend or relative? You can through our Kindred Spirits program. And if you'd like to contribute in a more structured way, our Planned Giving Office has suggestions about estate planning, annuities, and even gifts of stock that avoid capital gains taxes.

Maybe you have land that you would like to preserve as a lasting habitat for wildlife. Our Wildlife Land Trust can help you. Perhaps the land you want to share is a backyard— that's enough. Our Urban Wildlife Sanctuary Program will show you how to create a habitat for your wild neighbors.

So you see, it's easy to help animals. And The HSUS is here to help.

THE HUMANE SOCIETY
OF THE UNITED STATES.

2100 L Street NW • Washington, DC 20037 • 202-452-1100 • www.hsus.org

Dedication

This book is dedicated to Makoto Maeda.

Table of Contents

Foreword   11

Preface   15

Introduction   19

SECTION 1: UNDERSTANDING BONDS   21

The Concept of the Bond....................................23

Chapter 1: The History of
Bonds and Bond Investing   23

United States 24

Civil War...25

Federal Reserve System.....................................26

U.S. Savings Bonds 26

Late Twentieth Century.....................................28

Chapter 2: Why Bonds?   31

Inverse Relationship to the Stock Market..................31

Lower Volatility..32

Steady Source of Income....................................32

Expected Appreciation.......................................33

Preservation of Capital......................................33

Terminology 35

Chapter 3: The Fundamentals of Bond Investing   **35**

Types of Bonds 40

How Are Bonds Issued? 43

Bond Credit Ratings 46

Calculating Yield 49

The Primary Market 61

Chapter 4: The Basics of Buying and Selling Bonds   **61**

The Secondary Market 64

Chapter 5: Corporate Bonds   **67**

How Are Corporate Bonds Secured? 70

Other Types of Corporate Bonds 72

Credit Ratings 77

Corporate Bonds in Your Portfolio 78

Corporate Bonds and Your Taxes 80

Chapter 6: U.S. Treasury Securities, Agency Bonds, and U.S. Savings Bonds   **81**

U.S. Treasury Notes and Bonds 82

U.S. Treasury Bills 84

STRIPS 85

TIPS 87

U.S. Savings Bonds 89

I Bonds 90

Series EE Bonds 92

Series HH/H Bonds 93

U.S. Agency Bonds 95

Supranational and International Government Bonds 99

Chapter 7: Municipal Bonds   101

Tax Advantages 102

Categories of Municipal Bonds 104

Types of Municipal Bonds 106

Who Issues Revenue Bonds? 107

Types of Revenue Bonds 110

Short-Term Notes 123

Pre-Refunded or Escrowed Bonds 125

Call Provisions 125

Sinking Funds 126

Risks Associated with Municipal Bonds 127

Insurance 129

Municipal Bond Credit Ratings 131

Chapter 8: International Bonds   135

Additional Risks Associated with International Bonds ...135

Chapter 9: Mortgage-Backed Bonds   139

How Mortgage-Backed Bonds Work 140

Fannie Mae, Freddie Mac, and Ginnie Mae 142

How Mortgage-Backed Bonds Differ from Other Bonds .144

Prepayment and Average Life 145

Advantages of Mortgage-Backed Bonds 147

Disadvantages of Mortgage-Backed Bonds 148

Mortgage Bonds and Taxes..150

Mortgage-backed Bonds in Your Portfolio.........................151

Chapter 10: Bond Mutual Funds   153

How Are Bond Mutual FundsDifferent from Bonds? 154

Benefits of Bond Mutual Funds 154

Disadvantages of Bond Mutual Funds 156

Unit Investment Trusts...159

Closed-End Bond Funds 160

Open-end Bond Mutual Funds..164

Understanding Bond Mutual Fund Expenses 168

Share Classes..170

Net Asset Value (NAV)..173

Yield and Total Return..174

Actively and Passively Managed Bond Funds....................176

Bond Indexes 179

Bond Mutual Funds 180

Chapter 11: Exchange Traded Bond Funds   195

What is an Exchange Traded Fund?....................................195

Advantages of Bond ETFs...196

Bond ETFs 202

SECTION 2: CREATING YOUR BOND INVESTMENT STRATEGY   209

Define Your Financial Goals and Requirements.................211

Chapter 12: Choosing a Strategy   211

Chapter 13: Understanding
the Risks of Bond Investing   219

Predicting the Future 227

Chapter 14: Evaluating a Bond Investment   227

Your Taxes 231

Chapter 15: Doing the Research   241

Where to Find Information 242

Government Agencies 242

Professional Associations...244

Brokerage and Financial Sites 246

Prospectuses and Sales Literature 248

Planning Your Strategy...251

Chapter 16: Building Your Bond Portfolio   251

Rebalance Your Portfolio Regularly 256

Protecting Yourself from Risk.....................................257

Bond Strategies...259

Retirement..263

Chapter 17: Bonds as a
Source of Steady Income   263

Building a Fixed-Income Portfolio 264

Chapter 18: Bonds as Savings   269

Saving for Education 270

Education Savings Bond Program...............................277

Tax-Free and Tax-Deferred
Retirement Savings Accounts......................................279

401(k)s, Solo 401(k)s, and Roth 401(k)s.............................280

IRAs and Roth IRAs...281

Taxable and Tax-advantaged Accounts 283

Bonds and Estate Planning..284

Choosing a Brokerage..287

Chapter 19: Buying and Selling Bonds   287
Buying Bonds...290

Making the Most of Your Bond Portfolio 291

When to Sell Your Bonds..293

Active Trading with Bond Funds and Bond ETFs.............295

Chapter 20: What Is on the Horizon   297
New Investment Offerings 298

Globalization 298

Increased Transparency and Regulation.........................299

More Participation by Individual Investors......................301

New Methods of Bond Trading.....................................302

Demographic Changes..303

New Technologies...305

Passage of Time 306

Keeping Informed 307

Appendix A: Glossary   309
Web sites...329

Bibliography   329
Biography   333
Index   335

Foreword

Martha Maeda, in *The Complete Guide to Investing in Bonds and Bond Funds: How to Earn High Rates of Return – Safely*, provides a modern perspective on the fixed-income markets. Novice, as well as sophisticated, investors will find the information provided in this book helpful and informative. With the baby boomers being the largest segment of our population, many of them will transition from equity to fixed-income investments during their retirement years. This book is an excellent primer on the definitions, benefits, and potential dangers inherent in various fixed-income instruments. From the historical beginnings of the market to the most recent scandals involving the fixed-income rating agencies, it is an excellent read. I especially appreciate the highlighted tips and case study portions of the book, which reinforced excellent information on individual instruments and markets.

The vocabulary of the bond market can seem Greek to an investor who is more familiar with price earnings ratios than yield to maturity. This book has an emphasis on a practical and pragmatic approach to investing in the bond market. The sections on understanding the risks of bond investing and evaluating a bond investment give you the tools you need to make the right investment decision when weighing many variables in your portfolio. Important information on bond funds and exchange traded funds is timely in an environment where owning individual bonds can be more risky than usual. This risk is due to the exodus from the market by large players, like Lehman Brothers®, creating less liquidity in the marketplace.

This introductory perspective to the budding bond market is invaluable and creates opportunities for above-average rates of return. The text flows smoothly from one topic to the next, which is helpful in this often misunderstood nomenclature. As a veteran of the bond market for over 35 years, I also gleaned new information due to the modern approach and timeliness of this book. The first half of the book is devoted to the history of the bond market with definitions and explanations of the various terms and elements of the market. A more knowledgeable investor can skip to the second half of the book which concentrates on strategies for your portfolio and the various elements of return. Tax information relative to the various types of bond funds is helpful for understanding how your individual portfolio will impact your tax situation. There are many reasons for owning a bond portfolio, and author Martha Maeda covers each one in depth. Whether you are saving for your child's college education, buying a house, or looking for steady income, the various strategies employed by this book will be helpful to you.

Perhaps one of the most important chapters is the chapter titled "Doing the Research." In this chapter, the author gives you the tools you need to be more fully informed about your investment choices in today's world of information overload. This is not only a book for the buy-and-hold investor. To the reader's advantage, active bond market trading strategies are discussed as well. These are tools you truly need in today's marketplace.

In the bond market, you are dealing with a tremendous number of complicated variables. Author Martha Maeda simplifies the process and explains these terms in a concise and understandable way, which can lead to successful investing. As you travel from investing in the stock market to investing in the bond market, I think you will find it to be an exciting ride. As Maeda indicates, the bond market is much larger than the stock market and statistics prove that the market will grow even larger as our population ages, needs more income, and requires a safe return on limited assets. The bond portion of your portfolio will transcend to the largest portion as you age and that is why a book like this is so important.

Meri Anne Beck-Woods

Cofounder of Odyssey Advisors LLC

Chairman of the Board and Chief Operating Officer

Odyssey Advisors LLC

6033 West Century Blvd. Suite 1110

Los Angeles, CA 90045

310-568-4700

www.odysseyadvisors.com

Mabwoods@odysseyadvisors.com

Meri Anne Beck-Woods is Odyssey's chairman and chief operating officer. She is responsible for managing the fixed- income portion of Odyssey's balanced portfolios as well as the individual fixed-income portfolios. These portfolios include both taxable and tax-exempt bonds. She has over 35 years of experience in the investment industry, including balanced and fixed-income portfolio management.

Prior to cofounding Odyssey Advisors, Beck-Woods spent 14 years with Loomis Sayles & Co., L.P. as a senior partner and senior portfolio manager. While there, she managed $2 billion in fixed-income portfolios and balanced mutual funds. Prior to that, she managed $1 billion in fixed income and fixed income mutual funds as a senior portfolio manager and fixed income strategist for TSA Capital Management. Following college, Beck-Woods was a portfolio manager and research analyst for Norton Simon's $500 million in fixed-income and equity assets.

Preface

G iven the recent volatility in the financial markets, there could not be a better time to read this book. Many individual investors are rethinking their expectations on what they can earn on their investments. Gone are the days where cheap funding was available to invest in real estate, which partly fueled the housing boom. The credit crunch and the current economic dislocation will make it difficult for companies to grow their earnings and improve their stock prices in the near term.

This is the time to consider investing in bonds, or what experienced investors call fixed -income securities. The term fixed income, as it implies, means a locked-in flow of income. This income is derived from the interest payments on the bonds, which, unlike equity dividends, are contractual obligations that are payable as long as the bond issuer remains solvent.

At first sight, bonds seem much more complicated and harder to source than stocks. With the information in *The Complete Guide to Investing in Bonds and Bond Funds,* you will become familiar with the various types of bonds and how to add them to your portfolio. Author Martha Maeda focuses the book on helping the novice investor understand the different types of bonds and their pitfalls. Later on in the book, Maeda explains how the reader can determine what his or her appropriate investment objective should be and what types of fixed-income investments fit those objectives.

To maximize the information in this book, the reader should try to establish a list of characteristics about his or herself; 1) are you a buy-and-hold to maturity investor or an active trader; 2) what is your risk tolerance; 3) what are your return objectives; 4) What is your investment horizon and liquidity requirements; and finally, 5) how much available time can you devote to analyzing your investments and what resources are at your disposal.

As an individual investor in bonds, you may not be able to be an active trader, given that, unless you trade in large blocks (sometimes $1 million or more), the cost of transactions will be high. On the other hand, you may be looking at a bond as a vehicle for earning the coupon and getting your principal at maturity. The later type of bondholder is called a buy-and-hold investor.

From a risk perspective, there is a full spectrum from the "risk free" return of U.S. Treasuries to the high risk of below investment grade or "junk bonds," which require a significant amount of analysis. The reader needs to be aware of their return objectives and make sure they are consistent with their risk tolerance. As the famous Nobel Price winning economist Milton Friedman once said, "There is no free lunch." This is true for bond investing as well. If you reach for yields that resemble equity returns, then you are probably taking significant default or nonpayment risk. Remember, you are buying bonds to reduce your volatility, and in return for that, you are receiving a lower yield. The question you need to ask yourself is how much risk am I comfortable with.

Time frame may be one of the easier criteria to analyze. If you know that you will not need the specific pool of money for a 10-year period, then you can buy bonds with a 10-year maturity and receive the coupon payments and have a predictable return on your investment. However, if there is the potential need to call on those funds at anytime, you may need to buy liquid, short duration instruments like U.S. Treasury Bills. This book describes the levels of liquidity of all the various types of bonds.

Finally, you must ask yourself how much time can you devote to your research. If you are planning on investing in high-yield corporate bonds you will need to have a detailed understanding of the companies you are investing in. If you have a portfolio of equities as well, the time you spend on your high-yield bond research, will be time taken away from your equity research. You need to consider if this is a good trade-off. You will need to consider where you will get the greatest return on your effort, junk bonds or equities.

There is much to learn about investing in bonds. *The Complete Guide to Investing in Bonds and Bond Funds* is an excellent starting point. You will learn the terminology, risks, and considerations in investing in this important asset class.

James Lyman

Jim has been a fixed-income professional for 20 years having worked in a number of different areas of the market. He began his analytical career at Moody's Investors Service, a leading rating agency. While at Moody's, Jim analyzed, structured, and rated almost all types of municipal bonds from the basic general obligation credits to complex municipal bond derivatives. He then moved to Financial Guarantee Insurance Company (FGIC) where he was an assistant vice president of public finance underwriting.

In 1995, Jim segued to the institutional investment side of business when he joined Weiss, Peck & Greer Investments, LLC. (WPG) as director of municipal bond research. In this role, Jim was responsible for analyzing risk and making buy-and-sell recommendations on municipal bonds for client portfolios. In 2000, Jim moved over to the taxable fixed-income unit of WPG to run corporate bond research. More recently, Jim has been employed at Fischer Francis Trees and Watts as a portfolio manager trader running the U.S. dollar corporate component of the firm's client portfolios.

Introduction

Dependable, safe, reliable, predictable, steady — these are attractive words when you are looking for a way to invest hard-earned money. Bonds have a long-standing reputation for being stable and a predictable source of steady income, even in times when the economy is uncertain. Despite their unexciting public image, some bonds markets today are among the most vigorous speculative markets in the world.

Buying a bond essentially involves loaning your money to a government entity or a corporation for a specified time, and then receiving interest and the return of your principal when the bond matures. Though the bond market does not experience the volatility and related growth potential of the stock market, the average private investor invests approximately 50 percent of long-term savings in fixed-income assets. The public U.S. fixed-income market (nearly $30 trillion in 2007) is much larger than the public U.S. equity market.

The Complete Guide to Investing in Bonds and Bond Funds: How to Earn High Rates of Return Safely will help you to understand the many types of fixed-income assets, including Treasury notes, government agency issues, mortgages, corporate bonds, municipal bonds, asset-backed securities, and inflation-protected securities. You will learn how bonds are bought and sold, and how you can become involved in the bond market. You will find guidance on how to construct a portfolio and select bonds that will help you meet your financial goals.

The book is divided into two sections. If you are already familiar with bonds, you may want to use the first section on bond basics only for reference, and go directly into the investment strategies in the second section. The "TIP" sections point out important issues for your consideration. Definitions for terms in bold type can be found in the glossary at the end of the book.

No one is responsible for your money but yourself. There is no reason why, armed with a clear understanding of the risks and rewards of investing in bonds, you cannot achieve your goals and look forward to a successful and secure financial future.

SECTION 1: UNDERSTANDING BONDS

CHAPTER 1

The History of Bonds and Bond Investing

The Concept of the Bond

Early legal codes frowned on loaning money for interest; the Israelites prohibited usury. Credit was necessary, however, for merchant trade, and bills of credit allowed merchants to borrow money to buy goods and repay it after the goods were transported and sold. After Charlemagne (747 - 814) prohibited usury in Western and Central Europe, the Catholic Church developed a monopoly on lending, allowing nobles to borrow money and secure the debt with their lands. During the fifteenth century, European monarchs who needed to borrow money to finance their wars and political ambitions established merchant banks which rewarded lenders with special trade concessions or the privilege of participating in royal business monopolies. After the Protestant Reformation in 1517, the payment of interest became acceptable compensation for the risks involved in loaning money. The Roman Catholic Church did not formally endorse the payment of interest until the early nineteenth century.

Today's bond markets reflect a pattern established in Venice and other Italian towns and later in the Netherlands in Antwerp and Amsterdam. The modern concept of a bond was developed during the early 1800s, when England passed a new law allowing loans to become a negotiable instrument and establishing formal bond issues that stated how much was being borrowed, when the bonds would come due, and the terms under which the money was being borrowed. Subsequent issues of the same bond followed the same terms, and bonds were issued in large amounts to satisfy the needs of large-scale investors.

United States

European settlers brought their concepts of lending, interest, and raising capital to the United States. In 1690, Massachusetts became the first colony to issue debt notes to pay for its share of costs incurred by the Anglo-French War. The debt was successfully repaid from its tax revenues.

In 1776, private citizens purchased more than $27 million in government bonds to help finance the American Revolution, with no assurance that their money would be returned to them. After the war, the new government of the United States of America set a precedent by paying off its financial obligations, in full and on time, despite some opposition in Congress. American investors subsequently funded a number of projects, including the Louisiana Purchase, the acquisition of Alaska, the building of the transcontinental railway, the digging of the Panama Canal, and several wars.

State governments soon began issuing debt to finance the building of roads and public works. It was common for banks to assist in the formation of bond debts to finance development and expansion projects.

Civil War

During the Civil War, when the Confederate government found its tax revenues inadequate, it issued war bonds. Patriotic southerners quickly bought up the first bond issue of $15 million, but sales of the second issue of $100 million, in 8-percent-yield bonds, were dampened by a 12 percent rate of inflation and a shortage of cash. The Union government raised over 65 percent of its war revenue through bonds, enlisting Philadelphia banker Jay Cooke to administer the sale of war bonds. Cooke expected banks and wealthy citizens to purchase most of the bonds, but he launched a campaign of patriotic newspaper advertisements to market the bonds to the middle classes as well. An army of 2,500 agents persuaded almost one million northerners to invest in the war effort; bond sales topped $3 billion.

The Legal Tender Act of 1862, authorizing the issue of $150 million in Treasury notes, known as greenbacks, ensured an unrestricted supply of currency with which to purchase bonds. The law required citizens, banks, and governments to accept greenbacks as legal tender for public and private debts, except for interest on federal bonds and customs duties. Buyers of bonds were able to profit at the expense of taxpayers by purchasing them with depreciated greenbacks and receiving the interest accrued to them in gold valued at the prewar level.

Following the Civil War, the states that had issued bonds to pay for war expenses found themselves unable to repay their debts and turned to the federal government for help. Their requests were denied, triggering a widespread financial crisis. As a result, the federal government, though still encouraging states to raise capital for their own development, placed restrictions on the amount of debt that each state can incur at any given time, and established that it would not continue to bail out states that mismanaged bond issuances.

Federal Reserve System

In 1913, the Federal Reserve Act established the Federal Reserve System to act as a central bank, monitor inflation, manage interest rates, and oversee the overall health of the country's economy. At the outbreak of World War I, the Federal Reserve became the primary retailer of war bonds under the direction of the U.S. Treasury. After World War I, the Federal Reserve began to oversee the issuance of Treasury bonds.

Corporate bonds, which made their appearance during the early 1900s, offered significantly higher interest rates than Treasury bonds, and created stiff competition for the U.S. government. To raise money for the war, the U.S. government- issued Liberty Bonds and began an aggressive appeal to patriotic Americans. Posters were commissioned from well-known artists, and celebrities such as Al Jolson, Elsie Janis, Mary Pickford, Douglas Fairbanks, and Charlie Chaplin appeared at public rallies to promote the sale of Liberty Bonds. Even Boy Scouts and Girl Scouts sold them, under the slogan, "Every Scout to Save a Soldier." The sale of Liberty Bonds raised approximately $17 billion for the war effort.

U.S. Savings Bonds

During the Civil War and the Spanish-American War, the U.S. Treasury had discovered that person-to-person sales were an effective way of selling bonds and also that bonds in small denominations were attractive to investors. Early in 1935, the U.S. government was about to undertake public works programs to create jobs after the Great Depression and needed almost $5 billion in financing. The U.S. Treasury introduced legislation to allow the issuance of a new type of security, the U.S. savings bond.

The first U.S. savings bond, "Series A," was released on March 1, 1935. Unlike marketable securities such as Liberty Bonds, which could fluctuate in value, the savings bond was non-negotiable, could be replaced in case of loss, and was registered to the owner at purchase. The savings bonds sold at a discount to their face value and came with a fixed schedule of redemption values; after a brief holding period, they could be redeemed at any time prior to maturity for the full purchase price, plus accumulated interest. They were available in denominations from $25 (purchase price $18.75) to $1,000. The small denominations and the bonds' simplicity soon earned them the nickname "baby bonds."

U.S. savings bonds were sold only through the Office of the U.S. Treasury, and branches of the U.S. Post Office. The advertising budget was small, and the bonds were publicized mainly through direct mail to carefully selected lists of addresses. This method of selective advertising resulted in the sale of mostly larger denominations of $100, $500, and $1,000, rather than the use of bonds by "small savers."

In 1940, as World War II threatened, American factories began to employ large numbers of workers for military production, while at the same time, the war effort was diverting consumer goods from the market. To control price inflation, the U.S.

government saw a need to pull excess cash out of the economy and store it for future use. A decision was made to expand the U.S. Treasury's "small savers" initiative.

On the evening of April 30, 1941, President Franklin D. Roosevelt went on the radio to announce the issue of a new "Defense savings bond," the "Series E," and invited all Americans to join him in "one great partnership" to help finance the national defense effort. The next morning, he became the first to buy a "Series E" bond. A massive marketing campaign brought astonishing results. Over 85 million of the 130 million people in the United States bought war bonds, raising a total of $185.7 billion dollars during the time that they were offered for sale.

Late Twentieth Century

During the second half of the twentieth century, bonds, which had been the provenance of institutional investors such as insurance companies, banks and pension funds, became increasingly popular with individual investors.

In the 1980s, the term "junk bond" was applied to high-yield bonds issued by corporations with low credit ratings who needed immediate access to capital. The 1980s was characterized by corporate raids and hostile takeovers, funded with bond issues, and by rapidly increasing inflation that, by the end of the decade, brought in double-digit returns in the bond markets.

During the 1980s, new technology made bond information more easily accessible, and bonds easier to track. In 1983, legislation was passed requiring bonds to be registered prior to their issuance. As the bond market continued to expand, new forms of bonds were released, such as zero coupon and convertible bonds, and state and local governments increasingly turned to bonds to fund public works projects and budget shortfalls with future tax revenues as collateral.

During this time, bonds were issued on paper certificates, called "bearer bonds," each containing all of the relevant information for the investor's records. Today, bonds are traded electronically, offered in several formats, and a staple in any investor's portfolio. The expansion of the Internet has made bond information readily available, and bond trading can be done with the click of a mouse from the comfort of an investor's home.

CHAPTER 2

Why Bonds?

Inverse Relationship to the Stock Market

Bonds have historically exhibited an inverse relationship to the stock market; when the prices of stocks are falling, the prices of bonds are normally rising. The average private investor invests between 40 and 60 percent of his or her long-term savings in fixed-income assets to increase stability, provide diversification, and act as a buffer against adverse conditions in the stock market. Most bonds exhibit a slight negative correlation to the performance of stocks.

There is no guarantee that historical trends will always repeat themselves, but two factors affect the performance of bonds during periods of economic difficulty. Demand for bonds increases because they are considered a safer investment than stocks. Investors begin to divest themselves of their poorly performing stocks and re-invest their capital in bonds. The increasing demand for bonds raises their prices on the secondary market, allowing owners of bonds to sell them at a premium and realize a profit. During periods of economic decline, the interest rate is often lowered, increasing the value of older bonds that are locked into higher interest cash flow because of the higher coupon and causing the prices of these older bonds to escalate.

Lower Volatility

Bonds provide a safety net during difficult economic times because of their lower volatility. Volatility is an indicator of the possibility that, at the particular moment when you decide to sell your investments, you will realize a reasonable return on the sale.

Historically, investments in stocks have brought in higher returns than investments in bonds; over the past 80 years, the average annualized return of the S&P 500 Index® has been about 10 percent, while the average annualized return of long-term U.S. government bonds has been approximately 5.5 percent. Adjusted for inflation, the real return on stocks has averaged 7 percent, while the real return on government bonds has averaged 2.4 percent. Yet, during their worst year, in 1967, volatile U.S. government bonds returned -9.2 percent. In contrast, during its worst year, 1931, the stock market had a negative return of 43 percent. Someone who relies on investments for a steady income or who has to pull out of the financial markets at a particular date because of retirement or another life event can be confident that even during a time of economic crisis, a substantial portion of his or her capital will still be available.

Steady Source of Income

One of the most attractive features of a bond is its ability to produce a current stream of income for an investor. Although bonds are appropriate for most investors, individuals seeking income for retirement often select bonds for a significant portion of their portfolio. Bonds pay a fixed rate of interest at regular intervals, allowing the investor to predict his or her annual income with accuracy.

Though many stocks pay dividends and preferred stocks promise regular dividend payments, these may be eliminated or reduced if a company's board of directors finds it necessary. Dividend payments from stocks are taxable income, while interest from some types of bonds (municipal, agency, and Treasury) is exempt from federal or local taxes.

Expected Appreciation

Investors who expect overall interest rates to decline will look to purchase bonds in anticipation of this, and profit from selling the bonds at a premium once rates decline and bond prices go up. Additionally, the investor benefits from the annual interest payments. When the stock market is in a slump, as it was in the second half of 2008, active investors began to divert their capital into the bond market, increasing demand and raising bond prices. In times of economic crisis, there is a good possibility that interest rates will be lowered, raising bond prices.

Preservation of Capital

Bonds are issued with a promise to return the investor's original capital investment at maturity. Even if the holder of a bond does not realize a profit by selling it at a premium, he or she will have received regular interest payments over the life of the bond and will be able to redeem it at face value when it matures. If the issuer of a bond calls it in before it reaches maturity and returns the original capital, the investor will have profited from interest payments in the interim. Many bonds that are callable require the issuer to pay a slight "call premium" above the face value as a penalty for redeeming the bonds early.

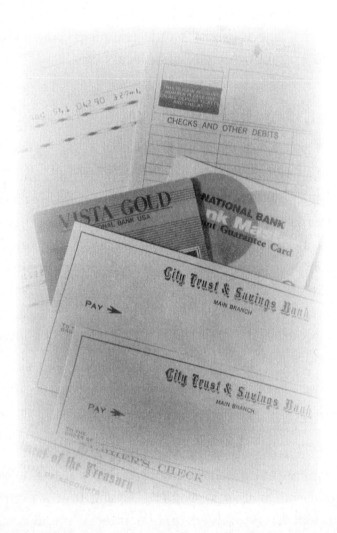

CHAPTER 3

The Fundamentals of Bond Investing

Terminology

Principal or Face Value

The principal, or face value, of a bond refers to the amount that an investor will receive at the bond's maturity. It is common for the principal to equal the original price of the bond, but there are exceptions, such as U.S. savings bonds that sell for 75 percent of face value, or new issues sold at a discount.

Issuer

The bond issuer is the organization, government entity, or corporation issuing the bonds to raise capital. The credit rating of the issuer affects the interest rate of the bond; an issuer with a high credit rating will pay a lower interest rate, while an issuer with a low credit rating must pay higher interest rates to compensate for the increased risk that it might default on the principal.

Coupon Rate

The coupon rate is the interest rate applied to the principal to calculate the annual interest payment for a bond. Most coupon rates remain the same over the life of the bond.

For example, a $5,000 bond with a 5 percent coupon rate will pay you $250 per year in interest. Depending on how often the bond issuer makes interest payments, your $250 could be received in quarterly, semi-annual, or annual installments. This bond may be referred to as a "5 percent coupon bond."

In the past, bonds were issued as paper certificates with coupons that an investor had to clip and mail in to receive an interest payment. Bond holders were called "coupon clippers." Today, bond ownership is registered electronically and the regular interest payments are deposited automatically into a brokerage or bank account.

A common rule is that the higher the yield, the higher the risk associated with the bond. Higher yields are intended to compensate the investor for taking a greater risk.

Maturity

Every bond has a date on which it is issued, and a date on which the investor will receive his or her initial capital investment back. A bond's maturity is the date on which the bond is scheduled for redemption. Most bonds have maturities of less than 30 years; there are a few exceptions, such as "Methuselahs," which are issued with maturities of 50 years. Although bonds can be bought and sold on the secondary market, the market value of a bond is irrelevant when it reaches maturity. The investor will receive only the face value of the bond.

Bonds with maturities between zero and two years are considered short-term, those with five- to ten-year maturities are considered intermediate-term, and those with maturities longer than ten years are considered long-term bonds. The maturity of a bond affects its value; a longer maturity increases the risk that inflation or rising interest rates will decrease the value of the investment.

Duration

Duration is an indicator of how much the price of a bond will increase or decrease if interest rates rise or fall. The duration of a bond fluctuates daily. Duration serves as a measure of interest rate risk, and can be used to compare the relative risks of two or more bonds with different maturity dates, coupon rates, and yields to maturity. A long duration is an indicator of a higher risk. The longer the duration of a bond, the greater the loss if interest rates rise and the bond is sold before its maturity date, and the greater the profit if the bond is sold when interest rates have gone down.

Duration is the number of years required to recover the true cost of a bond, expressed as a number of years from its purchase date. The calculation accounts for inflation in determining the present value of all future interest payments and of principal when it is paid out at maturity. The higher the interest rate, or coupon, of a bond, the shorter its duration, because more money will be paid out by an earlier date and the cost of the bond will be recovered faster. A bond with a long maturity has a longer duration, because the present value of interest payments spread over a long period will be gradually diminished by inflation.

The price of a bond with a duration of five years would go down about 5 percent if interest rates rose by 1 percent before the bond was sold. If interest rates went down 1 percent, the price of the bond would rise by approximately 5 percent.

The duration of a zero coupon bond is equal to its maturity; the prices of zero coupon bonds react the most when interest rates change.

Duration is a measure of interest rate risk and its impact on secondary market price and is not a concern if the bond is held to maturity. Because bond funds do not have a maturity date, duration is used to indicate how the bond fund net asset value will respond to interest rate changes.

Call Provision

A call provision is an option allowing the issuer to payoff a bond prior to its maturity date. Issuers often use call provisions when interest rates fall in order to refinance their debt at a lower rate. Bond investors do not lose their capital investment, but lose the interest payments that they were expecting to receive until the bond's original maturity.

Not all bonds contain a call provision. Those that do, however, generally have a higher yield or a call premium to compensate the investor for the potential of the bond being called and the risk of having to replace the coupon with the lower yields of the prevailing market.

TIP: Call Provisions Can Hurt Investors

Investors who rely on the steady income from bond interest suffer a loss of income when a bond is called in prematurely. They are forced to reinvest their capital, either in a bond paying a lower interest rate, or by paying a premium on the secondary market for another bond with a similar high interest rate and, most likely, higher risk. Before investing in a bond, consider whether or not it has a call provision.

Put Option

A few bond issues offer put options. A put option allows the bond purchaser to force the prepayment of the bond by the issuer prior to its scheduled maturity date. Put options act as insurance against rising interest rates, allowing an investor to sell a low coupon bond before its maturity and reinvest in a newer bond with a higher coupon.

Yield to Maturity

Yield to maturity (YTM) is a calculation of the return of a bond, based on its current market price, interest rate, and remaining time to maturity. YTM is the most common measure of a bond's return. It takes into account the gradual increase or decrease in the market price of the bond as it approaches maturity.

Several other methods of calculating the return of a bond are discussed later in this book.

Bond Credit Rating

A bond's credit rating is a measure of the risk that the bond issuer will default on the principal and interest or that the bond will decrease in value. Several independent credit rating agencies offer objective assessments of the risks associated with bonds and rate them according to a ranking system.

Premium

When a bond is selling on the market for a price higher than its face value, it is trading at a premium. Investors who purchase a bond at a premium are paying extra for the interest income expected from that particular bond. Bonds trade at a premium when the stock market is in a decline and investors want to move their assets into bonds that offer a secure income and preserve capital. Bonds without call provisions trade at a premium when interest rates fall because investors are willing to pay more to lock in a higher interest rate.

Discount

When a bond is selling for a price lower than its face value, it is trading at a discount. At times when interest rates are rising, outstanding bonds will begin to trade at a discount to compensate the investor for the fact that the outstanding bond has a lower coupon then the new bonds being issued. Certain types of bonds, such as zero coupon bonds, are sold below their face values on the primary market, and the difference between the purchase price and the face value is factored into the return.

Bid and Ask Prices

The ask price is the price at which a bond is offered for sale. The bid price is the price paid by the buyer. The difference between the bid price and ask price is called a spread. Bonds are bought and sold by bond traders and brokerages in an over-the-counter market; the spread is the profit traders receive from brokering the sale of a bond.

Accrued Interest

Accrued interest is the interest which has accumulated on a bond, but has not yet been paid. Bonds are not commonly sold on or even near the dates that interest payments are made. The amount of interest that has accrued since the last payment date is included in the price of the bond on the secondary market.

Types of Bonds

U.S. Treasury and Agency Bonds

U.S. Treasury and agency bonds currently make up the largest segment of the U.S. bond market. Treasury bonds are backed by the full faith and credit of the U.S. government. The U.S. Treasury issues a variety of bond types, including Treasury bills, Treasury notes, Treasury bonds, Treasury Inflation Protection

Securities (TIPS), and savings bonds. Each of these Treasury issues will be discussed in greater detail later in the book.

Agency bonds are bonds issued by federal government agencies, such as the Federal Home Loan Mortgage Corporation (Freddie Mac), Federal National Mortgage Corporation (Fannie Mae), and the Small Business Administration (SBA). They are not backed by the full faith and credit of the U.S. government, but are given the highest credit ratings because they are associated with the federal government and are considered to be fundamental to its operation. Agency bonds make up about 18 percent of the bonds held by individual households.

Corporate Bonds

Corporate bonds are bonds issued by corporations to raise financing for a variety of purposes, including expansion, the purchase of new equipment, and company acquisitions. Corporate bonds are rated according to the credit worthiness of the companies that issue them. Because corporations have a higher potential of default than a municipality, agency or the U.S. government, they tend to have lower ratings and pay a higher yield. Having said this, there are corporations rated in the highest rating category, General Electric being one of them.

Municipal Bonds

Municipal bonds are issued by counties, townships, cities, schools, or tax districts to finance public projects such as roads, bridges, stadiums, or sewage treatment plants. Municipal bonds fall into two categories: revenue bonds and general obligation bonds. Revenue bonds repay investors out of the revenues generated by the completion of the project, such as the tolls collected from a toll road. General obligation bonds are guaranteed by the taxing authority that is issuing the bonds. Interest paid by municipal bonds is generally, but not always, tax exempt, making them particularly attractive to investors in higher income tax brackets.

Zero Coupon Bonds

Zero coupon bonds are sold to investors at a deep discount to the bond's face value. They pay no regular interest, but at maturity, the investor is paid the face value of the bond. The difference between the discounted price and the face value equals the interest paid on the principal.

> ### TIP: Interest on Zero Coupon Bonds is Reported Annually
>
> You may be subject to taxation on the interest from zero coupon bonds, even though you are not receiving it annually. The IRS requires that the interest on zero coupon bonds be reported annually.

Mortgage-Backed Bonds

Mortgage-backed bonds are secured by deeds to real estate, equipment, or other hard assets. The mortgages are normally residential, but in some cases, they can be commercial.

International Bonds

International bonds are debt instruments issued by other countries. International bonds are subject to additional risks such as sovereign risk and currency risk.

Bond Mutual Funds

Bond mutual funds pool together investor capital to purchase individual bond securities. Bond mutual funds are managed by a professional portfolio manager and can have a variety of objectives related to risk, industry sectors, international investment, and length of maturity. Bond funds offer investors flexibility and diversification. They do not have a maturity date because, as bonds mature, they are replaced with new bond purchases. Bond funds incur management fees and may charge a load fee or an exit fee.

Bond Exchange Traded Funds (ETFs)

Bond ETFs are investment pools similar to bond mutual funds, but are sold as shares on the stock market and can be traded throughout the day like stocks.

How Are Bonds Issued?

A bond is issued when a federal or state government, municipality, or corporation decides that a bond is the most appropriate way to raise the funds needed for a particular purpose or project. These decisions are made with the assistance of a financial advisor or a consultant. The federal government and federal agencies use the services of internal financial advisors. Municipalities and local governments, who issue bonds only occasionally, characteristically hire outside consultants to work with their finance directors and legal staff in collecting all the necessary documentation and statistical information. Corporations rely on the services of their investment banks.

A government or municipality issues bonds to raise money for public undertakings, expecting to repay the debt using tax revenues or, in the case of a revenue-generating project such as a toll road or a university dormitory, from future income when the project is completed. A corporation may choose to issue a bond to finance an expansion of its operations or the acquisition of another business, expecting to repay the debt from the future income generated by its increased business activity.

The preparation of a bond issue is a highly orchestrated process requiring the participation of several legal and financial entities. Once it has been established that a bond issue is appropriate and a preliminary draft has been prepared, the contract (bond indenture) is reviewed by a bond counsel who gives a legal opinion. The bond counsel determines whether the bond issue is appropriate for the debt being incurred, the legal position of the bondholders relative to other creditors, and the tax status of the interest paid by the bond.

During the preparation of the bond indenture, the issuer must decide whether to include a call provision, and whether the bond issue will be paid off in increments or all at once. A call option gives the bond issuer the right to redeem the bond issue before its maturity date, more often than not when interest rates fall. Many bond issues have fixed call options, allowing the issuer to redeem the bond only after a certain period of time has elapsed. A municipal bond may have a call provision that is triggered when specific circumstances arise. A single issue consisting of bonds with different maturity dates is called a serial bond. A term bond is one with a fixed, long-term maturity date. Many U.S. government bonds and corporate bonds are term bonds.

A bond may have a senior lien, meaning that if the bond issuer declares bankruptcy, bond holders will be given priority over other creditors when cash is distributed. A holder of a bond with a junior lien will be placed in a subordinate position to other creditors.

Prospectus or Offering Statement

Before a bond issue goes on the market, the bond issuer must prepare an offering statement (OS), or prospectus, which is a public document detailing the type and structure of the bond, its special features, participants in the bond issue, the strengths and weaknesses of the issuer, and any liabilities. Offering statements are provided to every purchaser of a bond, and are often posted on Web sites such as **www.emuni.com** and **www.internotes.com**, and on the Web sites of individual bond issuers.

Setting the Interest Rate, or Coupon

The bond issuer then requests a bond rating from one or more of the major bond credit rating agencies. These agencies assign a credit rating to the bond, based on their evaluation of the financial strength, as well as other economic and qualitative judgments, of the issuer's ability to pay. The bond's rating assists in determining the minimum interest rate or coupon rate that will allow the bond to clear the market. The interest rate must be competitive, and is frequently set to equal the yield of similar bonds that are already on the secondary market so that the bond can be priced at its face value.

Most bonds have a fixed rate of interest that is set when the bond is issued and remains the same throughout the life of the bond. Floaters, or variable-rate bonds, have interest rates that are periodically reset, commonly in line with the market rates on specified dates. The interest on zero-coupon bonds accrues and is not paid out until the bond reaches maturity.

Setting the Price

Except for U.S. government bonds, bonds are not normally sold directly by the issuer. An investment bank or a large brokerage house, called an underwriter, buys the bonds from the issuer and resells them to investors. The underwriter takes on the risk that all the bonds may not be resold immediately. A large bond issue is handled by a group of underwriters, known as an underwriting syndicate. Underwriters use legal counsel to negotiate a contract with the bond issuer.

Underwriters purchase the bonds for a price lower than the face value of a bond, and make their profit by selling it to investors at face value. The price paid by an underwriter is based on the size of the bond issue, the reputation of the issuer, and the stability of credit markets. The underwriter might realize a profit of $15 per bond on a moderately sized bond issue, or $10 per bond on a large issue of $50 million or more. Several underwriting syndicates may offer competitive bids for a bond issue, which is then sold to the highest bidder. All members of an underwriting syndicate will re-sell bonds to investors at the same price.

Sometimes, an issuer bypasses underwriters and sells the entire bond issue directly in a private sale to the institutional investor, such as a pension fund, hedge fund, bond fund, bank, insurance company, or large brokerage, who offers the highest price. The bond is now ready to be placed on the market.

Bond Credit Ratings

Brokerages, bond insurers, underwriters, and institutional investors rely on independent bond credit analysts to assess the risk that a bond issuer may not be able to pay back its debt. Three major credit rating agencies, Standard and Poor's®, Moody's®, and Fitch Ratings, and two smaller agencies, Dominion Bond Rating Service of Canada and A.M. Best, are designated Nationally Recognized Statistical

Rating Organizations (NRSROs) by the SEC, and are closely monitored. The best-known agencies are Standard and Poor's and Moody's. Each agency uses a slightly different methodology to rate the creditworthiness of bonds, but their assessments are similar.

How Bonds Are Rated

Credit rating agencies charge bond issuers fees to evaluate their financial profiles. They are expected to provide impartial, unbiased assessments. To maintain their credibility, rating agencies continually monitor their larger clients, and occasionally perform an unsolicited upgrade or downgrade of a bond's rating when they detect a change in the issuer's financial situation.

Each bond is assigned a rating based on the bond issuer's financial strength and other qualitative factors affecting the ability to pay debt service. Rating agencies evaluate a number of factors, including the issuer's stability, potential for revenue growth, cash flow, size, existing debt obligations, and probability of being able to make interest payments on time. Each agency uses a slightly different methodology to rate the creditworthiness of bonds, but their assessments are essentially similar. Bonds with the highest rank, Aaa or AAA, are considered the safest investments. (*See Chapter 5: Corporate Bonds, Credit Ratings.*)

A Bond's Credit Rating Determines Its Interest Rate

A bond's credit rating strongly influences the interest rate that the issuer will have to pay. A bond with a lower credit rating must offer a higher interest rate to compensate investors for the increased risk they are taking when they buy the bonds. Bonds with the same maturity date and credit rating commonly offer the same interest rate.

A Bond's Credit Rating Affects Its Price

The price of a bond is determined by a number of factors including its coupon and the yield on the secondary market for bonds with a similar maturity and credit rating. If the price of a bond is not competitive, it will be difficult to sell.

Investors look both at the interest rate (yield) and the risk associated with a bond. At times when the stock market is declining, investors moving their capital out of uncertain stocks and into stable, investment-grade bonds may increase demand and raise the price of those bonds on the secondary market.

A change in the credit rating assigned to a bond may have a powerful effect on its price in the secondary market. From time to time, when the financial condition of the issuer deteriorates, rating agencies assign a lower rating to a bond. The rules followed by an index bond fund, or the client guidelines of a large institutional investor, may mandate the sale of bonds that drop from a BBB rating to a BB rating, releasing large quantities on the market and lowering prices. If a bond's rating is raised, its price is likely to go up because the coupon on the bond remains the same, while the risk associated with it has gone down.

Split Ratings

All ratings are based on some subjective judgments made by credit analysts. Though the ratings of the three major rating agencies coincide most of the time, there are occasions when agencies assign different ratings to the same bond. This situation is known as a split rating. The difference may be an entire category or only a variation within a category. A split rating reflects a disagreement over the bond issuer's ability to adapt to new circumstances, or whether it will have the cash necessary to make certain interest payments on time.

TIP: Bond Credit Ratings are not Infallible

Bond rating agencies constantly reiterate that the ratings they assign should not be used as signals by investors to buy and sell bonds. Downgrading the rating of a bond may hasten the collapse of a company in financial distress, so rating agencies frequently wait until after the market price has slumped before downgrading. Consequently, bond ratings lag behind market conditions.

TIP: Credit Rating Agencies are not Responsible for Detecting Corruption

Enron's bonds were rated as investment grade by both Standard and Poor's and Moody's until four days before it declared bankruptcy. WorldCom's collapse took everyone by surprise. A credit rating agency is not responsible for detecting fraud, illegal bookkeeping practices, corrupt management, or other hidden problems. Nevertheless, many investors wondered how two highly respected credit agencies could have been unaware of the true situation of these companies.

Calculating Yield

"Yield" refers to the rate of return on a bond investment. The term "yield" is used in several different contexts, and it is important for a bond investor to understand each one correctly. Yield tells an investor how much he or she can earn from the coupon payments of the bond. The concept of yield also allows an accurate comparison of different types of bond investments. There are five different ways in which yield is calculated.

Nominal Yield

Nominal yield is the bond's stated interest rate, or coupon, based on the face value of the bond. Nominal yield is established when a bond is issued, and remains unchanged until the bond's maturity. It is not affected by fluctuations in interest rates or in the market value of a bond. The nominal yield tells a buyer how much he or she will receive in annual interest payments during the life of a bond.

This formula is used to calculate the nominal yield:

$$\text{Nominal Yield} = \frac{\text{Annual Interest Payment}}{\text{Face Value of Bond}}$$

Nominal yield is often used to identify a bond issue; "8 percents of 09" refers to a bond issue with an 8 percent coupon maturing in 2009.

Nominal yield applies only to a bond which is purchased at a price equal to its face value and is held to maturity. It does not accurately describe the return on a bond purchased at a price lower than its face value, or on a bond purchased at face value and later resold at a higher or lower price.

For example, the nominal yield of a $1,000 bond paying 5 percent interest would be:

$$5\% = \frac{50}{1,000}$$

Current Yield

Current yield is a calculation of the actual return a buyer will receive on a bond, based on its current market price.

$$\boxed{\text{Current Yield} = \frac{\text{Annual Interest Payment}}{\text{Amount Paid for Bond}}}$$

The current yield for a bond purchased at face value would be equal to the nominal yield. A bond rarely sells at face value on the secondary market. If a bond is selling for less than its face value, the current yield will be higher, and if it is selling at a premium, the current yield will be lower.

Here are sample current yields for a $1000 bond selling for a price $100 below and $100 above its face value:

$$5.56\% = \frac{50}{900}$$

$$4.55\% = \frac{50}{1100}$$

To sell a bond on the secondary market, the seller must adjust the price of the bond so that its current yield matches the prevailing interest rate. When interest rates rise, the seller is forced to lower the price of the bond so that its current yield matches the higher interest rate offered by similar, newly issued bonds.

Current yields are quoted for bond mutual funds and bond ETFs, which have no date of maturity. The dividends from these funds include both interest payments and capital gains from sales of bonds held by the funds, so the current yield of a fund cannot be directly compared to the current yield of an individual bond.

Current yields are frequently quoted in the financial pages of newspapers, and are important to investors who are purchasing bonds as a source of fixed income. However, current yield does not provide an accurate picture of the total return on a bond investment because it does not account for the length of time the bond is held. When a bond reaches maturity, the investor will receive the face value of the bond. If, as in the previous example, the investor paid $100 less than the face value of a $1000 bond, at maturity, he or she will gain a profit of $100 in addition to the regular interest payments he or she has been receiving. For a bond maturing in 30 years, this would amount to an extra $3.33 per year in income. If the bond is maturing in two years, though, the investor would receive an additional $50 per year — a substantial consideration in deciding whether to purchase a bond.

Current yield also does not account for the income that would be received if the annual interest payment received from a bond were reinvested at the same interest rate.

Yield-to-Maturity

Yield-to-maturity (YTM) is the most commonly used calculation of the return on a bond investment. YTM accounts for both interest income, any difference between the price paid for the bond and its face value, and the changes in market value of a bond as it approaches maturity. The one flaw in YTM is that it assumes that each coupon payment will be reinvested at the same interest rate. So, if you buy a new issue at a YTM of 8 percent and interest rates decline to 6 percent, each coupon can only be reinvested at 6 percent. In other words, the 8 percent YTM is not actually achieved for the life of the bond.

YTM is an interest rate that incorporates the total retu an investor will receive on a bond purchase. When a analyst or investor speaks of a bond's "yield," they are generally referring to YTM. YTM is a complex and time-consuming calculation, so most brokers and investors now rely on financial calculators or investment software. You can find financial calculators on Web sites such as **www.investinginbonds.com, www.bloomberg.com, www.moneychimp.com,** and **www. kiplingers.com.**

YTM tells an investor how much return he or she will receive on a bond that is purchased at the current market price and held to maturity, if the interest payments are regularly reinvested at the same rate as when the bond is purchased. It provides a more accurate picture of the real value of an investment than the **current yield**.

For example, the YTM on the $1000 bond in the previous examples, with a 5 percent interest rate and a ten-year maturity, would be:

- Selling at face value: 5.07 percent (assuming the interest is reinvested at 5 percent)

- Selling for $900: 6.19 percent

- Selling for $1100: 4.08 percent

Taking into account the bond's maturity (ten years) and the income gained by reinvesting the interest at the same coupon rate (5 percent), the $1,000 bond selling for $900 offers a return of 6.19 percent rather than 5.56 percent — a much more attractive proposition.

The chart below illustrates how the total return on a bond with a face value of $1,000 is affected by its market price, the length of time it is held before it matures, and the income from reinvesting the interest:

Market price	Maturity	Nominal Yield	Current Yield	Yield to Maturity
$1,000	2 years	5%	5%	5.06%
	10 years	5%	5%	5.07%
	30 years	5%	5%	5.09%
$900	2 years	5%	5.56%	10.75%
	10 years	5%	5.56%	6.19%
	30 years	5%	5.56%	5.46%
$1,100	2 years	5%	4.55%	0.18%
	10 years	5%	4.55%	4.08%
	30 years	5%	4.55%	4.75%

For an investor who is using interest from bond investments as a source of regular income, the YTM is not an accurate indicator of the return on an investment, as the interest is not being reinvested.

TIP: Remember to Account for Taxation

Another factor affects the real return an investor will receive on a bond investment: the amount of taxes he or she must pay on the interest received from the bond and on capital gains realized through the sale of a bond before it reaches maturity. Taxes are determined by the type of bond, the investor's income bracket, and whether the bond is held in a tax-deferred account. Most financial calculators account for taxation in determining the return on a bond investment. (For more information, see the section on Taxation.)

TIP: Income from Interest Can Rarely be Reinvested at the Same Rate

The YTM calculation assumes that all the interest payments from a bond will be reinvested at the same yield as when the bond is purchased. In real life, the interest payment must be reinvested at the interest rate prevailing when the payment is distributed. The longer the maturity of a bond, the greater the likelihood that interest rates will fluctuate, making the YTM calculation increasingly less predictive of investment return. A small private investor may not receive enough cash from a single distribution to make an appropriate investment, and may have to wait until enough cash has accumulated in a money market account that offers a lower interest rate.

Yield-to-Call

YTM applies only when an investor holds a bond until maturity. Many bonds have call provisions allowing the issuer to redeem a bond at an earlier date. **Yield-to-call** measures the return on a bond that is likely to be redeemed at a **call price** before it reaches maturity. Sometimes the term **yield-to-worst** is used to describe the lowest potential return for a callable bond. If interest rates decline and an issuer can refinance at a new lower interest rate and, therefore, a call is likely, the yield-to-worst will reflect the yield to the earlier call date. If interest rates increase to a level above where the bond is issued, the issuer has no benefit to refinance and call the bond, so it is assumed it will go to maturity and the yield-to-worst will reflect the YTM.

Yield-to-call, rather than YTM, should be applied to any callable bond that is selling at a **premium** because it offers a coupon rate higher than the prevailing interest rate. Yield-to-call is the return that an investor can expect to receive on a callable bond because of the potential early redemption and should be used to evaluate the value of a bond whenever it is lower than the YTM. It incorporates the call price, which is generally slightly higher than the face value of the bond, and replaces the bond maturity date with the call date in the calculation. The call price is often high enough to raise the yield-to-call higher than the yield-to-maturity, particularly for bonds with shorter maturities.

Look at the chart below. The same bond from the previous examples now has a call date five years after its issue. If purchased at face value, it actually offers a higher rate of return than if it is held until maturity. If it is purchased at a premium, however, the yield-to-call is considerably less than the yield-to-maturity.

Market price	Maturity	Nominal	Current Yield	Yield to Maturity	Yield to Call*
$1,000	2 years	5%	5%	5.06%	n/a
	10 years	5%	5%	5.07%	5.56%
	30 years	5%	5%	5.09%	5.56%
$900	2 years	5%	5.56%	10.75%	n/a
	10 years	5%	5.56%	6.19%	7.80%
	30 years	5%	5.56%	5.46%	7.80%
$1,100	2 years	5%	4.55%	0.18%	n/a
	10 years	5%	4.55%	4.08%	3.56%
	30 years	5%	4.55%	4.75%	3.56%

*Call date is five years after bond is issued

Older bonds offering high coupons are likely to sell at a premium at a time when interest rates have fallen. Those are the same circumstances in which an issuer is most likely to call in a bond and seek financing at the new, lower interest rates.

TIP: Higher Returns May be Offset by Lower Interest Rates

Though an investor may initially receive higher returns when a bond is called in before it reaches maturity, the gains may be offset by the fact that the investor, faced with lower prevailing interest rates, may have to settle for a new investment with a lower rate of return.

TIP: Sales Literature May be Deceptive

Sales literature for bonds selling at a premium higher than the call price may promise attractive rates of return, without pointing out that if the bond is called prior to maturity, the investor will realize considerably less.

Realized Yield

A fifth calculation, **realized yield**, measures the returns realized during the period that a bond is owned. If the bond is held until maturity, the realized yield is the same as the YTM, and if the bond is held until the first call date, it equals the yield-to-call. An investor who plans to sell a bond before it is redeemed can calculate the realized yield by estimating the price at which the bond will be sold and the amount of time it will be held.

Yield-to-Average Life

Certain types of bonds, called **sinking fund bonds**, shave a specified maturity, but are subject to a random call before maturity. Corporate or municipal bonds that have **sinking funds** use a lottery to select some bonds for retirement at regular intervals. It is not known exactly when a specific bond might be called, so yield is calculated using the **intermediate point**, the point at which half of the bonds in the issue will have been called in. This is called **yield-to-average life**, or **yield to the intermediate point**. Mortgage-backed securities may also use this calculation, as it is not known exactly when specific mortgages will be paid off. **Yield-to-average life** assumes that cash flows will be reinvested at a similar interest rate as they come in.

Total Return

Institutional investors and bond traders look at bond returns in terms of **total return**. Total return incorporates the interest received during the time a bond is held, the difference between the purchase price and the selling price. Total return fluctuates along with the price of a bond on the secondary market.

Total return applies to individual bonds only if they are sold before they reach maturity. It is not appropriate for buy-and hold investments. The concept of total return always applies to bond mutual funds and exchange traded funds (ETFs) because they do not have a maturity date and their market prices and dividend payments continually fluctuate. An investor in a bond fund might decide to sell his or her shares if the total return drops below a set limit.

Basis Points

Changes in the yield of a bond, or differences among the yields of several bonds, are expressed in terms of **basis points**. A basis point is a unit equal to one-hundredth of 1 percent. Bond analysts often use **bp** or **bps** as abbreviations for basis points. For example, a bond whose yield increases from 5 percent to 5.5 percent is said to have increased by 50 basis points. Basis points are used because even a small change in a bond's interest rate can mean a significant difference in its yield. The use of basis points also avoids confusion in discussions of percentage change; the phrase a "1 percent increase" in a 10 percent interest rate could be construed either as an increase from 10 percent to 10.1 percent, or from 10 percent to 11 percent.

Basis points are also used to express the difference (**spread**) between the interest rate of a particular bond or bond fund and that of an underlying security or index. The difference between an interest rate of 4.5 percent and an interest rate of 5.27 percent is 77 basis points, or .77 percent.

TIP: It is Important to Understand which Concept of Yield Applies to an Investment

In making a comparison between two or more bond offerings, it is necessary to know which yield calculation to use. YTM is the most accurate prediction of the returns that will be realized if a bond is held to maturity; if the bond has a call provision, the investor should consider yield-to-call or yield-to-worst instead. Nominal yield or current yield is appropriate for an investor who intends to spend the interest rather than reinvesting it. Realized return or total return should be used when an investor plans to sell the bond before it reaches maturity. In every calculation, the investor should also consider taxes and brokerage fees.

CHAPTER 4

The Basics of Buying and Selling Bonds

Most bonds are still traded through **brokers** at large investment firms which both sell and issue bonds and maintain large inventories. Smaller independent brokers often specialize in a particular type of bond, such as municipal bonds for a specific geographic region.

Bond trading online has not achieved the same ease and affordability as online stock trading. Some of the large investment firms and brokerages offer their inventory online through their Web sites. Many smaller online brokers do not hold any inventory, but sell bonds through affiliate programs with companies such as ValuBond. There is no central clearing house for bond trades, and bonds offered for sale online may no longer be available by the time an order is placed. After reviewing online bond offerings, it is a good idea to call the brokerage and confirm the price and availability of the bonds you are interested in.

The Primary Market

When a bond is first issued, it is said to trade on the **primary market**. In the primary market, the investor frequently purchases the bond at close to face value, without a commission or markup. This is because the investment bank or brokerage is making their profit from the sale of the bond. They earn the difference between the price the issuer sold the bonds to the underwriter and the higher price (near face value) that the ultimate buyer pays the underwriter or broker. This differential is called the underwriters discount.

U.S. Treasury Bonds

New U.S. Treasury bonds can be purchased directly from the Treasury by establishing a Treasury Direct account with the Federal Reserve Bank, or from many banks or institutions for a small fee. Treasury Direct accounts can be easily opened online at **www.treasurydirect.gov**. An investor purchasing Treasury bonds through a stock broker normally pays associated markup and transaction fees.

Individual investors can also buy Treasury bills for a discount at auction. New Treasury bills (T-bills) are sold to brokerages and institutional investors at an auction every Monday. Individuals can enter non-competitive bids, specifying the amount they wish to purchase (up to $5 million) and agreeing to accept the discount rate, or yield, set at the auction. Institutional investors wishing to buy $500,000 or more place competitive bids specifying the discount rate they wish to receive. Based on the amount of money it wishes to borrow and the bids that have been submitted, the Treasury determines the highest yield that it can accept; any higher bids are rejected. Non-competitive bidders are then sold T-bills at a price determined by averaging the successful competitive bids. When all the noncompetitive bids have been filled, the remaining T-bills are allocated to the competitive bidders, starting with the lowest bid. No individual bidder can be allocated more than 35 percent of the total amount. Treasury bonds and notes are also sold at auction, but at less frequent intervals.

An individual investor can also place an order with a brokerage to purchase Treasury bills, notes, or bonds at an auction for a nominal fee.

Corporate and Municipal Bonds

New issues of corporate and municipal bonds are offered for sale to both institutional and individual investors through investment banks and brokerages. The yields on these new issues are calculated just before the bond goes on the market, and the bonds normally sell at prices close to their face values. If market interest rates change at the last minute, the coupon (interest rate) or price of the bond may be slightly adjusted to keep the bond competitive.

Sales personnel and brokers contact investors prior to the sale date of a new bond issue to take orders. Based on the perceived demand for the new issue, the bond manager may make adjustments to the yields or re-price the bond. An investor who has placed an order before the yield was adjusted downward is normally allowed to withdraw without penalty.

> **TIP: Learn about New Bond Issues from Brokers**
>
> Contact one or more brokers and let them know that you are interested in new bond issues. Be sure to specify the type and quality of bond you desire.

The Secondary Market

Once a bond has been issued, it is bought and sold in the **secondary market** or **over-the-counter (OTC)** market. Billions of dollars in bonds are traded in the secondary market every day. Bond traders buy and sell directly from each other. Individual investors have access to the secondary market only through brokerages and financial institutions, which are connected to one another through a sophisticated communications network. The secondary market allows investors to sell their bonds easily when they need cash, and also gives them access to a wide variety of bond investments.

The secondary market is also important to bond issuers because liquidity (the ability to sell a bond when needed) is one of the characteristics that attracts investors. When a bond issue is selling at a premium in the secondary market, it increases investor confidence in the financial stability of the issuer and affects the issuer's ability to borrow money in the future.

U.S. Treasury Issues

The secondary market for U.S. Treasury issues is by far the most liquid and highly traded, and also the most transparent. The average holding period for a 30-year U.S. Treasury bond is only about 30 days. A relatively small number of dealers ask for bids and provide quotes for all Treasury securities. They also work closely with the Federal Reserve in buying and selling its own Treasury securities. Prices of previously issued Treasury securities are quoted daily and tracked by financial journals, such as *The Wall Street Journal,* and on their associated Web sites. U.S. Treasury securities are bought and sold through brokerages and financial institutions for a commission.

Corporate Bonds and Municipal Bonds

Buying and selling corporate and municipal bonds in the secondary market can be challenging, as there is no single source of information on available bonds and prices. Regulators in recent years have tried to improve price transparency in these markets with mandated price tracking sources. In the case of the corporate market, The National Association of Securities Dealers (NASD), now called Financial Industry Regulatory Authority (FINRA), developed TRACE (Trade Reporting and Compliance Engine), and in the case of the municipal market, The Municipal Securities Rule Making Board mandated the RTRS (Real-time Transaction Reporting System). Unfortunately, these pricing sources are not easily available to individual investors. Most large brokerages maintain an inventory of bonds, purchased from their customers and also from competing dealers, which are available for sale. By contacting several brokers, it is possible to have access to a wide variety of bonds.

The same bond may be offered for different prices at different brokerages. It may be difficult to obtain up-to-date price information for bond issues that are infrequently traded. According to research cited in *Investing in Bonds*, by Ken Little, in the course of a year, less than 30 percent of all outstanding bonds trade on the market and less than 1 percent trade in a given day.

Municipal bonds are sold by numerous dealers who specialize in **tax-exempt bonds** and often maintain inventories that are mostly local. Many municipal bond issues are relatively small and appear infrequently on the secondary market. Institutional investors commonly buy up large portions of municipal bond issues and hold them until redemption.

Individual investors can buy and sell small quantities of bonds on the stock exchanges. However, this method of transacting is clearly not as liquid as trying to sell equities on the New York Stock Exchange® (NYSE®) or American Stock Exchange® (AMEX®). Over 2,000 bonds are listed on the NYSE, and about 400 on the AMEX). Most of these bonds trade on the OTC market, but there are a few, such as AT&T™, that trade often on the stock exchange. Information on bond trades is posted daily on the stock exchange Web sites and in the financial sections of newspapers, so it is possible to see whether a bond that you want to sell has traded recently and at what price.

TIP: Bond Prices Can Change Substantially on the Stock Exchanges

It is a good idea to enter a limit order specifying the highest price at which you will buy a bond, and the lowest price at which you will sell on the stock exchanges, to avoid an unpleasant surprise. Bonds that trade in small volume are subject to sudden price changes.

TIP: Investing Small Amounts in Bonds

Bonds are commonly traded in large quantities. If you are investing less than $5,000, consider buying shares of a bond mutual fund or bond ETF of the same type as the bond you are interested in.

CHAPTER 5

Corporate Bonds

C ompanies issue bonds to finance large projects, such as new buildings, new equipment, or corporate acquisitions. Bonds are often a less expensive way to raise capital than traditional lending sources. Capital that is raised with the issuance of bonds normally comes with longer repayment terms and more favorable interest rates than traditional lending sources. There are many situations in which corporations would prefer not to issue additional stock to raise the needed funds. Stockholders have ownership rights in the company and may interfere in business operations. Corporate managers strive to maintain an ideal balance of ownership equity (stocks) and outstanding long- and short-term debt.

Two major indexes, **Lehman Brothers** and **Dow Jones®**, track corporate bonds and categorize them into industry sectors. All the industries in a particular sector tend to be affected in the same way by changing economic trends.

The major corporate bond industry sectors are:

- **Industrials:** Manufacturing, energy, mining, and service companies.

- **Banks and Financial Institutions:** Banks, brokerage houses, insurance companies, mortgage companies, and Real Estate Investment Trusts (REITs). Banks do not always move in tandem with the other types of businesses in this sector and are sometimes placed in a separate category.

- **Transportation:** Airlines and railroads. The development of new technologies and government deregulation of the transportation industry have eroded the creditworthiness of this corporate bond sector. Railway bonds were once considered some of the safest bonds; today, railways have difficulty staying afloat because of the high costs of modernization and competition from other forms of transportation. Many airline companies entered bankruptcy between 2002 and 2006 due to rising fuel costs and poor management decisions.

- **Utilities:** Transmission companies, telecommunications, gas pipelines, electric power companies, water, and sewage-treatment plants. This sector has also been affected by government deregulation, as companies that were previously monopolies experience difficulties in the competitive private arena.

A corporate bond represents a legal business debt obligation. The issuer contracts to repay the principal by a certain date and to make regular interest payments according to the terms in the **bond indenture**. Corporate bonds commonly pay a higher interest rate than comparable Treasury issues or municipal bonds, for several reasons. Interest income from a corporate bond is taxed as income unless it is kept in a tax-deferred account, while municipal bonds are often tax-exempt. Corporate bonds carry greater risk, since they must be repaid from income generated by the business. Municipal and U.S. Treasury issues are backed by the government's authority to collect taxes; most corporate bonds are not secured by any kind of collateral.

Some corporate bonds are **secured** by hard assets such as real estate. Secured bonds include **equipment trust certificates** (secured by transportation equipment), **first mortgage bonds** (secured by real estate), and **collateral trust bonds** (secured by financial assets). Unsecured bonds are known collectively as **debenture**s. If the issuer of a corporate bond declares bankruptcy, secured bonds take priority over all other debts, followed by debentures, and finally, by stock equity. There are several categories of senior and junior unsecured debt that determine in what order bondholders will be repaid.

In 2008, the corporate bond market accounted for more than $4 trillion in outstanding debt. Daily trading volume in the corporate bond market exceeded $24 billion. Approximately 93 percent of all corporate bonds are owned and traded by institutional investors.

Most corporate bonds are sold in denominations of $1,000. An investor receives a single certificate for the total amount of a bond purchase; if he or she later wishes to sell a portion of that original purchase, a replacement certificate will be issued for the new amount. A corporate bond is issued at a price close to its face value. Once it has been issued and is trading on the **secondary market**, its price will fluctuate with changes in market rates of interest, and with changes in investors' perception of the issuer's ability to make interest payments as scheduled. Corporate bonds are issued with maturities ranging from 2 to 30 years, and are classified according to their maturities:

- Short Term: 1 to 4 Years

- Intermediate Term: 5 to 12 Years

- Long Term: 13 years+

The majority of corporate bonds make semi-annual interest payments that remain unchanged from the day the bond is issued until the day it is redeemed. The size of this interest payment affects the market price of the bond; a high fixed interest rate commands a higher price on the secondary market. Corporations sometimes issue floating rate notes (floaters) and bonds with interest payments that are periodically altered in accordance with a predetermined formula. Their changing coupon rates cause these bonds to sell consistently on the secondary market at prices close to their face values. The floating interest rate is tied to, and slightly higher than, the interest rate on a newly issued short-term U.S. Treasury debt. While the floating interest rate prevents an investor from calculating exactly how much income he or she will receive in the future, it keeps the market price of the bond stable and ensures the bond can be sold for almost its full value as it approaches maturity.

How Are Corporate Bonds Secured?

Secured Bonds

Secured bonds have a direct lien on specified assets of the issuer. These assets can include anything from real estate to electric generation plants.

Unsecured Bonds

Unsecured bonds only have a full-faith and credit obligation of the issuer, and the bondholder has no claim on physical assets or specific revenue sources.

Subordinated Debentures

In the event of a default or company bankruptcy, subordinated debenture bonds fall behind secured bonds in priority for repayment. Subordinated debenture bonds normally offer a higher interest rate to investors to compensate for their lower status.

Mortgage-Backed Bonds

Mortgage-backed bonds are among the newest form of bonds, offering security in the forms of deeds to real estate or other hard assets, such as equipment, that are financed with the capital raised from the bond issue. When a mortgage is the collateral, bondholders are not always in a first **lien position**. Depending on how the bond issue is structured, the bondholder could be in the second or even the third lien position. The lien position determines the order in which the **principal** will be repaid in the event of a default.

Guaranteed Bonds

A guaranteed bond is backed by a third party. Guaranteed bonds are a way for a less credit-worthy issuer to access the market. Often, they are issued by small companies that are subsidiaries of larger more credit-worthy entities and where the stronger parent company guarantees the small subsidiary.

Equipment Trust Certificates or Bonds

Railroads and airlines require large amounts of capital to purchase and maintain equipment. An equipment trust certificate or bond issue uses the equipment being purchased as collateral, to be released on the repayment of the bond.

Other Types of Corporate Bonds

Convertible Bonds

Convertible bonds allow the bondholder to convert the bonds into a predetermined number of shares of the issuing company's common stock. The bondholder, not the issuer, decides when and whether to convert the bond to shares of stock. Like other bonds, convertible bonds offer regular fixed interest payments until the bond reaches its maturity date and is redeemed by the issuer.

If a bondholder or broker submits bonds for conversion, the issuer is required to issue additional shares of stock to replace the debt. The bondholder receives ownership of the shares of stock and relinquishes all rights to further interest payments or future repayment of the principal. Once the transaction is complete, it cannot be reversed. The investor will now receive dividend payments from the shares of common stock, if the company pays dividends. The investor can sell the shares of stock or continue to hold them in a portfolio.

A convertible bond can be exchanged for a specific number of shares of stock, no matter how high the price of those shares might become. Convertible bonds can become extremely valuable if the business is successful. A $1,000 convertible bond, exchangeable for 50 shares of the issuer's common stock, could have a market value of $3,000 if the price of each share rose to $60. The market value of a regular bond, in contrast, will fluctuate somewhat as interest rates rise and fall, and then approach the face value of the bond as it reaches maturity.

Convertible bonds state the conversion rate, specifying how many shares of stock the investor can receive in exchange for the bond, in the **indenture**. The ratio (sometimes called a premium) is expressed either as a ratio or as a percentage.

A ratio of 25:1 means each bond unit can be exchanged for 25 shares of the company's common stock. This ratio can be used to determine a target stock price at which it would become profitable to convert the bond. A $1,000 bond, divided by 25 shares, would equal $40 per share. When the price of the common stock rises above $40 per share, the bond's market value becomes higher than its face value.

A convertible bond can also be expressed as a percentage, which can be used to calculate the premium that would be paid if the bond were converted to shares of stock at current share prices. For example, if the stock is currently trading at $20 per share and your purchase premium was 40 percent, you would be paying the equivalent of $28 per share, or 40 percent above market price, to convert the bond to common stock.

Convertible bonds are attractive to investors because they can receive regular interest income from the bond, and if the value of the predetermined number of shares of the issuer's stock surpasses the bond's face value, it can be converted to even more profitable stock ownership. A convertible bond can be regarded as an interest-paying bond with a stock option.

Convertible bonds nearly always offer lower interest rates than ordinary bonds; the trade-off is less income from interest, for the possibility that the company will do well and its share prices will shoot up. One of the investment risks associated with buying a convertible bond is that the value of the issuer's stock may not rise above the face value of the bond. In that case, the investor would have sacrificed the opportunity to earn higher returns from an ordinary bond. Another risk is **liquidity**; the convertible bond market is dominated by institutional investors trading in large quantities, and it may be difficult to find a buyer for a small number of convertible bonds.

The issuer of a convertible bond more often than not retains a call provision allowing the forced conversion of the bond if the price of its stock rises dramatically. This effectively caps the amount of profit that can be realized by converting a bond.

Prices of convertible bonds in the secondary market are affected by a complex combination of factors, including whether the bond has call or put options, and events such as stock splits or dividend payouts that might reduce the value of the company's common stock.

> ### TIP: Convertible Bonds are Unsecured Debt
>
> Convertible bonds are debentures, or subordinated debentures, and are not secured by any collateral. They expose the investor to considerable risk if the issuer encounters financial difficulties.

High-Yield or Junk Bonds

High-yield bonds, or **junk bonds**, are debt securities with credit ratings below Baa3/BBB (the lowest investment-grade ratings by Moody's and S&P®) and, therefore, higher risk of defaulting on repayment of the principal and interest. To compensate for the higher level of risk, they offer investors a higher interest rate. High-yield bonds may offer 2 percent or more above the interest rates of investment-grade bonds. They are attractive to investors who are seeking higher returns than the regular bond market and willing to accept the added risk.

The term "junk bond" came into use during the 1920s to describe bonds that no one wanted because they were below investment grade. They were also called "fallen angels" because they had once had high credit ratings that dropped when their issuers experienced severe financial difficulties. Many institutional investors were precluded from buying them because junk bonds were excluded by the rules of their investment policies. In the 1980s, the term was applied to established companies undergoing restructuring and also to companies that borrowed money to buy a controlling interest of their own stock, called leveraged buy-outs.

During the 1980s, the advent of modern **portfolio theory**, which promotes the concept that **diversification**, cushions the risks of volatile investments in a portfolio, made junk bonds with their higher rates of return desirable components of a well-balanced portfolio. During the 1990s, mutual funds increasingly purchased high-yield bonds for their portfolios.

High-yield bonds that have defaulted can be lucrative for knowledgeable investors who follow bankruptcy proceedings and buy, at very low prices, and receive higher post bankruptcy recoveries after they are reorganized. Defaulted bonds commonly trade without accrued interest. Because the issuer is not paying interest, the seller is not owed interest that has accrued during their holding period.

In 2006, Moody's began analyzing the protections for buyers that are written into the contracts of high-yield bonds, and assigning ranks to them before they went on the market. Bonds with the strongest protections for buyers are rated CQ-1, and the weakest are rated CQ-3. One protection that particularly strengthens a bond is a **change-of-control provision**, which allows the buyer of a corporate bond to return the bond at par if ownership of the company changes hands.

There are several important considerations in deciding whether or not to include high-yield bonds in your portfolio:

- High-yield bonds tend to be more **volatile** than other bonds. When there are fluctuations in the economy, changes in interest rates, or unsettling news reports in the media, high-yield bonds react more like stocks.

- High-yield bonds trade less frequently than other bond types. An investor who needs to sell high-yield bonds in a hurry may find it difficult to locate a buyer willing to pay an acceptable price for them.

- Junk bonds are likely to have call provisions. If the credit rating of a high-yield bond is upgraded over time, the issuer will call in the bonds and issue new bonds at a lower interest rate. The investor will no longer receive the expected high rate of return and will be forced to invest somewhere else at a lower rate.

- The interest rate paid by high-yield bonds is often not high enough to compensate for the significantly greater risk associated with the issuer not repaying the principal.

> ## TIP: High-Yield Bonds Might Have a Place in Your Portfolio
>
> In spite of the risks associated with high-yield bonds, they can have their place in specific portfolio allocations. Keep only a small percentage of your portfolio in high-yield bonds. Avoid them if your portfolio is not large enough to allow for diversification among many different issues.

Credit Ratings

Credit rating agencies employ hundreds of professional researchers and analysts to study every aspect of a corporation's business and financial status and determine to what extent it has the financial strength to meet its debt obligations on time. **Investment-grade bonds** are considered relatively safe investments. Any bond rated lower than BBB is an investment risk and, consequently, offers a higher coupon rate to attract investors.

Credit Ratings for Corporate Bonds

		Moody's	Standard & Poor's	Fitch
Investment Grade Bonds	Highest Quality	Aaa	AAA	AAA
	High Quality	Aa	AA	AA+
	Good Quality	A	A	AA
	Medium Quality	Baa	BBB	BBB

		Moody's	Standard & Poor's	Fitch
High-Yield Bonds	Speculative Elements	Ba	BB	BB
	Speculative	B	B	B
	More Speculative	Caa	CCC	CCC
	Highly Speculative	Ca	CC	CC
	In Default	------	D	D
	Not Rated	N	N	NR

From time to time, a bond's credit rating may be upgraded or downgraded as the corporation's circumstances change or earlier debt is paid off. An upgrade is likely to raise the price of a bond on the secondary market, as it now offers a higher yield than comparable bonds. A downgrade may lower the price because some bond funds and institutional investors that are mandated to hold only bonds of a certain credit rating will be forced to sell. A bond that has been downgraded may be a bargain if the company's business is still solid and there is a probability that it will be upgraded again in the near future.

Corporate Bonds in Your Portfolio

The greatest attraction of corporate bonds is their higher rates of return, and the fact that they provide a steady and predictable income. Corporate bonds are normally included in the conservative to moderately conservative portfolios of investors in retirement or close to retirement, who seek current income, or who are leaving an appreciation phase for a more income-focused investment phase. Corporate bonds are often a portion of an **all-bond portfolio**, offering higher yields than other types of bonds. Corporate bonds are also suitable investments for investors in lower tax brackets, and those who have tax sheltered retirement accounts.

The highest-grade corporate bonds are considered to be nearly as safe as U.S. Treasury bonds; the best protection against the risk involved in lower-grade bonds is diversification. Just as a stock portfolio should be diversified among many market and industry sectors, the corporate bonds in your portfolio should be divided among several bond types and industry sectors. Diversify by purchasing bonds from each of the four major sectors: utilities, transportation, financial, and industrials, including technology and oil and gas. If your portfolio is large enough, include some international bonds and high-yield bonds.

A quick way to diversify is to invest in a bond mutual fund, or purchase shares of bond **ETFs**. There are over 4,000 bond mutual funds and approximately 100 bond ETFs on the market. **Broad-market index funds** include a selection of bonds that represents a sampling of the entire bond market. Specialized funds offer exposure to a specific industry sector or type of bond, or employ customized investment strategies. If the size of your portfolio does not allow you to own a wide range of corporate bonds, a fund is a better option because it protects you from the risk of losing a large portion of your capital when a single bond issuer defaults.

The risk associated with lower-grade corporate bonds should be well-balanced with highly rated investment-grade bonds. Investing in corporate bonds requires more research than investing in municipal and U.S. Treasury bonds. Review bond credit ratings carefully and consider any particular knowledge you might have about specific market sectors or the corporations

issuing bonds. Most importantly, do not sink too much of your capital into a single bond issue or single corporation.

Different bond issues from the same corporation may have different credit ratings, based on what lien, such as secured, senior, or subordinated, the bonds are issued under.

Invest in bonds with different maturities so that all of your investment capital is not returned to you during the same time period. Staggering the maturities of your bond investments also protects your portfolio from the changes in interest rates; the prices of corporate bonds of different maturities respond differently to market fluctuations.

Corporate Bonds and Your Taxes

The interest received from corporate bonds is taxed as regular income by both federal and state governments. If the income from interest payments on corporate bonds bumps you into a higher income tax bracket, the increased taxes may erode any profit you have made. For this reason, it is preferable to hold corporate bonds in a tax-deferred account such as an Individual Retirement Account (IRA).

When corporate bonds are sold, you may be required to pay either a short- or long-term capital gains tax on the bond's appreciation. If a corporate bond is purchased at a premium, it is possible that the premium can be amortized on your tax return until the bond's maturity date. Consult a tax advisor before investing in corporate bonds.

CHAPTER 6

U.S. Treasury Securities, Agency Bonds, and U.S. Savings Bonds

When tax revenues are not sufficient enough to cover its expenses, the U.S. government issues bonds. Bonds help pay for operating expenses during times of shortfall, and for large infrastructure projects such as the building of highways. They also pay for the costs of going to war. During economic recessions the government's shortfall can be substantial, as tax revenues drop and the need for services increases. The U.S. government and its agencies issue a variety of high-quality bonds, bills, and debt notes, raising hundreds of millions of dollars every year.

The bonds, bills, and notes issued by the U.S. Department of the Treasury are backed by the full faith and credit of the U.S. government and are considered the safest investments in the world, with the lowest default, event, liquidity, and political risk. U.S. Treasury bonds, bills, and notes are **marketable**, or **transferable securities**, meaning that after purchase they can be resold to other individuals or entities.

All U.S. Treasury debt instruments are sold in **book entry** form. An investor's purchase is recorded under his or her name in the accounting records of banks or brokerages or directly with the U.S. Treasury if the bond is purchased through the **Treasury Direct program**, a book-entry system operated by the U.S. Bureau of the Public Debt. No certificate of ownership is issued, but the investor receives a statement confirming the purchase.

All Treasury securities are now issued with a minimum face value of $100 and in subsequent increments of $100. The three most common types of Treasury securities are:

- **Treasury Bonds**: 10- to 30-year maturity

- **Treasury Notes:** 2, 5, and 10-year maturities

- **Treasury Bills:** Under 1 year maturity

U.S. Treasury Notes and Bonds

U.S. Treasury notes and bonds both pay interest to bondholders every six months and are initially sold at auction. Monthly auctions are held for the two- and five-year notes. Auctions for the 10-year notes and for the 10- to 30-year bonds are held quarterly (See *Chapter 19: Buying and Selling Bonds*).

All fixed-income, buy-and-hold investors should consider owning Treasury notes and bonds because of their safety and liquidity. U.S. Treasury issues are in demand among investors all over the world and are highly traded on a daily basis. This trading frequency makes it easy to follow the prices of U.S. Treasury notes and bonds, which are posted in the financial pages of newspapers, on television, and on Web sites such as **www.investinginbonds.com** and **www.bloombergs.com**. The 10-year and 30-year Treasury bonds are quoted as benchmarks for all fixed-income securities.

The interest received from U.S. Treasury Bonds or notes are subject to federal income tax, but exempt from state and local income taxes. This makes them particularly attractive to investors living in states with high income taxes. Interest is taxable in the year it is received. The exception is zero coupon bonds where interest is paid at maturity, but the proportion of interest earned, but not paid, in a given year is taxed in that year. If a bond is purchased at a price lower than face value, the difference may be taxable as interest income over the period that the bond is held. If a bond is purchased at a price above face value, the difference may be deductible from the bondholder's taxable income over the period that the bond is held. Sellers of Treasury notes and bonds must report the interest accrued up to the date of sale on their federal income tax returns. The tax exemption increases the after-tax yield of U.S. Treasury securities compared to taxable bonds and allows the Treasury to offer lower interest rates.

Longer-term Treasury notes and bonds are more vulnerable to market risk and inflation risk. Interest rate fluctuations affect their prices in the secondary market. Inflation lowers the purchasing power of the principal over time. To compensate for these risks, long-term Treasuries offer higher interest rates. Thirty-year Treasury bonds have the longest maturity of any of the U.S. issues and typically offer the highest interest rates.

Prior to 1985, the U.S. Treasury issued 30-year bonds with call dates five years before maturity. In 2000 and 2001, when the government was running budget surpluses, these bonds were retired and bondholders were forced to give up an annual coupon rate of 14 percent. All Treasuries issued since 1985 have been non-callable. The size and frequency of long-term bond issues declined significantly in the 1990s and early 2000s. As the U.S. government used its budget surpluses to pay down the federal debt in the late 1990s, the 10-year

Treasury note began to replace the 30-year Treasury bond as the general, most-followed metric of the U.S. bond market. On October 31, 2001, the U.S. federal government stopped issuing the well-known 30-year Treasury bonds (often called **long bonds**). In response to demand from pension funds and long-term institutional investors, and to the need to spread the Treasury's debt obligations over a longer time period, the 30-year Treasury bond was re-introduced in February 2006 and is now issued quarterly. A lower interest rate also lowered the cost of long-term borrowing.

Treasury notes and bonds can be sold or transferred in partial lots; an investor holding $20,000 in Treasury bonds can sell $5,000 and keep $15,000 of them, as long as they are sold in $1,000 increments. They can also be used as collateral for a low-cost loan from a brokerage.

U.S. Treasury Bills

U.S. Treasury bills, known as **T-bills**, are used to finance the short-term needs of the U.S. government. Treasury bills have short maturities of 4, 13, 26 and 52 weeks, and though technically not bonds, they offer similar opportunities to investors. Treasury bills with maturities of 4, 13, and 26 weeks are sold at weekly auctions; those with maturities of 52 weeks are sold every four weeks. Treasury bills are issued on the Thursday following the date of sale, and mature on a Thursday. T-bills are sold at a discount to their face value. They are **zero coupon bonds**; they do not make interest payments like regular bonds. Instead, the investor is paid the face value of the bill at maturity, and the difference between the price paid for the bond and its face value, or the price received for the bill if it is sold before it reaches maturity, is treated as "interest income." Interest income from T-bills, like interest income from Treasury bonds and notes, is exempt from state and local income taxes. The overall yield of T-bills is low in comparison to other cash investments such as corporate bonds, certificates of deposit (CDs), and money market funds.

Treasury bills have such short maturities that they do not fluctuate much in price. An investor selling a bill before it matures will receive a price somewhere between what was paid for the bill and its face value; there is little likelihood of a loss. The four-week T-bills are probably the safest investment possible. Prices of T-bills are quoted in decimals rather than in fraction form. T-bills are popular with individual investors because of their simplicity and affordability. They are sold in increments as small as $100. In a single auction, an investor can buy up to $5 million in bills by non-competitive bidding or up to 35 percent of the initial offering amount by competitive bidding.

Cash management bills are issued for extremely short-term debt, usually only a matter of days.

STRIPS

STRIPS, or Separate Trading of Registered Interest and Principal of Securities, is a unique partnership between the private sector and the government. Brokerage firms buy eligible Treasury notes and bonds, and sell their individual interest and principal components separately to investors as zero coupon bonds. Each trade is registered with the Treasury, making STRIPS securities into direct debt obligations of the U.S. government.

For example, a Treasury note with a maturity of ten years consists of a single principal payment, due at maturity, and

20 interest payments, one due every six months for ten years. When this note is stripped (converted to STRIPS form), each of the 20 interest payments and the principal payment becomes a separate security. In the Treasury's commercial **book-entry** system, each interest payment and the principal payment becomes a separate zero-coupon security, with its own identifying number, and can be held or traded separately.

Brokers sell each component to investors at a discount to its face value. The investor is paid the face value when the interest payment or principal becomes due, and the difference between the price and the face value is the "interest" received. Prices are determined by market interest rates at the time of sale, and the amount of time remaining to maturity. For a bond to be "stripped," its components must have face values in increments of $100.

Interest earned on STRIPS must be reported in the year in which it is earned, and inflation adjustments to principal on **TIPS** (Treasury Inflation-Protected Securities) must also be reported in the year earned, even though the investor may not receive the funds until maturity.

STRIPS are attractive investments for tax-deferred accounts, such as IRAs and 401(k) plans, and for non-taxable accounts, including pension funds. They are popular with investors who want to receive a known amount of income on a specific date. Every investor in STRIPS receives a report each year displaying the amount of STRIPS interest income from the financial institution, government securities broker, or government securities dealer that maintains the account in which the STRIPS are held.

TIPS

To counteract the **inflation risk** associated with low-coupon **Treasury bonds, Treasury Inflation-Protected Securities (TIPS)** were introduced on January 29, 1997. The interest rate, which is set at auction, remains fixed throughout the term of the security, but the face value of the security is regularly adjusted for inflation, so that the amount of each semi-annual interest payment may vary. The inflation-adjusted principal will be paid at maturity.

TIPS are sold at auction in 5-year, 10-year, and 20-year maturities, in increments of $100. The five-year TIPS are auctioned in April, and as re-openings in October. The ten-year TIPS are auctioned in January and July and as re-openings in April and October. The 20-year TIPS are auctioned in January, and as re-openings in July. The reopened security has the same maturity date and interest date as the original security, but has a different issue date and usually a different price. Semiannual interest payments are based on the inflation-adjusted principal at the time the interest is paid.

The index for measuring the inflation rate is the non-seasonally adjusted U.S. City Average All Items Consumer Price Index for All Urban Consumers (CPI-U), published monthly by the Bureau of Labor Statistics (BLS). If the **Consumer Price Index** rises, the face value of TIPS increases and so does the amount of the interest payment. If deflation occurs and the Consumer Price Index drops, the face value of TIPS decreases. At maturity, TIPS will be redeemed at whichever is greater: the inflation-adjusted principal or the original principal.

The interest payments from TIPS are exempt from state and local income taxes. Federal income tax must be paid on the interest income in the year that payments are received. The inflation adjustment credited to the bonds is also taxable each year, even though the increased principal will not be paid out until the TIPS reaches maturity. This tax treatment means annual cash receipts from TIPS will actually be lower until the bond is redeemed. During a period of no inflation, the face value of a TIPS will remain the same, and the investor will receive the interest and pay federal income tax on it just as though it were a regular bond. If inflation causes the face value of the TIPS to rise, the investor will now receive a larger interest payment to account for the reduced purchasing power of the dollar. Nevertheless, the investor must pay income tax on the higher amount of interest as well as on the increase in the face value of the TIPS, lowering the overall cash flow received from the bond for that year. Investors in higher income tax brackets should hold TIPS in tax-deferred accounts to avoid unexpected surprises. When the TIPS reaches maturity, the investor will be paid a larger amount of principal to account for inflation.

The U.S. Treasury provides TIPS Inflation Index Ratios on the TreasuryDirect Web site (**www.treasurydirect.gov/instit/annceresult/tipscpi/tipscpi.htm**) to allow investors to easily calculate the change to principal resulting from changes in the Consumer Price Index.

Investors are attracted to TIPS as a hedge against inflation and as a means of preserving capital. A person nearing retirement, for example, could put $100,000 into ten-year TIPS and be secure that those savings will not lose purchasing power over time. The greatest investment risk associated with

TIPS, especially those with shorter maturities, is **opportunity loss**. TIPS have lower interest rates than other investments because they offer additional protection within their portfolios due to the inflationary protection that is offered. If there is little or no inflation during the life of the security, the investor will have forfeited the opportunity to make higher returns with another investment.

> ### TIP: TIPS Should Make Up No More Than 30 Percent of Your Investments
>
> Though TIPS offer protection against inflation, their low rate of return makes them a poor source of income. There are many other bond investments that offer a higher yield and are still relatively secure. Reduce inflation risk by putting a portion of your portfolio in short-term bonds with higher yields and regularly reinvesting.

In addition to offering protection against inflation for investors, TIPS serve as a useful information source for monetary policy makers: the interest-rate differential between TIPS and conventional U.S. Treasury bonds is what borrowers are willing to sacrifice in order to avoid inflation risk. Changes in this differential indicate that market expectations concerning inflation have changed. Because the market both contributes to inflation and responds to it, this information can help in making decisions about interest rates.

U.S. Savings Bonds

U.S. savings bonds are direct obligations of the U.S. Treasury. They can be purchased online directly from the U.S. Treasury, or from agents of the U.S. Treasury such as banks and brokerages. Unlike other government debt obligations, U.S. savings bonds are not marketable; they cannot be purchased from or resold to other investors. They can only be liquidated by having them redeemed by an agent of the U.S. Treasury. Investors can hold the bonds to maturity, or redeem them prior to maturity. There are several types of U.S. savings bonds: I Bonds, Series EE Bonds, and Series HH Bonds.

U.S. savings bonds are the most widely held security in the world. They have the reputation of being a simple, straight-forward investment, but in reality, they are quite complex. Their structure has changed numerous times over the years. The most recent change was in 1995, when EE savings bonds began to be issued with a fixed interest rate instead of a variable (floating) rate. Until then, it was impossible to predict exactly what the return on an EE bond would be. I Bonds still have a variable interest rate which can change every 6 months. The U.S. Treasury Web site (**www.TreasuryDirect.gov**) offers detailed information on all savings bonds.

Interest income from U.S. savings bonds is exempt from state and local taxes, but is subject to federal income tax in the year that the bond is redeemed.

I Bonds

"I" stands for "inflation." I Bonds are inflation-indexed savings bonds sold directly by the U.S. Treasury and through financial institutions and some payroll savings plans. I Bonds are sold at face value. Paper I Bonds are offered in $50, $75, $100, $200, $500, $1,000, $5,000, and $10,000 denominations, and can be bought electronically to the penny in amounts over $25 (for example, $35.25). An individual cannot purchase more than $60,000 of I Bonds in a single year.

Like TIPS, I Bonds have a fixed interest rate, but it is combined with an inflation rate adjustment linked to the **Consumer Price Index for Urban Consumers (CPI-U)** to produce a composite rate that determines the interest paid. Every May and November, the Treasury announces the interest rates for I Bonds to be sold during the following six-month period. The fixed rate that is in effect during the period when a bond is purchased remains in effect for the 30-year life of that bond. At the same time, the treasury announces an inflation rate adjustment which determines the interest paid on I Bonds for the next six months. I Bonds increase in value on the first of every month when interest is added to the principal, and compounded semiannually. Interest accrues until the bond is redeemed. In times of deflation, the composite rate may be lower than the fixed rate, and the value of the bond will increase slowly or not at all. A safety provision guarantees that the composite rate will never drop below zero.

I Bonds have a 30-year maturity, but can be cashed in anytime after the first 12 months of ownership. If the I Bond is cashed in before five years of ownership, the investor must forfeit the last 3 months of interest as a penalty.

Unlike the interest accrued on a zero-coupon bond, the accrued interest on I Bonds is not taxed as income until the bonds are redeemed. This makes them an attractive investment for a taxable account, since the interest income will compound unchecked until the bond is redeemed, like the interest in a tax-deferred IRA account. I Bonds are subject to federal and state gift tax, estate, and inheritance taxes.

> ## TIP: I Bonds Do Not Guarantee a Minimum Level of Earnings
>
> In times of deflation, the composite rate of return on an I Bond may drop. Deflation occurs only rarely, but when it does, the value of an I Bond will not increase in value, or will increase very little.

Series EE Bonds

Series EE savings bonds have a maturity of 30 years. Every May and November, the U.S. Treasury announces a fixed interest rate that will apply to all EE bonds purchased during the following period. EE savings bonds are sold electronically at face value in any amount of $25 or more. Paper EE bond certificates are sold at half their face value and offered in $50, $75, $100, $200, $500, $1,000, $5,000, and $10,000 denominations. Paper EE bonds will not be worth their face value until they mature. An individual cannot purchase more than $30,000 of EE bonds in a calendar year.

The rules regarding EE savings bonds are different depending on the date when the bonds were purchased. EE bonds purchased between May 1997 and April 30, 2005, earn a variable rate of return that is 90 percent of the average yield on 5-Year Treasury securities for the preceding six months. The interest rate is announced every six months, on May 1 and November 1. These bonds are guaranteed to reach their face value in a maximum of 17 years, and promise a minimum compounded interest rate of 4.2 percent for that 17-year period. The redemption value of the bond increases every month when the interest is added.

EE bonds purchased on or after May 1, 2005, earn a fixed interest rate for the 30-year life of the bond. The interest accrues monthly and is **compounded** semiannually. The interest rate for the first 20 years is fixed at the date of purchase, and will be automatically extended for the remaining 10 years unless the Treasury announces different terms. EE Bonds have a one year holding requirement and then a penalty of three months' interest if they are redeemed before five years from the date of purchase.

EE bonds are an attractive investment because they can be redeemed at any time after they have been held for 12 months, and never decline in value. The U.S. Treasury guarantees that an EE bond will at least double in value after 20 years. If this does not occur through applying the fixed interest rate for twenty years, the U.S. Treasury will make a one-time adjustment at maturity. Like I Bonds, interest on EE series savings bonds accrues and is not taxed as income until the bond is redeemed.

Series EE bonds are subject to federal and state gift, estate, and inheritance taxes.

Series HH/H Bonds

As of September 1, 2004, the U.S. Treasury stopped issuing Series HH savings bonds. HH bonds (20-year maturity) and H bonds (30-year maturity) could only be acquired by trading in at least $500 in EE bonds or reinvesting the proceeds of matured HH/H bonds. HH bonds pay out interest every six months at a rate fixed on the date of purchase. This rate was locked in for a period of 10 years, to be re-set on the tenth anniversary of the bond purchase. HH bonds can be redeemed at face value any time.

Interest from HH bonds must be reported as income in the year in which it is received and is not subject to state and local income taxes. Investors who exchanged EE bonds for HH bonds are allowed to continue deferring federal income tax on the interest from the EE bonds until they redeem the HH bonds. This could result in a large income tax liability in the year that the HH bonds are redeemed, if the EE bonds were held for a long time and accumulated a substantial amount of interest.

TIP: Consider Taxes Before Cashing in Your HH Savings Bonds

HH bonds acquired after January 1, 1993 are earning only 1.5 percent interest and should be cashed in so that the principal can be reinvested at a better rate. If you are cashing in HH bonds which you acquired by trading in EE series bonds, be careful that the interest accrued on the EE bonds does not bump you into a higher tax bracket.

TIP: Savings Bonds Could be as Tax-Efficient as Tax-Free Municipal Bonds

If you are able to meet all the requirements, EE or I savings bonds could be as tax-efficient as tax-free municipal bonds, and may bring in a higher rate of return. It is difficult, though, to anticipate whether you will be able to take advantage of the education benefit 10 or 20 years down the road. Will you or your spouse be enrolling for a college or postgraduate degree or certification 10 or 15 years from now? According to current IRS rules, a child who receives more than $3,300 in scholarships, job income, or work-study income in a calendar year cannot be claimed as a dependent on your tax return. A family with a lower income that qualifies for need-based financial aid, or whose child earns a merit-based scholarship, may not be able to take advantage of this tax exemption because their child does not qualify as a dependent.-

U.S. Agency Bonds

Bonds issued by U.S. government agencies or government-sponsored enterprises (GSEs) are called agencies or agency securities. GSEs, with the exception of Federal National Mortgage Association and **Federal Home Loan Mortgage Corporation** (which the federal government took over in July 2008), are private sector companies affiliated with, but separate from, the U.S. government. Five GSEs are currently active:

Federal Farm Credit Bank (FFCB)

Established in 1916, the **Federal Farm Credit Bank** provides loans, credit and services to farmers, homeowners in rural areas, and agricultural cooperatives. Bonds are sold for a minimum of $5,000, and above that in increments of $1,000. Bond issues are exempt from state and local taxes. (**www. farmcredit-ffcb.com**)

Federal Home Loan Bank (FHLB)

Founded in 1932, the **Federal Home Loan Bank** is a system of twelve regional banks regulated by the Federal Housing Finance Agency that facilitate extension of credit to provide access to housing and improve communities. Bond issues are exempt from state and local taxes. (**www.fhlbanks.com**)

Federal Home Loan Mortgage Corporation (Freddie Mac)

Founded in 1970, **Freddie Mac** is a corporation traded on the NYSE that provides a continuous flow of funds to mortgage lenders by purchasing mortgage loans and using them as collateral for mortgage-backed securities. Freddie Mac is chartered to provide a secondary market for residential mortgages. Mortgage interest passed through from mortgage-backed securities is fully taxable as income. (**www. freddiemac.com**)

Federal National Mortgage Association (Fannie Mae)

Fannie Mae was founded as a government agency in 1938 as part of Franklin Delano Roosevelt's New Deal to create a secondary mortgage market and provide liquidity to fund residential mortgages. In 1968, Fannie Mae was converted into a private corporation traded on the NYSE, and a new **Government National Mortgage Association (GNMA, Ginnie Mae)** became the guarantor of government-issued mortgages. Mortgage interest passed through from mortgage-backed securities is fully taxable as income. (**www.fanniemae.com**).

Tennessee Valley Authority (TVA)

The **Tennessee Valley Authority (TVA)** is a federally owned corporation created by congressional charter in May 1933, as part of the New Deal, to develop the Tennessee Valley region. Interest from TVA bonds is exempt from local and state taxes. TVA bonds are not obligations of the U.S. government. (**www.tva.com**).

Student Loan Marketing Association (Sallie Mae®)

The **Student Loan Marketing Association (Sallie Mae)** was a GSE until 2004, when it became a fully private corporation. Bonds issued by Sallie Mae before 2004 still have the status of agency bonds. (**www.salliemae.com**).

Government National Mortgage Association

The **Government National Mortgage Association (GNMA,** also known as **Ginnie Mae),** founded in 1968, is a U.S. government-owned corporation within the Department of Housing and Urban Development (HUD). Ginnie Mae provides guarantees on mortgage-backed securities (MBS) backed by federally insured or guaranteed loans, mainly loans issued by the Federal Housing Administration, Department of Veterans Affairs, Rural Housing Service, and Office of Public and Indian Housing. Ginnie Mae securities are the only MBS that are guaranteed by the U.S. government. (**www. ginniemae.gov**)

Most agency bonds pay a fixed rate of interest twice a year. About 75 percent of them are non-callable, or bullet bonds. Some agencies also issue **no-coupon discount notes**, called **discos**, with a maturity of one year or less. These are sold at a discount to their face value, and the investor receives no interest until maturity, when the face value is paid out. Discos are purchased mostly by institutional investors. Agency bonds with variable interest rates pegged to a benchmark such as the three-month T-bill are called **floaters**. Another type of agency bond, called a **step-up**, offers an interest rate that increases regularly according to a pre-set schedule. Step-ups offer protection against interest rate risk, but they are typically callable. Agency bonds are not sold at auction like Treasuries, but their issuers try to follow the Treasury market closely.

Only a few agency bonds carry the full guarantee of the U.S. government. The slightly higher credit risk means that these bonds offer slightly higher returns than Treasuries. Agency bonds offer some diversity because their underlying securities, mostly mortgages, behave differently from other industry sectors during economic fluctuations. Agency bonds are issued to fund government initiatives such as farming subsidies, but by far the largest portion are pass-through mortgage securities that support affordable-housing loans to middle- and low-income families. As of early 2008, Fannie Mae and Freddie Mac owned or guaranteed more than $5 trillion in mortgage-backed securities (MBS) and debt, almost half of the $12 trillion U.S. mortgage market.

GSE bonds do not carry the "full faith and credit" of the U.S. government, but they are considered almost as safe as U.S. Treasury issues. Because these issues play an important role in the economy, investors assume that the government will not let GSEs fail. This assumption was justified on September 7, 2008, when the director of the **Federal Housing Finance Agency (FHFA)** announced a decision to place Fannie Mae and Freddie Mac into a conservatorship run by the FHFA. At the same time, the U.S. Treasury made a commitment to invest as much as $200 billion in preferred stock and extend credit through 2009 to keep the GSEs, which had lost a combined total of $14.9 billion, solvent and operating. Concerns in the market about their ability to raise capital and finance additional mortgage debt threatened to disrupt the U.S. housing financial market. The Housing and Economic Recovery Act of 2008, signed into law on July 30, 2008, established the FHFA with expanded regulatory authority over Fannie Mae and Freddie Mac, and authorized the U.S. Treasury to advance funds, when necessary, to stabilize Fannie Mae, or Freddie Mac. The law raised the Treasury's national debt ceiling by $800 billion, to a total of $10.7 trillion, so that it would have additional capacity to support Fannie Mae, Freddie Mac, or the Federal Home Loan Banks if needed. (See *Chapter 9: Mortgage-Backed Bonds* for more information on pass-through mortgage securities.)

Other U.S. federally related agencies that issue bonds include the Private Export Funding Corporation (PEFCO) and Export-Import Bank (Eximbank). Eximbank is backed by the full faith and credit of the U.S. government and PEFCO bonds are guaranteed by Eximbank.

> ### TIP: Agency Bonds are More Expensive than Treasuries
>
> The returns from agency bonds are moderate, so it is crucial that expenses are kept low. Unlike U.S. Treasuries, which can be bought directly from **TreasuryDirect.com**, agency bonds must be bought and sold through a brokerage that charges a commission. If you are investing small amounts of $1,000 to $10,000 the sales commissions may be so large that they wipe out your returns for several years. If you are investing less than $50,000, a bond mutual fund or Treasuries are a better choice. If a large portion of your portfolio is devoted to fixed-income, though, you may be able to realize slightly higher returns with agency bonds than with Treasuries.

Supranational and International Government Bonds

Supranational and international institutions, such as the World Bank, also issue debt securities to raise funds for their lending activities. These agencies issue bullet (non-callable) securities, callable bonds, and floating rate debt through a variety of formats including formal debt issuance programs, competitive auctions, and negotiated underwritings. Many Yankee bonds are issued by foreign governments and government agencies.

Canadian bonds are issued by federal government agencies and Crown corporations. The federal government directly guarantees bonds issued by the Federal Business Development Bank (FBDB) and the Canadian Mortgage and Housing Corporation (CMHC). Provinces guarantee bonds issued by provincial Crown corporations such as Ontario Hydro and Hydro Quebec.

CHAPTER 7

Municipal Bonds

Municipal bonds are issued by state and local governments or by special public entities such as school districts, utilities, and water boards to pay for projects like the construction of schools and hospitals, power plants, toll roads, bridges, airports, and sewage treatment plants. Municipal bonds have a low rate of default and are considered second only to securities issued by the federal government as safe investments.

Interest received from municipal bonds is exempt from federal income tax and, in many cases, from state and local taxes. This feature makes them popular with individual investors. Municipal bonds are the only sector of the bond market that is dominated by private investors rather than institutional investors. According to the December 2007 Federal Reserve Flow of Funds Report, at the end of 2007, including indirect ownership through mutual funds and closed-end funds, 54 percent of the total U.S. municipal bond market ($1.4 trillion out of $2.6 trillion) was held by individual households.

In addition to security and exemption from taxes, municipal bonds offer a predictable stream of income and a wide selection of maturities, bond qualities, and issuers in different geographical locations. Most municipal bonds (munis) are issued at face value with a fixed coupon rate and maturity and make semi-annual interest payments. They are typically issued in denominations of $5,000. Municipalities tend to issue what are called serial bonds. Instead of a single maturity in an offering like a corporate term bond, a serial offering splits the amount of the financing into separate annual maturities with bonds typically maturing annually over a 30 year period, so that the municipality does not have all the debt coming due at the same time. The advantage to the investor is that there is more choice of maturities to ladder the portfolio.

Tax Advantages

The exemption of interest on municipal bonds from federal income tax makes them particularly attractive to investors in the highest income tax brackets and retirees who are not able to claim other types of tax deductions. In most states, interest income received from securities issued by government entities within the state is also exempt from state and local taxes. Some states extend that exemption to income from municipal bonds issued in other states. Interest income from securities issued by U.S. territories and possessions is exempt from federal, state, and local income taxes in all 50 states. This allows state and local governments to pay less to borrow money.

Municipal bonds typically offer lower interest rates than corporate bonds, but when tax benefits are taken into consideration, the municipal bonds yield greater after-tax income. Municipal Spotlight (Municipal Market Commentary, January 2008, (**http://financialservicesinc.ubs.com/staticfiles/ pws/adobe/municipal_bond_market_commentary.pdf**) calculates that an investor in the highest federal income tax bracket would receive more after-tax income from a municipal bond offering 65 percent or more of the yield of a taxable bond with a similar maturity and credit risk.

Several Web sites offer calculators to help you compare the returns on taxable and non-taxable bonds. You can use the following formula to calculate the **tax equivalent yield**, which incorporates the savings from not paying taxes, of a municipal bond:

Tax Equivalent Yield =	$\dfrac{\text{Tax-free yield of municipal bond}}{1 - \text{Your income tax rate}}$

U.S. Treasury bonds are exempt from federal taxes, but are subject to state and local income taxes. To compare a U.S. Treasury bond to a municipal bond, it is necessary to calculate the tax equivalent yield of the Treasury bond:

Tax Equivalent Yield =	$\dfrac{\text{Tax-free yield of U.S. Treasury bond}}{1 - \text{Your state or local income tax rate}}$

Not all interest from municipal bonds is tax exempt. During the 1980s, tax reforms restricted the tax exemption to bond issues that fund "essential" projects. The interest on bonds issued to finance projects such as the construction of sports arenas or convention centers is subject to the **Alternative Minimum Tax (AMT)**. Some of these bonds may be exempt from state income taxes in the state where they are issued. Most issues of taxable municipal bonds are bought up by institutional investors and are, therefore, difficult for private investors to buy and sell.

> ## TIP: Munis Are Not for Everyone
>
> Investors in low income tax brackets, and those holding their investments in tax-deferred accounts, do not benefit in the same way from the tax savings offered by municipal bonds, and should look for investments that offer a higher rate of return.

Categories of Municipal Bonds

Municipal bonds can be categorized according to their purpose. Public purpose bonds are issued directly by state or local government entities to fund projects such as schools, sewage treatment plants, and roads. Nongovernmental purpose bonds fund projects that are associated with the private sector or serve a more restricted segment of the public, such as hospitals or university dormitories. Interest income from both of these categories is exempt from federal, state, and local taxes.

Private activity bonds are associated with projects that are not managed by state and local governments, such as airports, stadiums, and industrial parks. If more than 10 percent of the proceeds from a bond issue will be used for private trade or business, or if more than 5 percent of the proceeds will be loaned to private entities, the interest is subject to the Alternative Minimum Tax (AMT). Taxable munis offer yields similar to comparable corporate bonds, and are a good choice for investors who are not subject to the AMT.

Knowing which category a bond belongs to helps you to better understand the risks associated with the bond, and to maintain diversity in your portfolio by making sure it does not overlap with other investments.

CASE STUDY: MUNICIPAL BONDS AND BOND COUNSEL

The following is an excerpt from Public Bonds (**www.publicbonds.org**), a project of the Corporate Research Project of Good Jobs First. The Corporate Research Project helps non-profit organizations understand the worlds of business and finance. Good Jobs First promotes openness and accountability in economic development practices. The creation of Public Bonds was made possible by a grant from the Open Society Institute.

Public Bonds is edited by Philip Mattera, Research Director of Good Jobs First and Director of the Corporate Research Project.

"Every municipal security must be reviewed by a lawyer or law firm known as bond counsel. The legal opinion is an authorization of the debt and covers two main issues:

1. It ensures that the bonds are legal, valid and binding obligations of the issuer.

2. It verifies the tax status of the debt; that is, interest on the bonds is exempt from federal income taxes (as well as state and local taxes in some cases.

The practice of including a legal opinion developed after the massive defaults on municipal bonds issued for financing railroads in the late nineteenth century. Issuers who wanted to avoid their debt repayment obligations justified their actions by saying that the bonds had not been properly issued or authorized under existing laws. After the railroad defaults, issuers and underwriters started to include the opinion of bond counsel to restore investor confidence, which later became a requirement as capital markets became more complex.

Valid authorization of debt is one of the most important functions in the process of issuing and managing debt. The opinion of bond counsel is a form of assurance, in theory, for issuers and investors that all legal requirements are met. In reality, there have been cases in which bond counsel has been held liable for authorizing questionable debt.

In the case of the Washington Public Power Supply System's (WPPSS) 1983 default on $2.25 billion in bonds, bond counsel Wood Dawson Smith and Hellman as well as special counsel Houghton Cluck.

CASE STUDY: Municipal Bonds and Bond Counsel

Coughlin and Riley were held liable. A report by the Securities and Exchange Commission found that despite signs of legal difficulties with some of the provisions in the issuance and the lack of legal precedent on the issue, the firms issued an unqualified opinion on the bonds without determining the legality of the agreements. What also shocked the bond world was that the Wood Dawson agreed to pay bondholders only $500,000 to settle its portion of the massive class action lawsuit. The sum was considerably smaller than the $7.25 million that special counsel Houghton Cluck agreed to pay. The difference in the figures was because Houghton Cluck had malpractice insurance but Wood Dawson did not."

Types of Municipal Bonds

General Obligation (GO) Bonds

General obligation bonds are issued by states and municipalities that have the authority to raise taxes. They are considered the safest municipal bonds because they are backed by the full faith, credit, and taxation authority of the issuer. Some issuers of GO bonds, such as large metropolitan areas with low levels of debt and many sources of income, have a stronger economic foundation than others. Unlimited tax GO bonds (UTGO bonds) are backed by a state or municipality's full taxation authority. Limited tax GO bonds (LTGO bonds) have a limited taxation authority, such as when voters agree to a small raise in real estate tax to support school construction.

General obligation bonds are ranked among the safest bonds and typically have high credit ratings. GO bonds are most secure when the economy is doing well because the government collects more tax revenue. The greatest risk associated with GO bonds is that overall tax revenues will decrease during an economic recession.

Revenue Bonds

Revenue bonds are backed by the revenue, such as tolls, user fees, or leases, which will be generated by the project funded by the bond issue when it is completed. Revenue bonds are considered to entail more risk than GO bonds, but each bond should be considered on a case-by-case basis. A revenue bond issued to support an electrical utility owned by a large city may have a better credit rating than a GO bond issued by a small town with a weak tax base. Revenue bonds issued to support private institutions, such as hospitals, are more risky, because the revenue base of the obligor and their power to raise revenue is more limited than a government's tax raising ability. Many revenue bonds are issued through a municipality, by the ultimate obligor. Make sure you confirm the ultimate obligor on the bond you buy. If it is a hospital bond being issued by a city, which is acting as a conduit, and the hospital goes bankrupt, the issuing city is not responsible for payment.

The credit rating for a revenue bond takes into account the economic conditions that might affect the project's future ability to generate revenue, and the business risk involved in that particular industry.

Who Issues Revenue Bonds?

Authorities

Municipal revenue bonds are issued by various agencies and entities. Authorities are governmental conglomerates that issue bonds for transportation, housing, water and sewage, and other purposes. The first authority to issue bonds in the United States was the Port of New York Authority (now known as the Port Authority of New York), formed in 1921. During the 1960s, they became prevalent as revenue bonds began to replace GO bonds for many purposes.

Bond Banks

State bond banks are financial entities organized to help smaller municipalities within a state sell bond issues and lower their financing costs. Bond banks sell their own bonds and use the proceeds to purchase the bonds of the smaller municipalities; the bonds of the smaller municipalities typically secure the bonds of the bond bank.

Lease Rental Bonds and Certificates of Participation (COPs)

Some municipal bonds are issued to build facilities which are then leased to a municipality such as a school district, city, or even a State. The income from these leases is sufficient to pay interest and principal on the lease-backed bonds or COPs. At maturity, the state often has the option to purchase the facility for a nominal fee. Unlike general obligation bonds, the funds to pay the underlying leases need to be appropriated annually. There may be times when budgets are tight or political opposition may prevent the money from being appropriated. In these cases, the revenue stream for these securities goes away.

Certificates of Participation (COPs)

COPs are similarly backed by lease payments, though they are legally different from bonds. A COP is a tax-exempt lease purchase agreement, created to finance capital improvement projects or to purchase essential equipment that is divided and sold to multiple investors in fractions, typically in $5,000 denominations. Each certificate represents a proportional interest in the payments that will be made by the county government. Most COPs receive investment ratings from a rating agency. Occasionally, a county may insure its COPs rather than seek a credit rating.

Special Tax Districts

Special tax districts are sub-governmental entities created to provide specific services such as sewage, water, libraries, garbage collection, and fire protection to residents of a particular community or area. The special taxes are included in residents' property tax bills. Special tax districts are administered by elected commissioners. Bonds issued by special tax districts are more prone to default than traditional munis because the issuing entity is small and has less economic resources to pay its debt then a typical municipality.

CASE STUDY: GOVERNMENT BORROWING FOR PUBLIC CAPITAL AND DEFERRED TAXATION

The following is an excerpt from Public Bonds (**www.publicbonds.org**), a project of the Corporate Research Project of Good Jobs First. The Corporate Research Project helps non-profit organizations understand the worlds of business and finance. Good Jobs First promotes openness and accountability in economic development practices.

The creation of Public Bonds was made possible by a grant from the Open Society Institute. Public Bonds is edited by Philip Mattera, Research Director of Good Jobs First and Director of the Corporate Research Project.

"Rather than being financed by current taxes, public sector capital is often financed by borrowing through capital markets. The most common means of borrowing for the government is by issuing bonds that are sold to the public (individuals and institutions). General obligation bonds are backed by the full faith and credit of the government, require voter approval, and are subject to statutory debt limits. The other widely used bonds for public capital are lease-revenue bonds, which are payable exclusively from the revenues generated by the project and are an extension of the pay-as-you-use philosophy. Lease-revenue bonds do not require voter approval and are not subject to statutory debt limits.

CASE STUDY: GOVERNMENT BORROWING FOR PUBLIC CAPITAL AND DEFERRED TAXATION

When a government borrows money from the public by selling bonds, the government makes a commitment to repay the principal and the interest accrued over the life of the bond. In order to fulfill its obligation of repayment, the government will need future sources of revenues.

This could come from future taxes or additional borrowing. But eventually some taxes or fees will have to generate the needed revenue for repaying the bond debt. In this sense, bond financing for public capital or other forms of public spending is actually deferred taxation, which shifts the burden of taxation for financing public goods to future taxpayers. The level of government debt is particularly important because interest payments on debt constitute a significant share of total expenditures at all levels of government.

In other words, expenditures in a government budget arising from bond debt repayment (both principal and interest) are obligations on present taxpayers that were decided in the past. If a government decides to renege on its payment obligations for debts incurred by a previous government or defaults on its payment for some other reason, the public project would continue to provide public benefits to all current and future generations. Because of these equity and efficiency concerns, bond financing is politically sensitive."

Types of Revenue Bonds

Revenue bonds are issued for many purposes by a variety of issuers. All revenue bonds are not the same. Each type of revenue bond offers unique advantages, has its own structural characteristics, and is associated with certain types of risk.

Education Bonds

Education bonds are issued to fund charter schools, school construction, and university and college expansions. Charter schools are private schools that receive funding from local school districts and from the federal Department of Education. Their purpose may be to relieve overcrowding in public schools or to serve a special group of students, such as students with disabilities or students pursuing a particular field of study. As of 2008, over one million students were enrolled in more than 3,500 schools in 40 states plus the District of Columbia and Puerto Rico. (See **www.uscharterschools.org/ pub/uscs_docs/o/history.htm**). Unlike public schools, charter schools sometimes go out of business due to fiscal disorder or poor management. Charter schools may fund construction through a lease issued by a building corporation or a local authority. Funds are raised through student fees and local and federal government grants.

College and university bonds are typically issued through the auspices of a state authority, and are secured by various sources of income: government grants and private endowments, student housing rents, research contracts, and income from sporting events or entertainment. The issuing authorities are issuing conduits and provide no credit support to the bonds; they are simply a vehicle for issuing bonds and/or receiving tax-exemption. The most highly-rated bonds are those issued by well-known universities with sizable endowments.

Higher education bonds are considered an essential part of any conservative portfolio. Schools offer diversity because they have little correlation with other types of bonds or with the stock market. The greatest risk for higher education bonds is fiscal management and the possibility that, for whatever reason, student enrollment will decrease, cutting back on tuition, state funding, and revenue from fees. For colleges and universities, there is also the risk that during an economic decline, people will no longer be willing to pay the high costs of tuition. Small private colleges may see a decline in enrollment. Public state colleges and universities, which charge lower tuition and are able to offer more scholarships and financial aid, can also rely on indirect taxpayer support through contributions from their respective states.

> **TIP: Junior Colleges Are Not the Same as Community Colleges.**
>
> Community colleges are public, while junior colleges are private institutions. The privately funded debt of a junior college is not as strong a credit risk as the publicly funded debt of a community college.

Entertainment Industry

Entertainment debt, which is one of more speculative sectors in the municipal market, funds the construction of convention centers, sports arenas, golf courses, casinos, and cultural centers, and is repaid with usage fees and, in some cases, dedicated tax revenues. Local municipalities undertake projects such as these as a means of attracting visitors and stimulating local business, which in turn results in increased tax revenue.

The risk is that during an economic slump, income from both user fees and tax revenues will decrease. The successful operation of entertainment facilities is tied to the economic strength of business as a whole, so entertainment bonds have a substantial correlation to the stock market. Another risk is that local officials, excited by the publicity surrounding an entertainment project, may overestimate the economic impact of the finished project on the community and the revenue it will generate. For example, in recent years, the convention business has begun to decline as companies use new forms of communication to sell their products and achieve their goals. A completed convention center may not attract as much business as anticipated and fall short of its revenue projections.

Entertainment bonds are also issued to build tribal casinos. Because Native American tribes have the legal status of sovereign nations, it may be difficult to collect a debt if a dispute arises.

Health Care and Hospital Bonds

Bonds to build new health facilities, such as hospitals, nursing homes, and **continuing-care retirement communities (CCRCs)**, and to upgrade and buy new equipment for existing facilities, are issued through conduit authorities much like lease rental and some higher education debt. Just like lease rental and higher education bonds, responsibility for repaying debt rests entirely with the health care facilities for whom the bond was issued. Nursing home and CCRC bonds are frequently unrated.

Health care debt is considered risky. The health care industry is unstable because of rising costs, the health insurance crisis, and the rise of managed care programs. If a hospital goes into default it will probably be liquidated or sold, resulting in almost total loss of bond value. Standard & Poor's® study of defaults on bonds during the 1990s revealed that nursing home bonds had the highest rate of default. At the same time, aging baby boomers are creating an increased demand for CCRCs, and America's elderly population is growing.

Health care bonds often contain extraordinary call provisions, in addition to regular calls, and may have sinking funds. This exposes buy-and-hold investors to higher reinvestment risk.

> ### TIP: Research Non-Rated Bonds Carefully
>
> Bond issuers normally pay one or more credit rating agencies to rate a bond. Many bonds issued for CCRCs and nursing homes are unrated, either because they are below investment grade, or because the issuers are creditworthy borrowers but do not want to face the time and expense of being reviewed by a rating agency. Without the input of a credit rating agency, the burden is on the investor to learn as much as possible about the issuer of an unrated bond and the health service industry as a whole.

Housing Bonds

Three kinds of bonds support the creation of single- and multi-family housing units for the poor and elderly. State housing agencies issue bonds, some of which are federally insured, for builders of multi-unit apartment buildings for the elderly. Those without federal insurance may be risky.

Bonds are also issued by state agencies to purchase single-family mortgages from banks. These are backed by mortgage revenue and insured by the Federal Housing Administration (FHA) or the Department of Veterans Affairs (VA). Since 1944, the VA has backed more than 18 million home loans worth $911 billion. In 2007 alone, loans valued at nearly $24 billion were issued to approximately 135,000 veterans, active-duty service members, and survivors. The FHA has been insuring home loans since 1934 and is the largest mortgage insurer in the world. Some single-family mortgage bonds are further backed by a moral obligation pledge from the state that issues them. In some cases, the bond also carries insurance against damage and loss of the purchased properties, and contractors insurance to protect the investment from any errors made by contractors during construction. This insurance, coupled with the rigorous underwriting standards of housing agencies, minimizes the risk of default.

Local housing authorities issue bonds for the building of multi-family apartments. The U.S. Department of Housing and Urban Development (HUD) subsidizes rent payments for qualified individuals. Many of these bonds for multi-family housing are also backed by federal insurance and sometimes private insurance, and are given an A to AA rating. There is always a risk that HUD may suspend rent subsidies if apartments remain unoccupied for more than a year or if the housing authority fails to comply with HUD regulations. If a housing bond is issued in anticipation that HUD will pay a certain amount in subsidies, and the full amount is not appropriated, there might not be enough funds available for interest payments. A highly rated bond has safeguards against this eventuality.

As with any mortgage-backed bonds, there is always the risk that housing bonds may be called prematurely and because of this risk, investors require a moderately higher yield to compensate for the risk of having to reinvest the call proceeds at lower rates. Housing bonds are subject to extraordinary calls that may be exercised at any time, for example, if the issuer does not use all the funds raised by the bond issue, or if mortgages backing the bond are paid off. When interest rates drop, many mortgages may be retired and refinanced at lower rates. When mortgages are paid off, the bonds are called in. Housing bonds with maturities of 20 to 30 years that are likely to be called in much sooner are known as "**supersinkers**."

Housing authorities also issue some taxable debt that is subject to the AMT. Taxable bonds offer a higher coupon rate in compensation. Investors who are prepared to handle early and unpredictable calls may be attracted by the higher coupon rates of long-term housing bonds. If the bond is not called early, the ample interest payments will continue over a long period of time. When interest rates begin to decline, certain areas of the United States will experience early calls sooner than others, depending on economic factors and the policies of state housing authorities.

> ### TIP: Do Not Buy Housing Bonds at a Premium
>
> Housing bonds should be bought at close to or below face value because of the possibility that they may be called in early. If a bond is paid off soon after it is purchased, the buyer may not receive enough interest payments to make the investment profitable.

Public Power Bonds

A public power bond is debt issued by a public power agency such as the Municipal Electric Authority of Georgia. Interest on public power bonds is typically exempt from federal income tax. Interest and principal payments are derived from revenues generated by the sale of electricity.

Moody's gives some 300 public power electric utilities an average rating of A2, citing the historical stability of the credit quality of the public power sector. U.S. public power electric utilities are rated according to a number of factors: market position, local government credit characteristics, governance and management, financial position and performance, debt and capital plan, and covenants and legal framework, including debt service reserve and other required reserves.

Utility bonds fund a basic need to supply communities with power. Power agencies have a near-monopoly as providers of electricity, and are able to set their rates to meet debt obligations. They are supported by the local governments that sponsor them and are not under pressure to make a profit, as a private company would be. The ability to issue tax-exempt bonds gives them low-cost sources of financing.

Public power bonds are somewhat vulnerable to political changes and the enactment of government policies that might limit the rates they charge for electricity or impose other restrictions. They are also subject to extraordinary calls, like other revenue bonds, that could result in principal being returned much earlier than expected.

Tobacco Bonds

On November 23, 1998, 46 states, the District of Columbia, and various U.S. territories, cities, and counties entered into a **Master Settlement Agreement (MSA)** with the four largest U.S. tobacco manufacturers: Philip Morris, R.J. Reynolds Tobacco, Brown & Williamson Tobacco, and Lorillard Tobacco. To compensate the states for the cost of medical care related to illnesses caused by smoking, the tobacco manufacturers agreed to make five initial payments, ranging from $2.4 billion to $2.7 billion per year through 2003, and annual payments ranging from $4.5 billion to $9 billion per year, beginning in 2000 and continuing in perpetuity. The amount of the annual payments is determined by several factors, primarily domestic cigarette consumption.

State governments wanted immediate access to the funds promised by the tobacco settlement, so they created special authorities to **securitize** the anticipated revenue by issuing tobacco bonds. As of April, 2008, public borrowers had sold more than $32 billion of these bonds backed by the 1998 settlement. In 2007 alone, approximately $16 billion of tobacco bonds were issued as states looked for ways to make up shortfalls in their budgets. Interest and principal on **tobacco**

bonds is repaid either wholly or in part with income from the tobacco settlement. States use the money from tobacco bond issues to fund health care and to pay for other essential items in the state budget when tax revenues are not sufficient.

Governments that issue bonds against their future MSA receipts benefit by receiving a large sum of money that can be used for capital spending or any other purpose. The issuance of tobacco bonds is not subject to voter approval or debt caps. Depending on how the debt is structured, rating agencies usually exclude tobacco bond debt from a government's normal debt ratios, as long as the there is no legal recourse back to the state.

Tobacco bonds, which do not have a supplemental source of security, tend to be rated in the Baa/BBB range because the bondholder is, in essence, directly taking on the business risks faced by the tobacco companies, such as litigation, competition from smokeless products, and reduced demand resulting from negative advertising and smoking cessation programs. There is a risk that the MSA payments may diminish or be interrupted if Americans smoke less or a tobacco manufacturer goes into bankruptcy. If U.S. cigarette consumption decreases, so do the payment obligations of the tobacco manufacturers. If one tobacco manufacturer defaults on a payment, the others are not required to make up the difference. If an individual or a group wins large punitive damages in a lawsuit against a tobacco company, that loss will reduce the company's profits for that year. A provision of MSA is that the states themselves are responsible for collecting compensation from tobacco companies that are not part of the settlement. There is a danger that the tobacco companies may have legal grounds to break the agreement if they determine that the states have not complied with this requirement.

Not all tobacco bonds rely entirely on MSA receipts to pay the interest on a bond issue. Arkansas, for example, has issued revenue bonds that depend on tobacco revenue for only 5 percent of their interest payments. The stronger revenue stream for these bonds resulted in the bonds being rated in the AA category. California issued tobacco bonds that are rated in the A category. This rating reflects a supplemental annual appropriation pledge of the state which is not as concrete as the supplemental pledge in the Arkansas bonds, thus, the lower rating. Remember that annual appropriation is not an irrevocable guarantee. The state legislature still has to vote annually to appropriate funds to pay the bonds if the MSA revenue is insufficient.

Tobacco bonds typically offer a higher yield than many other revenue bonds because they are secured by a more risky revenue stream and have litigation risk. Some tobacco bonds have extraordinary call features that may result in early and unexpected redemption, and individual investors that do not have the sophisticated analytics to value the call probability, should not buy bonds trading above the potential redemption value which is usually the face value. Tobacco bonds tend not to be as liquid as other types of revenue bonds.

Transportation Bonds

Transportation authorities issue revenue bonds to finance every aspect of transportation, including the construction and upgrading of airports, ports, roads, and highways, and the establishment of bus systems and commuter train lines. Transportation bonds cover a full range of credit quality, from start up toll roads without any revenue generating history, to mature urban transportation systems like the New York City Metropolitan Transportation Authority. The most important factor in evaluating a transportation bond is how the bond will be repaid.

There are two types of highway revenue bonds: toll road bonds and public highway improvement bonds. Toll road bonds are repaid from the revenues collected at tollbooths set up along the highways. Public highway improvement bonds are repaid with a combination of gasoline taxes and fees charged for automobile registrations and driver licenses. While costs of construction and maintenance have rapidly increased, taxes and fees have failed to keep pace, and states and localities must look elsewhere for financing to solve their traffic problems. Recently, some states have formed private-public partnerships to build and finance roads.

The Federal Highway Administration (FHWA) administers the Federal-Aid Highway Program, which distributes federal funds, mostly from the federal gasoline tax, to state Departments of Transportation for the construction and maintenance of the National Highway System. Since 1995, the Federal Highway Administration has expanded the circumstances under which it will reimburse states for debt that finances eligible highway projects. Federal reimbursements cover many aspects of debt financing, including insurance and the costs of preparing the initial bond issue. Many states now issue bonds called Grant Anticipation Revenue Vehicles (GARVEEs) or Grant Anticipation Notes (GANs), backed by future disbursements of federal funds. These bonds are guaranteed by the fact that the projects for which they have been issued are eligible for federal funds, and not by the U.S. government itself. Because Congress appropriates funds for the Federal Highway Administration every six years, GARVEEs with shorter maturities are considered better credit risks than those with longer maturities.

Once a highway project is selected for bond financing, it is submitted to the responsible FHWA Division Office for approval as an advance construction (AC) project under section 115 of Title 23. A project with the AC designation that follows correct Federal-Aid Highway Program procedures will preserve its eligibility to receive future Federal-Aid funds to reimburse debt-related costs. At the time the project agreement is signed, the state decides whether to seek federal reimbursement for debt-related costs, or reimbursement for construction costs.

Train and bus systems rely on usage fees and on federal grants and local government subsidies to repay debt. Typically, train fare collections can only support less then 50 percent of the operating budget of one of these systems. Therefore, the federal and local government grants are an important source of revenue. Given the importance of many of these transportation systems to their local economies, there is a high probability that these grants will be annual appropriated; however, in tough economic times, when tax revenues go down, these subsidiaries may come under pressure. An investor should make sure that the system issuing the bonds is essential and that there are no political controversies surrounding the issuer which could hurt their ability to get the necessary governmental subsidies.

Revenue to repay airport bonds comes from ticket fees paid by airline passengers; usage fees including those paid by airlines, airport restaurant and concession fees, parking fees, and fueling fees; and rent paid for the use of hangars and terminals. Since 2000, a series of airline bankruptcies and restructurings has reduced the traffic at some airports. The uncertain future of the airline industry has increased the cost of financing for airports and increased the yield on airport bonds.

The transportation industry is subject to a number of vulnerabilities, including a drop in revenue during economic slowdowns, escalating costs, competition from new technologies and from neighboring facilities, and fluctuations in government policy. Some public projects such as commuter bus and rail systems are unable to pay for themselves and depend on subsidies. Each transportation bond must be judged on its own merits.

Water and Sewer Bonds

Water and sewer bonds are generally regarded as being among the safest municipal bond investments because they support services that everyone needs and expects to pay for. A municipality or group of closely associated municipalities normally issues these bonds, but they may also be issued through an authority, a state bond bank, or a water conservancy district. Revenue to repay water and sewer bonds comes from usage fees, connection fees, and assessment fees. Sometimes these bonds may have an additional pledge of tax revenue. These are called double-barreled bonds, because of the two revenue sources. If the project is funded by a federal grant or a state bank, it will be subject to federal and state oversight of the project.

The credit ratings of water and sewer bonds are determined by the economic strength of the service area as well as the financial flexibility and management of the system. Debt issued for new systems are more of a risk than existing ones which issue debt for projects to repair or upgrade the system, reflecting the unknowns and lack of operating history of the new system.

Water revenues can be affected by conservation programs, or by legislation that lowers consumption fees. Utilities may also be affected by natural disasters such as drought or flooding which force them to seek additional sources of water.

Short-Term Notes

Anticipation notes, or **short-term notes**, are issued when municipalities need to raise interim financing until a future (anticipated) source of revenue is secured. They are usually issued at face value and pay interest when they reach maturity. Most anticipation notes mature in less than a year; a few mature in 18 months and offer an interim interest payment before maturity. Common types of anticipation notes include **tax anticipation notes (TANs), revenue anticipation notes (RANs)**, tax and **revenue anticipation notes (TRANs)** and **bond anticipation notes (BANs)**.

Moody's and Standard & Poor's rate short term notes using a different scale than is used for longer term municipal funding:

Credit Ratings for Short-Term Municipal Notes	
Moody's	
MIG 1	Superior credit quality. Excellent protection is afforded by established cash flows, highly reliable liquidity support, or demonstrated broad-based access to the market for refinancing.
MIG 2	Strong credit quality. Margins of protection are ample, although not as large as in the preceding group.

Credit Ratings for Short-Term Municipal Notes	
MIG 3	Acceptable credit quality. Liquidity and cash-flow protection may be narrow, and market access for refinancing is likely to be less well-established.
SG	Speculative-grade credit quality. Debt instruments in this category may lack sufficient margins of protection.
Standard & Poors and Fitch	
SP-1 and F-1 SG	Strong financial backing; Will be given a SP-1+ or F-1+ rating if financial backing is undeniably strong.
SP-2 and F-2	Issuer has satisfactory, but not outstanding, capacity to pay principal and interest
SP-3	SP-3 Issuer has only speculative capacity to pay principal and interest.
F-3	Issuer has merely adequate capacity to pay principal and interest, and changes in relevant conditions could easily cause these issues to be of speculative quality.
F-S	Capacity of issuer to pay principal and interest is speculative.
D	Fitch assigns this rating to issues which are in actual or imminent payment default

A **variable-rate demand note**, also called a **floating-rate note** or **floater**, is a very short-term note with typically a 7-day or 28-day effective maturity, but sometimes longer through the ability of the investor to irrevocably put the bonds back to the issue. These notes are meant for institutional investors like tax-exempt money market funds. The interest rate on the notes are reset periodically based on prevailing rates in the money market for similar duration instruments.

Pre-Refunded or Escrowed Bonds

Just like you would refinance the mortgage on your home, municipal bond issuers can take advantage of lower interest rates and issue new lower coupon bonds to replace the existing bonds previously issued in the higher interest rate environment. Even if they are not callable, the bonds can be refinanced by what is called pre-refunding or escrowing the bonds. This involves the issuer taking the proceeds from the new issuance, or what is called the refunding bond, and buying U.S. Treasuries or Agencies directly guaranteed by the U.S. government. These securities are placed in an irrevocable escrow which is held by a third-party trustee. An accounting firm is hired to verify that the cash flow off of the securities is adequate to pay the principal and interest on the bonds and a Bond Counsel is retained to verify that the structure meets all legal requirements. Once this is done the bonds now assume the credit quality of the U.S. government and can be rated AAA by the rating agencies.

If a BBB bonds gets pre-refunded, and is now of AAA quality, the price will appreciate noticeably and the holder will profit.

Call Provisions

Many revenue bonds have call provisions that give the issuer the option of refinancing their debt in the future if interest rates drop. Some municipal bonds have **fixed call options**, with a first call between five and ten years after their date of issue, after which they can be called with a 30-day notice. Some have **extraordinary calls** that are exercised only if specific catastrophic situations arise or if funds become available early to pay off the debt. Housing bonds can be called at any time if mortgages are paid off early.

As discussed in the section on risk, call provisions mean reinvestment risk: the possibility that the income you expect to receive from regular interest payments will end prematurely if the bond is called before its maturity date, and that you will be forced to reinvest your capital at a lower interest rate. This is especially significant for the type of investor most likely to invest in municipal bonds: an individual in a higher tax bracket who wants to preserve capital while receiving a regular stream of income.

Sinking Funds

A municipal bond issuer may have a sinking fund, into which it regularly deposits funds with a trustee to pay off a bond issue. Each year, the trustee uses the sinking fund to retire a portion of the bond issue. The trustee purchases bonds in the secondary market if their price is below face value. If the market price is above face value, the bonds are redeemed from bondholders at a predetermined price. The bondholders whose bonds are to be recalled are selected by a lottery. An investor in a bond with a sinking fund cannot know whether he or she will hold the bond until it reaches maturity or be forced to redeem it an early date.

There is a high likelihood that holders of bonds with sinking fund provisions will be forced to redeem their bonds prior to maturity, even if market-wide interest rates remain unchanged. In contrast, a bond with a call provision will only be called if interest rates drop.

A sinking fund call is much like the principal component on your home mortgage. It is a way for the issuer to gradually pay-down debt instead of having a lump-sum or "bullet payment" at the end of the loan. From a debt management perspective, it is important to have sinking funds, or serial maturities which were previously mentioned in Chapter 7, so that a municipal government does not have to dramatically increase taxes in the case of a general obligation or fees in the case of a revenue bond to pay off a maturity.

Risks Associated with Municipal Bonds

Municipal bonds secured by a general obligation pledge or taxes and related revenues are a comparatively low-risk investment. Default rates on municipal bonds have been historically low because state and federal governments frequently provide assistance to municipalities in risk of default. Recent government reforms require oversight of troubled municipalities, the implementation of generally accepted accounting principles (GAAP), and tighter controls on funds raised through bond issues. Small issuers like special tax districts are the riskiest in the tax-backed category, given their small size. Health care related and start-up toll-roads bonds can be the riskiest in the revenue bond area. Additionally, there are enterprise bonds issued in the municipal market for such things as aquariums, water parks ,and convention centers. These tend to be the riskiest types of municipals given their nonessential nature.

Uncertainty Regarding Support from State and Federal Governments

There are no specific guidelines defining exactly how a state or federal government can or should assist a financially troubled municipality. During difficult economic times, state budgets may be depleted and resources may not be available for bailouts or temporary financing. Federal decisions on whether to intervene may be based on whether the financial crisis is perceived to be a threat to national economic stability.

Dependence on a Restricted Source of Revenue

A bond issue backed by revenue from a specific source or a restricted tax initiative is vulnerable to the effects of a natural disaster, political event, or economic downturn. For example, the September 11th attacks caused a decline in tourism and in airport revenues, and bonds in those industries were consequently downgraded. Hurricanes, floods, or forest fires may completely disrupt the economy of a municipality, and diminish its tax base. A political candidate may raise opposition to a sales tax and cause voters to demand a tax cut.

Fiscal Imprudence and Excessive Debt

Politicians are generally not experts in finance. They may make unwise decisions or cave in to demands from employee unions, overspending, and mismanage local finances, leaving their successors to deal with the consequences.

A municipality may take on a greater load of debt than its tax base or revenue source is capable of paying for. Mounting overall debt and interest payments are a sign that a municipality is in trouble. Its bonds may be **downgraded**, affecting their price on the secondary market.

Insurance

As of September 30, 2007, more than half of all U.S. municipal bonds ($1.5 trillion) were insured. Bond issuers purchase insurance from one or more of nine U.S. companies that provide protection against credit defaults. **Municipal bond insurance** guarantees that interest and principal will be paid as scheduled, should the issuer default. Each guarantee is unconditional and irrevocable and covers 100 percent of interest and principal for the full term of the issue. A bond may be insured in the **primary** or **secondary market**. If an insured bond defaults, the insurer will immediately step in and make the scheduled payments. Bond insurance shields investors not only from defaults and downgrades, but from other risks such as environmental hazards and natural disasters, including hurricanes, earthquakes, floods, and tornadoes that might affect a municipality's ability to meet its debt obligations.

Purchasing bond insurance automatically raises the **credit rating** of a municipal bond, lowering the interest rate which the issuer must pay to sell the bond, and making the bonds attractive to a wider range of investors. Bond insurers carefully assess the financial health of bond issuers and typically insure only higher-grade bonds. They also limit the amount of insurance that an individual bond issuer can purchase. Two bonds from the same issuer may have different credit ratings; one rated AAA because the bond is insured, and one reflecting the underlying credit quality of the issuer. The most secure bonds are those that are insured and also have a high underlying credit rating.

Bond insurers are themselves rated on their financial strength and ability to pay out claims. Before the stock market slump of 2007 and 2008, most of the bond insurance companies had the highest AAA-credit rating, and this rating transferred to the municipal bonds insured by them. During the first half of 2008, as the value of their holdings declined, some of these companies suffered financial losses and their credit ratings were downgraded. This affected the market price and **liquidity** of the municipal bonds they guarantee. Because municipal bonds are a comparatively safe investment, even without insurance, these credit downgrades should not affect investors who intend to hold municipal bonds until maturity.

TIP: Insurance does not make a Bad Investment Good

While insurance protects an investor from loss and raises the credit rating of a bond, it does not improve the quality of the underlying investment or reduce the risk of default.

Insurer	Claims Paying Ability as of 7/29/2008		
	Moody's	S&P	Fitch
AMBAC Assurance Corporation	Aa3	AA	na
Assured Guaranty Corp. (AGC)	Aaa	AAA	AAA
CIFG Assurance North America, Inc.	Ba2	A-	CCC
Financial Guaranty Insurance Company (FGIC)	B1	BB	CCC
Financial Security Assurance Inc. (FSA)	Aaa	AAA	AAA
MBIA Insurance Corporation	A2	AA	na

Insurer	Claims Paying Ability as of 7/29/2008		
XL Capital Assurance	B2	BBB-	CCC
Radian Asset Assurance	A3	A	na

Municipal Bond Credit Ratings

Municipal bonds are assigned ratings similar to those assigned to corporate bonds. Most municipal bonds are rated investment-grade, though the quality varies. Credit rating agencies use different criteria to assess municipal bonds than are used for corporate bonds. Many factors are taken into consideration, including historical growth of tax receipts, stability of cash flow to pay expenses, regional economic conditions, existing debt, and any past defaults.

It would take years of experience to understand all the variables that affect a particular municipal bond's credit quality and to compare it to other available municipal bonds. Despite the expertise of the rating agencies, individual investors should do their homework on the issuer of the bonds and get comfortable with the issuer's financial stability.

Interpreting the Data

Municipal bonds are sold to individual investors in the **over-the-counter** market, through a network of brokerages. Your broker may notify you when a municipal bond that fits your investment criteria becomes available, or you can request a broker to purchase municipal bonds of a particular type.

Information on bonds offered for sale is available directly from brokerages, or you can search the listings that brokerages post online. The following page shows an example of a listing of municipal bonds.

State	Moody	S&P	Qty	Description	Coupon	Maturity Date	Yield to Maturity
1-FL			65	BAKER CNTY FLA HSP AUTH REV	4.8	12/01/2009	4.79
2-AL	Aaa	AAA	25	JEFFERSON CNTY ALA SWR REV CAP	5	8/1/2012 PRE	3.10
3-PR	Aa3	AA	5	PUERTO RICO COMWLTH INFRASTRUCT	5.5	7/1/2015	4.00
4-GA	Aaa	AAA	15	ACWORTH GA HSG AUTH REV MULTI-	6.125	3/1/2017 AMT	5.82
5-CA	Baa1	BBB+	435	CALEXICO CA UNI SCH DIST G.O.	0	8/1/2028	6.00
6-PR	Aaa	AAA	25	PUERTO RICO COMWLTH HWY/ TRAN REV	5	7/01/2032	5.00
7-CA	Aa3	AA	20	RIALTO CALIF REDEV AGY TAX ALLOC	7.5	9/01/2037	7.37
8-MO	A2	AA-	755	KANSAS CITY MO SPL OBLIG DWNTWN	5.25	4/1/2040	5.40

AMT=Subject to   AMT C=Yield to Call   PRE=Pre-Refunded

The **State** column tells in which state the bond was issued. This is important because you may be exempt from taxes on income from municipal bonds issued within your state. The **Moody** and **S&P** columns show the credit ratings assigned by those two agencies. Bond #1 is unrated; Bond #5 has the lowest credit rating on the list. The **Quantity** column tells how many of the bonds are held in the brokerage's inventory. The **Description** tells whether the bond is issued by a state, city, or other authority. The end of each description tells something about the type of bond. For example, bond #5 is a **general**

obligation bond (GO), bond #6 is a transportation revenue bond, and bond #1 is a hospital revenue bond. On a brokerage Web site, each bond name or description links to a page with details including the bond's **CUSIP** number, information about call provisions, insurance, settlement date of the trade, and the way in which the bond sale will be documented.

Maturity date is the date on which the bond will be retired and the principal returned to the investor. "PRE" next to the maturity date for Bond #2 tells that it is **prefunded**, meaning that the investor is certain to receive interest and principal because funds have already been set aside for this purpose. "AMT" next to the maturity date of Bond #4 indicates that interest income from this bond is subject to federal **alternative minimum tax.**

The coupon is the fixed interest rate, expressed as a percentage of the face value of the bond. Bond #5 is a zero coupon bond, which will make no interest payments until maturity, when the investor will receive both principal and accrued interest. Yield to Maturity is the expected return on the bond if it is purchased at the current market price and held to maturity (See Chapter 3: The Fundamentals of Bond Investing: Calculating Yield). **Yield to Worst** is the expected return on the bond if it is purchased at the current market price and redeemed at the earliest call date. Notice that the Yield to Worst for Bond #4 is -6.89. More detailed information reveals that the first call date is only a month away and that the call price is 101, lower than the current market price for this bond. An investor who purchases this bond today would receive no interest payments and would lose money on the purchase price if the bond is called on its first call date. The "C" next to **Yield to Worst** shows that this bond has a call provision. Bond #6 also has a call provision, but it is selling at par (face value), first call is four years away, and the call price is equal to face value.

An investor who bought the bond today would receive eight semi-annual interest payments, amounting to exactly 5 percent of face value, before the first call date. Its **Yield to Worst** is therefore equal to its **coupon rate**.

Price: Bonds sold in the over-the-counter market are usually sold in $5,000 denominations. In the secondary market for outstanding bonds, prices are quoted as if the bond were traded in $100 increments. Thus, a bond quoted at 98 refers to a bond that is priced at $98 per $100 of face value. The price you see on a municipal bond listing, especially one that is not actively traded, is a price that is derived by industry pricing providers, rather than the **last-trade price** (as is customary with stocks) or the exact price that you will pay for the bond. Actual bond prices include fees or commissions and vary from broker to broker.

The Securities Industry and Financial Markets Association (SIFMA) displays a detailed history of each bond's trading activity on its Web site **(www.investinginbonds.com/ marketataglance.asp?catid=32)**. Information about a specific bond can be found by entering its CUSIP number in the search box. Click on the number of trades to see the dates on which trades occurred, the quantities that were traded, the prices at which they traded, and whether the trade took place between dealers or with a customer. The trading history gives a better idea of the price an investor will pay for the bond. The calculations page shows yields and the exact amount of interest a bondholder will receive while the bond is held.

CHAPTER 8

International Bonds

I nternational bonds are fixed-income securities that are issued by foreign entities to international investors. They are normally structured similarly to U.S. debt securities.

Many investors now include international bonds in their investment portfolios to increase diversity, hedge against the devaluation of the U.S. dollar, and capitalize on the growth of developing economies.

Additional Risks Associated with International Bonds

Though international bonds present attractive investment opportunities, bonds issued by entities outside the United States are subject to additional risks that investors must take into consideration.

Sovereign risk is the risk that a foreign government will default on its bonds. The U.S. government guarantees repayment of its bond obligations, based on its authority to tax the people of the United States. Other governments may not have the same authority, or their economies may become so constrained that they do not have the resources to meet their obligations.

Currency risk is the risk that the value of a foreign currency will rise relative to the U.S. dollar, causing the investment to lose value in U.S. dollars, even though the interest rate and price of the bond remains the same. The reverse is also true; if the value of a foreign currency falls against the U.S. dollar, the value of an investment in that currency will increase.

Political risk is the risk that political developments such as civil strife, war, a change of government, or a coup d'état will weaken an economy or undermine contractual agreements. There is no guarantee that a new government will honor the debt issued under a previous regime to which it is hostile.

Banking risk is the risk associated with foreign banks, and includes the possibility that banks in other countries may fail due to bad management or poor fiscal policy, or that the banks in a foreign country may not have enough liquidity in U.S. dollars to make payments to American investors.

Economic structure risk is the risk that the economic structure of a country will jeopardize the development of its economy or that changes in economic structure will affect business. Bonds issuers may default if it becomes impossible to complete the projects that the bonds were intended to finance.

Emerging Market Bonds

Emerging market bonds are issued by foreign companies and countries with limited financial markets and an increased risk of political crisis and economic instability. Emerging market bonds are characteristically not issued in U.S. dollars and are, therefore, subject to additional currency risk. Bonds issued by the governments of nations in Latin America, Southeast Asia, and Eastern Europe carry an increased sovereignty risk and offer higher yields as compensation.

Yankee Bonds

Yankee bonds are bonds issued by foreign companies, governments, and supranational organizations in U.S. dollars and trade in the U.S. markets. Yankee bonds include bonds issued by Canadian provinces and utilities, supranational agencies like the World Bank, and sovereign bonds issuers such as Mexico and Sweden, in addition to corporate bonds. Yankees offer diversity and less correlation to the U.S. stock markets, while offering a wide verity of names and levels of credit quality and potential yield.

Supranational Bonds

Supranational bonds, issued in U.S. dollar denominations, are designed to promote the economic health of developing countries and are backed by a minimum of two other foreign countries.

CHAPTER 9

Mortgage-Backed Bonds

Mortgage-backed securities (MBS) have increased in popularity over the past few years. In 2000, the MBS market overtook the market for U.S. Treasury notes and bonds and, with over $4.5 trillion of securities outstanding, is now the largest fixed-income market sector in the world. Most major fixed-income investors allocate a significant portion of their portfolios to MBS.

There are three sectors in the MBS market: loans backed by residential mortgages, loans backed by mortgages on multifamily residences, and loans backed by mortgages on commercial properties. Bonds backed by mortgages on commercial properties are typically sold only to institutional investors. Residential MBS can be categorized by their credit rating, and by their issuer/guarantor. Approximately 75 percent of MBS are guaranteed by the government-sponsored enterprises Fannie Mae and Freddie Mac, or by Ginnie Mae, and consequently have AAA ratings. (See *Chapter 6: U.S. Treasury Securities, Agency Bonds, and U.S. Savings Bonds: Agency Bonds*). The other 25 percent are issued by private financial institutions or brokerages and are guaranteed either by their issuers or by subordination to a more senior debt obligation. Most of these also have AAA ratings, although some have lower ratings due to the types of mortgages of which they are constituted, or the financial status of the issuer.

How Mortgage-Backed Bonds Work

Individuals take out mortgage loans from banks to purchase homes or multi-family residences. Rather than simply collecting the monthly payments of interest and principal, banks package a quantity of mortgages with similar interest rates and maturities into a **mortgage pool** and sell the collective debt to government agencies or brokerages. Mortgage pools commonly range from $25 million to $50 million, although some are smaller and some are much larger. In this way, banks recoup their capital immediately and are able to offer more loans to their customers.

The agency or brokerage then sells shares of the mortgage pool on a **secondary market** to individual investors in increments of $1,000 or more with a coupon rate that is typically 50 basis points (0.5 percent) lower than the interest rate on the mortgages. Each investor receives his or her share of the monthly interest and principal payments. The agency receives its commission of .05 percent.

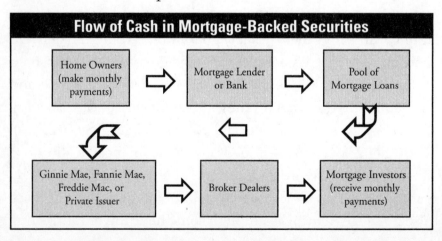

Flow of Cash in Mortgage-Backed Securities

Mortgage bonds are structured either as **pass-throughs** or as **collateralized mortgage obligations (CMOs)**, also known as **real estate mortgage investment conduits (REICs)**. The majority of mortgage-backed bonds are pass-throughs that pass monthly interest and principal payments from underlying loans directly to the investor. Collateralized mortgage obligations (CMOs) were first created in 1983 by investment banks Salomon Brothers and First Boston. Legally, a CMO is an independent, special purpose entity that owns a mortgage pool. A CMO mortgage pool is much larger than a pass-through, typically $300 million to $500 million, and consists of a variety of mortgages with different interest rates, maturity dates and credit ratings. A CMO typically sells between 60 and 100 different share classes, providing a way for investors to customize their income stream.

There are nearly 40 types of CMOs, but the majority of individual investors purchase only two types, **sequential bonds** and **planned amortization class (PAC)** bonds. These are both considered **plain vanilla** (the most basic or standard) bonds. A sequential bond has class shares (**tranches**) that absorb principal payments in a sequential order. For example, all payments of principal in the mortgage pool go to holders of Class A shares until those shares are completely paid off. Then, principal payments begin to go to the investors who own the Class B shares, until they are paid off, and so on. Each share class pays interest according to its **average life**. During the period before a share's first principal payment, known as the **lockout**, only interest payments are passed through to the investor. Sequential bonds may have a non-interesting paying, or zero-coupon, Z tranche holding mortgages with the longest maturities. Interest is not passed through to the investor, but accrues until the face value of the bond is reached. When the lockout period ends, both principal and interest are paid out. These bonds have the longest average lives, of 20 years or more, and offer the highest returns.

TIP: Z-Class Securities are Nicknamed "Toxic Waste"
In the bond trade world, Z-class securities are sometimes referred to as "toxic waste" because they contain what is left over after the sounder, short-term mortgages in a pool have been paid off. They are more volatile than other mortgage securities and have poor liquidity. Their risks are difficult to analyze and have complicated tax consequences. Salespeople at brokerages may promote Z-bonds because it is difficult to determine ask and bid prices and they are able to take higher commissions. Be cautious when you are encouraged to buy into a Z-bond investment. Though Z-bonds promise higher returns, they should be regarded as speculative investments.

PAC bonds distribute cash flow according to a fixed principal redemption schedule, reducing investment risk for investors. This is accomplished by transferring nearly all prepayment risk to another class of bonds in the CMO, called **companion bonds** or **support bonds**. The scheduled payments will be met as long as prepayments on the underlying mortgage collateral remain within a specific percentage range, which is called a **prepayment protection band**. The companion or support bonds absorb prepayment excesses from other classes of the PAC or make up for shortfalls. They offer higher yields, but are highly volatile and quickly affected by changes in interest rates.

Fannie Mae, Freddie Mac, and Ginnie Mae

Fannie Mae, **Freddie Mac**, and **Ginnie Mae** guarantee approximately three-fourths of all mortgage-backed securities, and two-thirds of all CMOs. The Federal National Mortgage Association (Fannie Mae) was created in 1938 as part of the

Federal Housing Administration (FHA) to make more money for long-term, fixed-rate mortgages available to prospective homeowners by purchasing these mortgages from banks and creating a **secondary mortgage market**. For the first 20 years of its operation, Fannie Mae purchased mostly mortgages issued to low-income home buyers. By the late 1960s, banks were selling a large portion of their mortgages to avoid interest rate risk. In 1968, the U.S. government split the Federal National Mortgage Association into two legal entities — a share-holder owned, privately managed public corporation that became known as Fannie Mae and the Government National Mortgage Association (Ginnie Mae), a government-owned corporation within the **Department of Housing and Urban Development (HUD)**. In 1970, Congress increased mortgage lending by chartering the Federal Home Loan Mortgage Corporation (Freddie Mac) as a participant in the secondary mortgage market. In 1989, Freddie Mac also became a share-holder owned, privately managed public corporation. The names "Fannie Mae" and "Freddie Mac" were legally sanctioned in 1997. As of 2008, Fannie Mae and Freddie Mac owned or guaranteed about half of the $12 trillion U.S. mortgage market.

In 2008, due to the credit crisis affecting the financial sector, Fannie Mae and Freddie Mac were taken over by the federal government due to concerns over their capital adequacy. How these entities will function going forward and what level of support from the federal government they will receive remains to be seen.

Ginnie Mae does not form mortgage pools, but guarantees, for a fee of six **basis points** (0.06 percent) of the outstanding principal balance, mortgage pools created by approved lenders. These mortgage pools are then sold to a bond dealer in the form of a "GNMA certificate." If a home buyer defaults on mortgage payments, GNMA pays the bond coupon, as well as the scheduled principal payment each month, until the property is foreclosed and makes up for any shortfall. Ginnie Mae's debt obligations are backed by the full faith and credit of the U.S. government. All mortgages in Ginnie Mae pools are insured by the FHA, the Veterans Administration (VA), or another government entity. Ginnie Mae bonds are considered extremely safe investments.

Approximately 25 percent of mortgage-backed bonds are issued by financial institutions such as investment banks. These offer a slightly higher rate of return to compensate for the lack of a direct or implicit guarantee from the U.S. government. They are considered fairly safe when the mortgage originators properly research the ability or mortgage-holders to repay loans and lend only to those who are credit-worthy.

How Mortgage-Backed Bonds Differ from Other Bonds

Other than having a face value and a coupon rate, mortgage-backed bonds behave differently from other types of bonds.

- The owner of a mortgage-backed bond receives monthly payments instead of annual or semi-annual payments. These payments consist of both interest and principal, passed through from the underlying mortgage payments. Mortgage bond yields are converted to semiannual (**bond equivalent**) yields so that they can be compared to other types of bonds.

- The amount of the monthly payments varies as holders of the underlying mortgages make prepayments or pay off their mortgages. As mortgages age, mortgage holders pay larger amounts of principal. When mortgages are paid off, the stream of interest from them ends.

- The prices of mortgage-backed bonds on the secondary market are more vulnerable to changes in interest rates than the prices of other bonds. When interest rates fall, prices of mortgage-backed bonds do not rise as much as Treasuries because prepayments of mortgages increase, shortening their average life. When interest rates rise, price of mortgage-backed bonds fall lower than Treasuries because prepayments of mortgages slow and the average life of mortgage bonds becomes longer. This is called "**negative convexity**." (See the following section *Prepayment and Average Life*.)

- A mortgage-backed bond does not have a fixed maturity date on which all the principal will be returned in a single payment. Instead, it has a fluctuating **average life**, the estimated date by which the principal will all have been repaid.

Prepayment and Average Life

The price of a corporate or a municipal bond is determined by the amount of **credit risk** and **interest rate risk** associated with the bond issue. Mortgage-backed securities are associated with a third risk, **prepayment**. Because prepayment risk is so closely linked to interest risk, it is difficult to create a mathematical model that can be used to accurately determine the value of a mortgage-backed security.

The interest and principal of the mortgage loans underlying a mortgage-backed bond are scheduled to be paid at regular intervals over a specified time. Individual homeowners do not necessarily follow the schedule. In the United States, holders of residential mortgages have the option to pay more than the required monthly payment (**curtailment**) or to pay off the loan in its entirety (**prepayment**) before the maturity date. When interest rates drop, large numbers of homeowners secure a new loan with a lower interest rate to pay off their mortgages, triggering a **refinancing** wave.

Early return of principal reduces the size of the mortgage pool, lowering the amount of interest generated and causing the returns on the investor's original investment to decline. The rate at which prepayment will occur cannot be known with certainty, so bond traders analyze historical data and use an estimated prepayment speed to assign a **weighted average life**, or **average life**, to each bond. **Average life** is the estimated time that it takes to return half of a mortgage pool's principal to the investor.

Most bond traders use the **PSA** (**Public Securities Association**, now called the Securities Industry and Financial Markets Association or SIFMA) standard, or "**prepayment speed assumption**," to calculate average life. The PSA assumes that newer mortgages are less likely to be prepaid than older ones, as new buyers are less likely to move to a different home, less likely to refinance, and less able to make additional payments on their principal. The standard PSA model ("100 percent PSA") starts with an annualized prepayment rate of 0 percent in month 0, increasing by 0.2 percent each month, until it peaks at 6 percent after 30 months; starting with the 30th month, an annual constant prepayment rate of 6 percent is assumed.

Bonds are tested in empirical models that predict how their prepayment rate will vary with interest rate fluctuations. Variations of PSA are expressed in percentages: a 150 percent model means a monthly increase 0.3 percent higher than the standard model, until the peak of 9 percent is reached after 30 months. When interest rates go down, the prepayment speed increases rapidly as homeowners refinance their mortgages, and the average life of a mortgage bond drops. If interest rates go up, homeowners are likely to hold on to their mortgages longer, and the average life increases. Weighted average life is a measure of credit risk; the longer the average life of the bond, the greater the possibility of capital loss through default.

Advantages of Mortgage-Backed Bonds

Mortgage-backed bonds are attractive to investors for several reasons:

- The yield on mortgage-backed securities is often higher than the yield on U.S. Treasuries or other agency issues. Non-agency bonds and CMOs offer even better rates to compensate for the additional perceived risk.

- Mortgage-backed bonds are considered to be some of the safest investments available. Ginnie Mae bonds and CMOs are fully backed by the U.S. government, and government support of Freddie Mac and Fannie Mae is an implied guarantee. Even non-agency bonds are considered safer than other types of bonds because they are backed by real estate as collateral.

- Mortgage-backed bonds pay investors both principal and investment on a monthly basis, unlike other bond types that only pay interest until the bond reaches maturity. They provide a higher current income stream instead of a lump-sum repayment of capital.

- Mortgage-backed bonds provide a degree of diversity in a portfolio because real estate has a lower correlation with the stock market than other industry sectors.

- CMOs are structured to provide a more stable income than regular pass-through bonds. Class A or B shares of a CMO behave almost like regular short-term bond, providing a predictable high monthly income.

- Though CMOs were originally created as investment vehicles for institutional investors and financial institutions, individual investors prefer to invest in them directly rather than indirectly through the CDs and money market accounts offered by these financial institutions.

Disadvantages of Mortgage-Backed Bonds

- The amount of monthly cash flow from mortgage-backed bonds is variable and unpredictable because it is a combination of scheduled interest payments and repayments of principal. Income from mortgage-backed bonds behaves as erratically as the homeowners who hold the mortgage loans.

- **Reinvestment risk** is higher for mortgage-backed bonds because repayment of principal can take place at any time. When interest rates drop, repayment may occur at a rapid pace, and you will be forced to reinvest your capital at lower interest rates. An increase in interest rates causes **extension risk**, the risk that homeowners will extend their mortgages and your capital will remain tied up at the old lower interest rate longer than anticipated. A short-term investment can be lengthened by many years.

- The income from a mortgage-backed bond decreases over time as the mortgages are repaid and the size of the mortgage pool decreases.

- The unpredictability of a mortgage-backed bond makes it difficult to calculate the yield accurately or compare it to the yield-to-maturity of other bonds. An investor purchasing a mortgage bond at a **premium** could lose money if the mortgages are prepaid unexpectedly before enough interest income has been generated to make up the price difference.

- The **collateral** for mortgage-backed securities is mortgage loans taken out by millions of individual homeowners. Mortgage pools are diversified by including thousands of loans of similar size and quality, assuming that only a few individuals in a particular loan sector will default. If a homeowner defaults on a loan, presumably the home can be sold to recoup the capital. This is not necessarily the case, as illustrated by the U.S. **subprime mortgage** crisis of 2008. A number of factors can trigger a wave of defaults on similar mortgages, such as the housing bubble of 2006 - 2008 that artificially inflated home values. Banks are no longer able to find buyers for foreclosed properties. Defaults also incur costs such as foreclosure expenses and bank fees that must be subtracted from the principal.

The primary challenge of investing in mortgage-backed securities is understanding how they work in general, as well understanding the structure of the particular security being purchased. So many simultaneous factors are at work that it is impossible to predict the future of any particular investment. Brokerage salespeople may misrepresent or omit disclosing the dangers of a CMO investment or quote past performance as an indicator of future success. It is very difficult to find information about mortgage-backed bonds and CMOs, even in financial newspapers like *The Wall Street Journal*. Regular daily pricing information is not available.

TIP: Make Sure You Understand What You are Buying

Before buying a mortgage security you should thoroughly understand how it is structured and the risks involved. If you need a steady income stream, the varying monthly payments of a mortgage bond may not be the most suitable investment. Your capital will be returned to you as mortgages are paid off and not in one lump sum at maturity like other bonds. Inexperienced investors may not realize that part of each monthly payment is repayment of capital and may, unwittingly, spend their capital and have little left to reinvest.

Mortgage Bonds and Taxes

Interest income from both agency and privately issued mortgage securities is subject to federal and state income taxes. The **original issue discount (OID)** on zero coupon bonds sold at a discount to their face value is also taxable as income. The portion of a mortgage bond payout that represents repayment of principal is tax free. Your broker will report interest and OID income to you on forms 1099-INT and 1099-OID.

CMOs are complex; the portion of income that is treated as interest is subject to state and federal income taxes and the portion treated as principal is not. If the CMO is originally sold at a discount (OID) part of the discount may be taxed as interest income and part may be taxed as capital gains. Because brokerages receive reports on the tax consequences of CMOs from outside sources, there is a possibility that you might not receive the information in time to prepare your tax returns by April 15th.

> **TIP: Remember to Subtract Trading Costs and Taxes from Yield Calculations**
>
> When comparing the yield of a Treasury bond with that of a mortgage-backed bond, remember that mortgage bonds must be purchased from a brokerage or bond dealer, while Treasuries can be purchased directly from Treasury Direct at no charge. To get an accurate comparison of the two yields, you must take trading costs into consideration. Interest income from mortgage bonds is subject to both federal and state income tax, while income from Treasuries is not subject to state and local taxes.

Mortgage-backed Bonds in Your Portfolio

Mortgage bonds issued by Freddie Mac and Fannie Mae can be purchased for $1,000. Ginnie Mae certificates are sold for a minimum of $25,000. CMOs can be purchased in increments of $1,000, though those created for institutional investors may require a much higher minimum purchase.

Mortgage bonds are considered safe because of the direct or implied guarantee from the U.S. government that their debt obligations will be met, and they offer slightly higher returns than U.S. Treasuries. Unlike Treasuries, the monthly income payments from mortgage bonds can vary widely as principal is prepaid and interest income diminishes. For this reason, they are not suitable if you need a regular fixed monthly income, but might be attractive if you don't care when the money comes in and have the discipline to reinvest your capital instead of spending it. The higher classes of CMOs are structured to offer a predictable regular income, more like other types of bonds.

A considerable investment is needed to properly diversify individual mortgage bonds in a fixed-income portfolio, and they are complex and difficult to understand. If you do not have a large amount to invest in mortgage bonds, or are investing smaller amounts at regular intervals, a bond mutual fund or ETF is a better choice. Whether you are investing in individual bonds or funds, always look carefully at trading costs, load fees, and fund expenses.

Some investors prefer to buy individual $25,000 Ginnie Mae bonds for a large flow of current income. A number of Ginnie Mae mutual funds are available, that offer diversification among Ginnie Mae securities and allow investments in smaller amounts and regular increments.

CHAPTER 10

Bond Mutual Funds

The easiest way to buy bonds is to purchase shares of a bond mutual fund. A bond mutual fund is an **investment pool** in which investors pool their money to purchase a portfolio of bonds. The portfolio is managed by a professional fund manager who buys and sells bonds to maintain the portfolio's investment objectives. Bond mutual funds can be purchased directly from the company sponsoring the fund, or through a broker.

There are four categories of bond funds: **unit investment trusts (UITs), closed-end funds, exchange traded funds (ETFs)** and **open-end mutual funds**. According to the Investment Company Act of 1940, only open-ended funds can call themselves "mutual funds." ETFs are the newest product on the market and are treated separately in Chapter 11.

How Are Bond Mutual Funds Different from Bonds?

When you purchase a bond, you receive annual or semi-annual interest payments until the bond reaches **maturity** or its **call date**, and your capital is returned to you. If you want to cash in your bond before it reaches maturity, you must sell it to another investor on the **secondary market**.

A share of a mutual fund represents a share of ownership in the perpetual portfolio of bonds held by the fund. When you purchase shares in a bond mutual fund you receive monthly pay-outs of interest from bonds in the portfolio and income from the sale of bonds. A bond fund does not have a maturity date; when you want to recover your **capital**, you sell the shares back to the mutual fund. The value of mutual fund shares fluctuates and may be higher or lower on the day you redeem them than on the day you bought them.

When you purchase a bond from a brokerage, you pay the brokerage a one-time commission which is typically included in the price of the bond. If you decide to sell the bond before it reaches maturity, you may also pay a commission to the brokerage to sell it for you. Many mutual funds have a **load fee** or an **exit fee**, essentially a sales commission for the fund company, and incur regular annual expenses such as management fees.

Benefits of Bond Mutual Funds

Diversification

To achieve a **diversified** bond portfolio, an investor must purchase a variety of individual bonds of different types, credit qualities, maturity dates, and industry sectors. Purchasing a bond mutual fund or several bond mutual funds provides instant diversification. A mutual fund may offer a totally diversified bond portfolio, or it may be focused on a particular bond type, industry sector, or investment objective.

Except for U.S. Treasury bonds, most bonds are sold in $5,000 increments. An individual investor must invest a considerable amount of capital to achieve a diversified portfolio. By purchasing shares of a mutual fund rather than a small number of individual bonds, a small investor is protected from losing a large portion of his or her capital if one bond defaults.

Professional Management

The bond market is complex, and successful bond investing requires considerable knowledge of economic factors and research to find the best opportunities. Bond funds are managed by professionals who make day-to-day decisions to ensure that the fund meets its investment objectives.

Low Cost

Bond funds purchased directly from the fund company can be less expensive than purchasing individual bonds when trading costs and brokerage fees are factored in. Look for no-load funds, or those which are specifically designed to be low-cost.

Dollar Cost Averaging

When you purchase individual bonds through a broker, you may be charged a one-time trading fee regardless of the amount being invested, or the broker's commission may be hidden in the price of the bond. Mutual funds charge an expense ratio which is a fixed percentage of the amount being invested. This makes them well-suited for **dollar-cost averaging**, an investment strategy in which a specific amount of capital is invested at regular intervals, instead of as a one-time lump-sum investment. The same amount of money buys more shares when prices are low and fewer shares when prices are high, so that in the long run you pay the average price for all of your shares. Dollar-cost averaging offers protection from the possibility that fund shares will suddenly drop in market value just after you have made a large purchase, although historically, that occurs very rarely.

Mutual funds also allow you to make small, regular investments such as monthly payroll deductions.

Liquidity
An individual bond may be difficult to sell quickly if you need the capital or want to rebalance your portfolio. Shares of a mutual fund can be redeemed at any time.

Reinvestment of Dividends
Bond funds present the opportunity to have interest payments and other income automatically and immediately reinvested in the fund. Owners of individual bonds may have to keep their interest payments in a money market account and receive a lower rate of interest until they accumulate enough capital to reinvest. (Some funds charge a fee for reinvestment.)

Consolidated Investment Statements
Bond mutual funds provide a consolidated statement of your account, including all of the relevant expenses and taxable income to make reporting simple for income tax returns.

Disadvantages of Bond Mutual Funds

Taxes
Capital gains realized from a mutual fund's sale of its bond holdings are passed on to the investor, even if those gains have

been used to purchase additional shares of the fund. Funds sell bonds to raise cash to pay off investors who are redeeming their shares of the fund, or to trade them for other bonds that will better meet its investment objectives. You must pay taxes on any gains realized by the fund during a calendar year, in addition to taxes on the interest income you receive from the fund. A fund with a high **turnover rate** (a measure of annual portfolio change) is more likely to generate capital gains. You may get an unpleasant surprise when your annual statement arrives. Fund losses are not passed through to individual investors.

> **TIP: Hold Mutual Funds in a Tax-Deferred Account**
>
> You can avoid unexpected annual capital gains taxes by holding a bond mutual fund in a tax-deferred account such as an IRA. You will have to pay the taxes eventually when you withdraw funds from the account.

Expenses

Mutual bond funds incur annual management fees and other expenses. Some mutual funds are more cost effective than others. The overall return of the fund must be adjusted downward to account for the expenses.

No Income Guarantee

Bond mutual funds typically pay dividends on a monthly basis, but the amount varies from month to month. You cannot predict exactly how much income you will receive from the fund, as you can with individual bonds.

Alternative Minimum Taxes

If your bond mutual fund invests in municipal bonds, the income received from them may be subject to the alternative minimum tax (AMT).

No Maturity Date

When you purchase an individual bond, you know that you will receive your original capital investment on a specific date. Except for UITs, bond funds do not have a maturity date because, as bonds in the fund mature, they are replaced with new investments. When you are ready to liquidate your investment, you will have to sell your shares at the market price. If the price is lower than what you paid for the shares, you will lose some of your capital. On the other hand, the price may have increased, giving you additional profit.

Investment Risk

Bond funds are subject to market risk, because their prices are affected by interest rate changes and by supply and demand in the market. If you purchase Treasury bonds, you are guaranteed to receive your original investment at maturity. If interest rates go up, a bond fund holding U.S. Treasuries will experience a drop in price that could last for years. You might lose some of your original investment if you sell shares of the fund while prices are lower.

Taxes

Like investors in any mutual fund, you are liable for taxes on any taxable income generated by the underlying investments of a bond fund. This can include taxable interest income, and capital gains tax on the sale of bonds held by the fund. Some funds pay out income that is subject to the AMT. Each fund provides an IRS Form 1099 to its shareholders annually with a summary of the fund's dividends and distributions. When you sell shares of a fund, you will realize either a taxable gain or a loss.

Unit Investment Trusts

Unit Investment Trusts (UITs) are closed-end funds that sell units of a fixed portfolio of bonds. UITs are assembled by a sponsor and sold through brokers to investors. Each unit typically costs $1,000 and can be resold in the secondary market. When all the units of a UIT have been sold, the primary offering period is closed. The portfolios of bond UITs contain ten or more bonds, often a mixture of high-coupon bonds and **zero-coupon bonds**. UITs dissolve on a mandatory termination date when all the bonds have matured.

Bond UITs became popular with investors during the 1950s, when tax laws prevented municipal bond mutual funds from passing tax-free income through to investors. After changes to tax laws in 1976 allowed open-ended mutual funds to do the same, brokers continued to promote UITs because they could earn high commissions from selling them.

UITs pay a relatively consistent income until the first bond in the trust is called or matures. When this occurs, the funds from the redemption are distributed to the clients. The trust then continues paying the new, reduced monthly income until the next bond is redeemed. This continues until all the bonds in the trust have been liquidated. Once the high-coupon bonds have all been redeemed, the trust continues to hold the zero-coupon bonds until they mature. You no longer receive monthly income, but will be handed all the accrued interest from the zero-coupon bonds, plus the principal, on the UIT's termination date. You will normally have the option of selling the units back to the sponsor prior to the termination date, but may be penalized for early redemption.

> ### TIP: UITs May Not be the Best Choice for Your Investment Strategy
>
> Before considering a UIT, read the prospectus carefully to determine whether it really meets your investment objectives. High load fees (ranging from 4 to 5.5 percent) eat into your returns. Your capital will be returned to you at intervals, while the monthly income from the UIT diminishes, and finally, you may be left holding zero coupon bonds for years until they mature.

Closed-End Bond Funds

According to the Investment Company Institute (**www.ici.org**), at the end of 2007, $89.3 billion was invested in 271 domestic tax-exempt municipal bond closed-end funds, $63 billion in 131 domestic taxable bond closed-end funds, and $15.8 billion in 34 global and international closed-end bond funds, a total of $168.4 billion.

Closed-end bond funds have a fixed number of shares, like UITs, but there the similarity ends. While UITs purchase and hold a specific portfolio of bonds until a termination date, closed-end bond funds are a pool of investment capital managed by professionals who buy and sell bonds to achieve the fund's stated objectives.

Closed-end funds raise money through an initial public offering (IPO) by offering a fixed number of shares at an offering price. After the IPO, shares of the closed-end fund are traded daily on an exchange like stocks. The underlying assets purchased with funds raised by the IPO remain under the control of the fund manager. Closed-end fund managers are therefore given a fixed amount of capital to invest and do not have to deal with the daily inflows and outflows of money that characterize an open-ended bond fund. This unique structure allows fund managers to use strategies to increase the yield of the fund portfolio.

> ### TIP: Buy Shares of a Closed-End Fund on the Exchange Instead of as New Issues
>
> A brokerage commission is embedded in the price of new issues of a closed-end fund. Once the shares begin to trade on the exchange, their price declines. To avoid the commission, wait to purchase shares of a closed-end fund in the secondary market.

Advantages of Closed-End Funds over Open-End Funds

Low Cash Reserves Allow More Investment

Open-end mutual funds must keep cash available in a low-yield money market account to redeem the shares of existing investors. Because closed-end funds do not accept new money from investors and do not redeem the shares of existing investors, they can stay fully invested in higher-yield investments.

Slower Response to Decreasing Interest Rates

Open-end funds are continually receiving new money and creating new shares. At times when the interest rate is declining, they are forced to invest new money at the prevailing lower interest rates, dropping the average yield of the portfolio. Closed-end funds do not have new money coming in and can retain the income level of older, higher yielding bonds for a longer time. Some investment risk still exists, as bonds in the portfolio are more likely to be called early and capital from bonds that mature must be reinvested at the lower rate.

This characteristic makes closed-end funds attractive to investors when interest rates decline, and increases their market prices. In 2001, when the Federal Reserve reduced interest rates eleven times, some closed-end bond funds were selling at 130 percent of the value of their underlying bonds (net asset value or NAV).

Leverage: Higher Returns (and Increased Volatility)

Managers of closed-end funds use leverage to enhance the fund's performance by borrowing money at low rates or creating and issuing **auction-rate preferred stock (ARPS)**, which pay variable short-term interest rates reset by auctions at regular intervals. The borrowed money is invested in longer-term bonds that yield a higher rate than the borrowing costs. The difference between the investment rate and the borrowing rate adds to a fund's earnings, and increases the fund's dividend payout to shareholders. Leveraging magnifies the gains or losses of a fund's portfolio, and increases the **volatility of the fund's net asset value (NAV)**.

When short-term interest rates rise and increase the cost of borrowing, dividend payments are reduced and the fund's value decreases rapidly. A recent disruption in the auction rate preferred market due to the credit crisis is an example of this risk. The increased volatility of a leveraged fund may impact its market price, making the risk of **capital loss** higher if you need to sell your shares.

Discounts

One of the advantages of investing in closed-end funds is the potential to purchase them at a discount to their **NAV**. The NAV of a closed-end fund is calculated in the same way as that of an open-end bond fund: the current market value of all the underlying bonds, minus any outstanding liabilities of the fund, divided by the number of outstanding shares. Investors in open-end funds redeem their shares by selling them back to the fund sponsor at NAV. Shares of closed-end funds are sold on an exchange at market prices. These prices reflect the supply and demand balance between buyers and sellers of the closed-end fund's stock and do not necessarily reflect the underlying value of the assets in the fund. Therefore, the trading levels of the shares are not equal to the fund's NAV. Many factors affect market prices, including the condition of the economy, the rise or decline of the stock market, media announcements, and investor demand for a particular industry or market segment. Lack of advertising, a decline in yield, or loss of investor interest, may cause a closed-end fund's market price to fall below its NAV so that it is trading at a **discount**.

The yield of a closed-end fund purchased at a discount is enhanced in the same way as the yield of an individual bond purchased at a discount to its face value. The interest income from the fund is based on its NAV and not on the lower purchase price. By buying the fund at a discount, you can realize a higher yield than by buying an identical open-end fund at NAV.

> **TIP: Look for Discounted Closed-End Funds Whose Market Prices are likely to Rise in the Near Future**
>
> When you purchase shares of a closed-end fund at a discount, the goal is not only to benefit from a higher yield on your investment, but to profit by selling your shares later at a price close to, or higher than their NAV. The market prices of some funds, however, never rise above their NAVs. Look for a closed-end fund that is currently selling at a discount significantly greater than its average discount for the past five years.

Income from Closed-End Bond Funds

The yield on a leveraged closed-end fund can be much higher than the yield-to-maturity of an individual bond, but the two should not be compared. The income from a bond consists of straight interest, with the capital returned at maturity or when the bond is sold on the secondary market. The income from a closed-end fund consists of interest payments, capital gains realized from the sale of bonds in the fund, and on occasion, distributions of paid-in capital. When interest rates drop, bonds in the fund are called in and replaced with lower-interest bonds, reducing the amount of annual income you receive from the fund. In addition, if you sell your shares of the fund at a market price that is less than you originally paid for them, you lose some of your capital.

Management

The skill (and luck) of the fund managers, combined with market conditions, ultimately affects the performance of closed-end funds. In the first three quarters of 2008, the average one-year NAV return of high-yield closed-end bond funds ranged from +11.24 to -76.67 percent. Many listings for closed-end funds include information such as the manager's name and how many years the manager has been directing the fund.

Open-end Bond Mutual Funds

An **open-end bond fund** is an investment pool that holds a portfolio of bonds, but unlike closed-end funds, the number of ownership shares is not limited. Once the fund is launched with an initial number of shares, investors can purchase additional shares at the fund's NAV plus any load fees. The money from sales of new shares is invested in more assets for the fund.

Open-end funds are bought directly from the fund company or through a broker acting as an agent for the company. When you cash out of an open-end fund, you receive the NAV of your shares minus any fees. The NAV at which a fund's shares are bought and sold is calculated at the end of every day by dividing the total assets of the fund, minus any liabilities, by the number of outstanding shares.

The NAV of an open-end fund fluctuates from day to day; if it is higher when you redeem your shares than when you bought them, you will realize additional profit, but if it is lower you will lose a corresponding amount of your original investment capital.

An open-end fund pays monthly dividends consisting of interest income from the underlying bonds, capital gains, and sometimes pay-outs of capital. The size of the dividend is affected by interest-rate changes. When interest rates decline, bonds held by the fund may be called early and the capital reinvested in new bonds offering the lower prevailing interest rate. Declining interest rates often accompany a weakening economy; as investors sell off their stocks and move their capital into bond funds, the fund will purchase more new bonds, reducing the fund's overall yield as these new assets that are bought will pay the lower prevailing interest rates in the marketplace. As is the case with popular equity mutual funds, it is always possible for a bond mutual fund manager to close the fund to new investors if the relative growth or size of the fund make it difficult to manage the fund and generate good performance.

Managers of open-end funds, like managers of closed-end funds, buy bonds, reinvest principal, sell bonds to implement the fund's investment strategy, and sometimes liquidate assets to redeem shares when investors exit the fund. Capital gains realized by these activities are passed on to investors as taxable income. Open-end funds must maintain a reserve of cash, which is typically held in a lower-interest money market account, to pay out dividends and redemptions.

Comparison of Bond Funds					
	Individual high-grade bonds	UITs	Closed-end Funds	Open-end funds	ETFs
Taxable capital gains	Only if bond is sold before maturity at a premium	Yes, unpredictable	Yes, unpredictable	Yes, unpredictable	No
Taxable interest income	Depends on type of bond	Depends on type of bond held by fund	Depends on type of bond held by fund	Depends on type of bond held by fund	Depends on type of bond held by fund
Steady income	Yes, annual or semi-annual	Monthly, diminishes over time	Monthly, unpredictable, diminishes when interest rates drop	Monthly, unpredictable, diminishes when interest rates drop	Monthly, unpredictable, diminishes when interest rates drop
Principal can be lost	All principal returned at maturity	Principal returned gradually	Yes, if price goes down	Yes, if NAV goes down	Yes, if price goes down
Can be resold in secondary market	Yes	Yes, but rare.	Yes	No	Yes
Leverage	Your choice	No	Sometimes	No	Sometimes

Comparison of Bond Funds					
	Individual high-grade bonds	UITs	Closed-end Funds	Open-end funds	ETFs
Cost to purchase	Difference between face value and price of bond, brokerage commission	Possible commission	Commission, transaction fee or load fee	For no-load funds, no; for load funds, yes	Commission or transaction fee
Cost to sell	None if held to maturity, brokerage commission if sold on secondary market	Commission, transaction fee or exit fee	Commission, transaction fee or exit fee	For no-load funds, no; for load funds, maybe	Commission or transaction fee
Price	Can sell at premium or discount to face value in secondary market	May trade at price higher or lower than NAV	May trade at price higher or lower than NAV	Sells at NAV minus fees	Market price fluctuates throughout the day
Ongoing fees and expenses	No	Yes	Yes	Yes	Yes
Duration decline	Yes	No	No	No	No
Offers diversification	Not necessary	Yes	Yes	Yes	Yes
Credit risk	Minimal	Yes, depends on portfolio holdings	Yes, depends on portfolio holdings	Yes, depends on portfolio holdings	Yes, depends on portfolio holdings

Comparison of Bond Funds					
	Individual high-grade bonds	UITs	Closed-end Funds	Open-end funds	ETFs
Interest risk	Regular fixed interest payments	Uncertain	Uncertain	Uncertain	Uncertain

Understanding Bond Mutual Fund Expenses

Financial companies create and sell mutual funds because it is a profitable business for them, not because they have your best interests at heart. All mutual funds incur some expenses which are either paid out of fund assets or deducted from the investor's capital. These costs must be subtracted from the fund's promised returns to provide an accurate evaluation of the returns on your investment. Before purchasing shares of a bond fund, it is essential to have a thorough understanding of its expenses. Bond funds are required to disclose all of their expenses in their prospectuses.

Load

Load funds charge a one-time fee for entering the fund. It is essentially a sales commission earned by the financial broker or advisor who sells you the fund. A **front-end sales** load is paid when you purchase fund shares. You immediately lose money, as the **load fee** is deducted from your initial investment, leaving less money to purchase shares of the fund. At one time, load fees were as high as 8 percent; they now average 4 or 5 percent. (FINRA does not permit mutual fund sales loads to exceed 8.5 percent.) Competition among funds has brought load fees down, and some funds, known as **low-load funds**, charge smaller load fees ranging from 1.5 percent to 3.5 percent.

Criticism of front-end load fees has led to some fund companies allocating the load fee over a number of years, or charging a **back-end** or **deferred sales** load when you redeem your shares. The amount of a back-end sales load is typically calculated based on whichever amount is lower: the initial investment or the price at which the shares were sold. You should carefully read a fund's prospectus to determine whether the fund calculates its back-end sales load in this manner. A **contingent deferred sales load (CDSC, or CDSL)** is calculated based on the length of time that you hold the fund shares and typically decreases to zero if you hold them long enough.

No load funds are offered directly by the fund company to investors without the front end fee. These funds advertise themselves extensively and may charge significant **12b-1 fees** to cover their marketing costs. If a broker sells a no-load fund, a small load may be attached to it to pay the broker's commission.

12b-1 Fees

12b-1 fees get their name from an SEC rule that authorizes a mutual fund to pay fees out of fund assets to cover the expenses of marketing and selling the fund, such as compensation for brokers and sales people, advertising costs, the printing and mailing of prospectuses to new investors, and the printing and mailing of sales literature. The SEC permits a fund to pay distribution fees out of fund assets only if the fund has adopted a "12b-1 plan" authorizing their payment. Some 12b-1 plans also authorize "shareholder service fees," which pay for a staff to respond to investor inquiries and provide investors with information about their investments.

Under FINRA rules, 12b-1 fees for marketing and distribution expenses cannot exceed 0.75 percent of a fund's average net assets per year.

Other Fees

A fund may pay shareholder service fees out of its assets without adopting a 12b-1 plan. Some funds charge investors additional fees for reinvesting dividends, fees for exchanging shares of one fund for shares of another, frequent transaction fees, and accounting costs. All of this information is available in detail in the fund **prospectus**.

Share Classes

Many funds group buyers into "classes" within the same fund, according to the amount they are investing. Fees on larger investments are lower.

- **Class A shares**: Buyers are charged a high front-end load fee, but long term 12b-1 fees and other annual expenses are low. Consider these if you are planning to stay in the fund for the long haul. Some mutual funds reduce the front-end load as the size of your investment increases. Be sure to inquire about **breakpoints**.

TIP: Breakpoints Must be Disclosed in the Fund Prospectus

Each fund company establishes its own formula for how they will calculate whether an investor is entitled to receive a breakpoint. If a fund offers breakpoints (discounts for specific levels of investment), the SEC requires that they be disclosed in the fund prospectus. Be careful to make sure the broker does not size the share purchase just below a breakpoint simply to enhance their commission.

- **Class B shares**: These shares are also for investors who intend to stay in the fund for an extended period. Class B shares typically do not have a front-end load fee; instead, the load fee is distributed and declines over a six-year period, and there is a hefty penalty for early withdrawal. Eventually, 12b-1 fees also diminish.

- **Class C shares**: Class C shares typically have no front-end load fee and a lower back-end load if you exit before one year. To compensate, the 12b-1 fee may be one percent or higher. Class C shares generally do not convert to another class.

- **Class D shares**: Class D shares may have the lowest fees and are typically sold directly to investors.

Some funds also have a special share class for 401K funds or IRAs, which over time may charge the highest fees of all. Some fund companies have special low-cost funds for high volume investors, such as Vanguard Admiral Funds, T. Rowe Price Summit Funds, and Fidelity Spartan Funds.

The FINRA (previously known as the NASD) Web site (**www. finra.org**) offers tools under Investor Information to calculate and compare the expenses of two or more funds and to research possible sales discounts and fee reductions on specific mutual funds. A "Mutual Fund Breakpoint Information" tool allows you to compare the discounts offered by different funds and to look up their **breakpoints**, the amounts you must invest in each one to become eligible for a price break.

CASE STUDY: CALCULATING MUTUAL FUND EXPENSES

A mutual fund's fees and expenses may be more important than you realize. Advertisements, rankings, and ratings often emphasize how well a fund has performed in the past. But studies show that the future is often different. This year's number one fund can easily become next year's below average fund.

On the other hand, independent studies show fees and expenses can be a reliable predictor of mutual fund performance.

Of course, selecting a mutual fund involves more than just picking one with low fees and expenses. Before you invest in any mutual fund, decide whether the investment goals and risks of the fund are a good fit for you and determine how it will affect the diversification of your entire portfolio. You can read about a fund's goals, risks, and costs in its prospectus.

Fees and expenses are an important consideration in selecting a mutual fund because these charges lower your returns. Many investors find it helpful to compare the fees and expenses of different mutual funds before they invest.

You can compare the fees and expenses of up to three mutual funds, or the share classes of the same mutual fund on the NASD's Mutual Fund Expense Analyzer (**http://apps.finra.org/Investor_Information/ EA/1/mfetf.aspx**). You can also compare the fees and expenses of up to three ETFs using the same tool.

With just some basic information, you can use the tool to compare the costs of different mutual funds in a manner of seconds. That is because the tool automatically provides fee and expense information for you. Simply enter each fund's ticker symbol or select the fund through the drop down menu. If you cannot remember the full name of the fund, you can also search for the fund using keywords.

CASE STUDY: CALCULATING MUTUAL FUND EXPENSES

The SEC's online, interactive Mutual Fund Cost Calculator can also help you compare the costs of different mutual funds and understand the impact that many types of fees and expenses can have over time. You can find this classic calculator at: **www.sec.gov/investor/tools/ mfcc/mfcc-intsec.htm**. Unlike NASD's Mutual Fund Expense Analyzer, you'll need to enter fee and expense information manually from a prospectus or other disclosure document when using this tool.

An excerpt from the U.S. Securities and Exchange Commission publication, Calculating Mutual Fund Fees and Expenses, is available on their Web site at **www.sec.gov/investor/tools/mfcc/mfcc-int.htm**.

TIP: Highest-Yielding Funds Are the Most Volatile

Managers of funds that charge high front-load fees are hampered by having less capital to invest and often compensate by buying non-rated or lower-rated bonds with higher yields. A fund that performed very well last year may tumble next year because of changing economic conditions. Lower-cost funds have the best and most consistent track records.

Net Asset Value (NAV)

Shares of open-end bond mutual funds are bought and sold at their net asset value (NAV), calculated by subtracting expenses and liabilities from the total assets of the fund, and dividing that amount by the number of outstanding shares. Fund companies calculate NAVs at the end of every business day, and they are posted on fund company Web sites and in the financial pages of newspapers.

The NAV of an open-end fund is determined both by the market value of its holdings and is simply a sum of the market value of all the fund's holdings. The value of one share is the NAV divided by the number of shares outstanding. Open-end mutual funds are required to provide their shareholders with daily liquidity, meaning that shares can redeemed for cash whenever the shareholders request it. A large-scale redemption could lower a fund's NAV per share by forcing the fund to sell to fast and at distressed levels to meet the large outflow. This is a particular concern with bond funds verse equity funds, given that the bonds trade in a less liquid market then equities. New investors purchasing shares and pouring cash into the fund may force it to buy bonds when interest rates are low, reducing the overall return of the fund and the amount available for reinvestment. Mutual funds are also required to make an annual distribution of 90 percent of their realized capital gains and dividends to shareholders. A fund's NAV dips after it has made this distribution.

As explained in the section on closed-end funds, their shares are bought and sold on a stock exchange after the initial issue, and prices are determined by market sentiment and investor demand. Shares of closed-end funds typically sell at prices higher or, most frequently, lower than their NAV.

Yield and Total Return

A bond mutual fund does not have a maturity date as the underlying assets are continually rolled over into new investments.

The interest earned on a bond mutual fund's portfolio is passed through to the investor as dividends, which can be taken in cash or reinvested in the fund. This component of a bond mutual fund's earnings, less fund expenses, is called its **yield**. A mutual fund's yield is determined by the credit quality and the maturity of the bonds in its portfolio. A higher yield means that the fund's underlying bonds have longer maturities or lower credit ratings and, therefore, entail greater risk.

Interest alone does not account for the income (or loss) that can be realized from a bond fund investment. The fund's share price, or NAV, can fluctuate daily. Your **total return** on a bond fund includes the difference in the price you paid for a share of the fund and the price at which you sold it, plus any income earned from interest and capital gains distributions, minus management, administrative, and 12b-1 fees and other costs automatically deducted from fund assets. If the share price (NAV) of a fund drops significantly between the time you buy it and the time you sell it, your capital losses may offset and even exceed the income earned from the fund.

The total return of a fund is typically reported for a given evaluation period and includes interest, capital gains, dividends, and distributions realized over that period. Morningstar^{SM} calculates the total return of a bond fund by taking the change in a fund's NAV, assuming the reinvestment of all income and capital gains distributions (on the actual reinvestment date used by the fund) during the period, and then, dividing by the initial NAV. Total return may be calculated for a calendar year, or on a quarterly basis. Comparing the total returns from different quarters gives you an idea of how volatile the fund might be. The total return for a calendar year may exceed the sum of the quarterly returns because interest and capital gains have been reinvested throughout the year. A bond index, such as Lehman Brothers Aggregate Bond index, is used as a benchmark to measure the amount by which a fund over- or underperformed its primary index during a given calendar year.

Your personal total return on a bond fund may not be the same as the reported total return, because it is based on the NAV on the particular days when you bought and sold your shares. Unless total return calculations are marked as "load-adjusted" they do not include the sales charges or redemption fees you may have paid to buy and sell your shares. When comparing two bond funds, you must also consider how each will affect your tax status. The tax-adjusted total return on a high-yield corporate bond fund might not be much different from the return on a tax-exempt municipal bond fund with a lower yield. A high-yield fund is subject to greater risk that some of the underlying bonds may default, lowering its total return.

Actively and Passively Managed Bond Funds

Passively managed, or **index bond funds,** hold a portfolio of bonds that closely resembles one of the major bond indexes. Their NAVs and rates of return typically rise and fall with the fluctuations of the indexes they are tracking. **Actively managed bond funds** employ professional fund managers who use various investment strategies in an effort to outperform bond indexes or to achieve a particular investment goal. A fund's prospectus will tell you whether a fund is actively or passively managed, its investment objectives, and the rules that govern its manager's activities. UITs are completely passively managed and do not make any changes to their portfolios after the initial offering of shares.

Index funds are a better choice for a buy-and-hold or long-term investor, for several reasons.

Lower Expenses

Bonds are less volatile and more predictable than stocks; funds holding bonds of a similar credit quality and average maturity will have a similar **gross yield** (the yield before fund expenses are deducted). In the end, a fund's expenses determine whether it will outperform similar funds. High expenses mean that a fund manager has less money to invest. Index funds have lower expenses because they require a much smaller management staff. They rely on the research done by the companies that supply the indexes, rather than hiring research analysts. Low-cost index funds do not have a large budget for sales and marketing.

Index funds can have expense ratios as low as 0.18 percent, while actively managed funds can have expense ratios over 3.0 percent.

Consistent Performance

Historically, the performance of bond index funds has remained consistently superior to that of actively managed funds. An actively managed fund may experience some good years but is rarely able to sustain its lead.

Diversification

Bond index funds are frequently more diversified than actively-managed bond funds. And, fund tracking the Lehman Brothers Aggregate Bond Index, as many bond index funds do, will hold a wide range of government and corporate bonds and mortgage-backed securities.

Less Tax Liability

Actively managed funds buy and sell bonds more frequently than index funds, generating capital gains that are passed on to the shareholders who must then pay income tax or AMT. Index funds are more likely to hold bonds to maturity and to sell only when necessary.

All bond index funds are actively managed to some extent. It is not possible, for example, to buy all of the more than 5,000 bonds included in the Lehman Brothers Aggregate index. Some of the bond issues in an index are not actively traded, or liquid enough to be purchased in sufficient quantities. Bond funds also aim to buy large enough quantities to take advantage of volume discounts. Many index bond funds hold approximately 80 percent of their assets in bonds from the Lehman Brothers index. The remaining 20 percent is invested in bonds outside the index that have similar characteristics to bonds in the index. Some index funds invest as much as 35 percent of their holdings in bonds outside the index they are purporting to track. The bonds may be public issues or medium term notes too small to appear in an index. A technique called "sampling" is used to achieve results that correspond to the performance of the index being tracked.

Index fund managers also buy some money market instruments and derivatives in order to manage cash flow, to reduce transaction costs, or to take advantage of arbitrage opportunities when they arise.

> **TIP: Bond Index Funds Outperform Inflation-Indexed Bonds When Inflation is Low**
>
> When inflation is low, the principal of an inflation-indexed bond will remain the same and the yield will decrease. The yield of a bond-indexed fund will also decrease, but its NAV will increase.

Bond Indexes

Most **bond indexes** were created as a means for economists and financial analysts to measure the activity of the fixed-income market, and also as a way to measure the performance of active bond management strategies. They were not intended as benchmarks for bond mutual funds and ETFs, and it is difficult for funds to track most of these indexes with precision. Many of the bonds included in traditional indexes are not available on the market, and there is a high turnover of the bonds in an index as they mature, are redeemed, or leave the index because of default or credit ratings changes.

Fund managers are not able to replicate a bond index exactly; instead, they use a complicated **sampling** methodology. Each bond in an index is assigned to a quadrant, based on a number of factors including credit rating, issue size, industry, maturity, and bond coupon. A few **liquid** bonds (bonds which are easily available on the market) are then selected to represent each quadrant. After a portfolio of bonds has been created and optimized, it is tested to see if the past performance of those bonds followed the performance of the index closely enough. If there is too great a discrepancy (tracking error) between the performance of the selected bonds and the actual index, the bonds in the portfolio are replaced with other bonds and more tests are done. The process is repeated until the performance of the portfolio mimics the index within an acceptable margin of error. A few hundred bonds are sufficient to create a portfolio that tracks the index.

Bond Mutual Funds

Taxable Bond Funds

Investment-Grade Corporate Bond Funds

Investment-grade corporate bond funds contain corporate bonds with the top four credit ratings, and are grouped into those with short-, medium-, and long-term maturities. Read the prospectus carefully to see if the fund includes any junk bonds to boost its returns.

Corporate bond funds with long-term maturities are especially sensitive to interest rate changes that may cause bonds to be called early. A slump in a particular market sector may cause the credit ratings of bonds in that sector to drop below the fund's selection criteria, necessitating a sell-off.

Investment-grade corporate bond funds are available as closed-end and open-end funds and as ETFs. They are a good choice for tax-deferred retirement accounts.

High-yield (Junk) Corporate Bond Funds

The style and composition of high-yield bond funds varies widely. Some are designed to provide high income, others to generate a high total return. The annual turnover rate of a high-yield portfolio may vary from 20 percent to 80 percent. It is important to read the prospectus of a high-yield fund carefully and understand its investment style.

Two types of risk are associated with high-yield bond mutual funds: the risk that corporations may default on payments of interest or principal, and the risk that investors in the fund may lose confidence during an economic slump and redeem large quantities of fund shares.

High-yield bond funds are available as closed-end and open-end funds, and as ETFs. (See *Chapter 5: Corporate Bonds: High-Yield Bonds* for detailed information on the bonds contained in these funds.)

> **TIP: High-Yield Bond Funds Should be Part of a Diversified Portfolio**
>
> High-yield bond funds offer higher returns at considerably higher risks. They should never be the primary holding in a portfolio, or the main source of income. Held in conjunction with safer, more conservative bonds or bond funds, their role should be to increase savings or provide extra income.

Convertible Bond Funds

Convertible bond funds behave more like stocks than bonds because of their underlying securities. (See *Chapter 5: Corporate Bonds: Convertible Bonds* for a detailed explanation.) Convertible bonds can become very valuable if the price of the issuing corporation's stock rises, but they offer lower returns in exchange for this benefit. They are a good investment when the stock market is doing well and prices are rising, but during an economic slump, other investments offer better returns. Convertible bond funds are available as open-end funds.

Foreign Bond Funds

International bond funds hold only foreign bonds; **global bond funds** may hold U.S. securities as well. Some funds specialize in a particular market sector, geographic area, or in **emerging markets**. Balanced funds may contain a mixture of U.S. and foreign bonds.

Foreign bond funds have higher fees than U.S. bond funds, and higher risk. (See *Chapter 8: International Bonds.*) They can be used to diversify a portfolio without investing a large amount of capital. Foreign bond funds are available as closed-end and open-end funds, and as ETFs.

Index Bond Funds

Index funds hold a selection of bonds representing one of the bond indexes. (See the section on *Bond Indexes* earlier in this chapter.) **Broad market, or total market index funds,** contain a broad array of government and corporate bonds of different maturities and market sectors. Short-, intermediate-, and long-term indexes are also used. The nature of the fund is indicated by its name. Index funds have the advantage of lower expenses because they require less management. The past performance of the bond index gives an indication of how the fund will behave even it is relatively new and has little historical data. Index bond funds are available as open-end funds and ETFs.

Stable Value Funds

Stable value funds are a way to generate interest income, without having the duration risk. In a stable value fund, the manager purchases a contract from a bank or other financial institution to guarantee the value of the original investment. So, if there is a significant increase in interest rates, the guarantor will make up the difference in the lower market value of the assets and the original investment. Stable value funds make up more than one fourth of the assets held in 401(k) plans and employer-sponsored retirement plans. They typically invest in asset-backed securities, government bonds, and **Guaranteed Investment Certificates (GICs)**, but may adopt riskier strategies to boost their returns.

The stable value funds in **401(k) plans** are regulated by the Department of Labor, which oversees retirement plans, and do not register with the SEC. As a result, they are not subject to the same rules as mutual funds regarding disclosure of their holdings.

The returns on stable value funds are used to purchase additional shares. Unlike bond funds, whose prices change every day, stable value funds maintain a constant price, usually $1 or $10 per share. Stable value funds can maintain a constant share price by smoothing their gains and losses over a long period, typically two to three years. This is because they buy insurance contracts, or **wrappers,** that guarantee to repay investors' principal plus accumulated interest.

Half of all 401(k) plans include stable value funds, and over $431 billion was invested in them by early 2008. Stable value funds are run by many of the same companies that run mutual funds, including Fidelity Investments®, INVESCO℠, Vanguard®, and T. Rowe Price®, and each fund is designed in collaboration with the sponsoring employer.

> ### TIP: Stable-Value Funds Should Not Make Up the Bulk of a Retirement-Savings Portfolio
>
> Stable value funds emphasize principal protection and are appropriate for short-term holdings or as a fixed-income portion of a balanced portfolio. They should not make up the bulk of a worker's long-term investment for retirement savings because their returns, though stable, are not as high as other types of investments.

Strategic or Sector-Rotation Funds

Strategic or sector-rotation funds attempt to achieve a better return than the market as a whole by employing a specific investment strategy, outlined in the fund prospectus. Sector fund managers use formulas and analysis to identify the market sectors that are doing best and regularly shift the fund's assets into those sectors. Strategic funds may invest in high-yield (junk) bonds and use **leverage** to boost returns.

Ultra-short Bond Funds

Ultra-short bond funds invest in a variety of short maturity bonds and/or **floating-rate** securities whose interest rates are periodically reset. The definition of "ultra-short" may vary from fund to fund, from maturities of one year to maturities of five years or less. Some ultra-short funds aim for high current income; others also aim at capital preservation and high liquidity. They are available as open-end mutual funds and may be called "adjustable rate," "variable rate," "short term," "capital preservation," or "ultra-short" funds.

Bond Alternatives

Bond alternatives are funds that do not necessarily hold bonds in their portfolios, but offer a fixed income stream similar to that of bond funds.

Buy-Write Funds

Buy-write funds purchase securities and simultaneously sell **call options** on them. Investors who purchase the call options have the right to buy the stocks when the price rises to a specified level. The funds produce income from the sale of the call options and from the difference between the price at which the stocks are bought and the price at which they are sold. Income potential is limited because the call options are exercised and the underlying stock is sold off when its price reaches the specified amount. The funds can lose money if the prices of the underlying stocks decline. Buy-write funds are sold as closed-end funds and have expense ratios greater than 1 percent.

Loan-Participation Funds

Loan-participation funds invest in bank loans made to companies with low credit ratings. They are also called **bank-loan funds, floating-rate funds, prime-rate funds,** or **senior loan funds**. Loan-participation funds do well when interest rates rise because the bank loans they hold are subject to variable interest rates pegged to a major benchmark like the U.S. prime rate or the London interbank offered rate (Libor). They also respond quickly when the Federal Reserve raises rates. The value of the underlying bank loans can also increase because they are traded, like bonds, on a secondary market.

Loan-participation funds typically carry less risk than corporate junk bond funds because the underlying loans rank higher in the capital structure of the company and will get better treatment in bankruptcy. The loans are treated as **senior secured debt** that is backed by collateral and is repaid first in case of default.

The main purpose of these funds is to provide income, but there is a substantial risk of capital loss. The loans in these funds are frequently used by companies for risky financial activities, such as leveraged buy-outs, mergers, and acquisitions, and liquidity disappears when the economy slumps. Rising interest rates may trigger defaults, causing loss of both principal and income.

Loan-participation funds are often leveraged to boost their yield and compensate for their high expenses. During an economic slump, an unleveraged fund may experience a loss of as much as 30 percent; a leveraged fund will experience greater loss. These funds must keep a substantial cash reserves and liquid securities to maintain liquidity, reducing the amount available for investment. Early payment of loans may result in taxable capital gains for the investor.

These funds can be used to balance the interest-rate risk of long-term or government bonds in a portfolio. They can also be used to provide a high current income if you can afford the risk that you might lose some of your capital. They should not be a major component of any portfolio. Loan-participation funds are sold as closed-end funds.

Dividend–Paying Stock Funds

Dividend-paying stock funds, or **equity-income funds**, hold stocks that pay regular dividends to investors. The expenses of these funds are typically equal to almost half of their dividend pay-outs, because they are actively managed and because fund managers incur trading fees by buying and selling stocks in an attempt to outperform other funds. Their average annual turnover is 51 percent. All this activity also results in taxable capital gains, which are passed on to the investor.

The annual yield from these funds is lower than the yield on bonds, but there is always the possibility that the value of underlying stocks will appreciate, causing the fund shares to rise in value. Dividend-paying stocks funds are sold as closed-end and open-end mutual funds and as ETFs.

TIP: Before Buying, Find Out When a Fund Makes its Annual Distribution

You are liable for capital gains taxes on a fund's annual distribution whether you have held the fund for a day or for twelve months of that year. Once a year, a fund is legally required to pay out 90 percent of its realized capital gains and dividends to its shareholders. The fund's NAV drops immediately after the distribution, usually in December, to reflect its lower value. Before buying shares of a mutual fund, find out when the fund makes its annual distribution. After the pay-out, shares of the fund will cost less, and you will not be saddled with a year's worth of taxable income from a fund that you owned for only a few days.

Municipal Bond Funds

Municipal bond funds are designed to provide a stream of **tax-exempt** interest income. State-specific bond funds may also be exempt from state and local income taxes if you live in the state where they are concentrated. Some municipal bond funds purchase bonds that are subject to the **AMT (Alternative Minimum Tax)** because they offer higher returns; if you are subject to the AMT (See Section on the Alternative Minimum Tax in *Chapter 14: Evaluating a Bond Investment: Your Taxes*), review the fund's portfolio carefully before buying.

Just as with individual bonds, the yield on municipal bond funds must be compared with the after-tax yield of comparable corporate bond funds. Historically, municipal bond funds have tended to outperform corporate bond funds because their expenses are lower and they are less volatile.

National and State Municipal Bond Funds

National municipal bonds funds include bonds from all the states and typically hold either investment-grade bonds or high-yield (**junk**) bonds. The name of the fund indicates its character. National municipal bond funds area available as UITs, closed-end funds, and open-end mutual funds.

If you are living in a state that taxes you on income from out-of-state bonds, you will receive an annual statement detailing what percentage of the fund's holdings are invested in each state, and any income that is subject to the AMT. For example, if 15 percent of the fund is invested on your state, you will not pay taxes on 15 percent of the interest income from the fund.

If your state tax on income from out-of-state municipal bonds is high, you should invest in state-specific funds. State funds are also available as UITs, closed-end funds, and open-end mutual funds, and always have the name of the state in their title. Compare the returns of a state-specific fund to its national counterpart before buying. State-specific funds may be more volatile than national funds because they are sensitive to local events such as natural disasters, job losses, or economic failures that may affect credit ratings. Income from a state-specific fund may be subject to AMT.

High-Yield (Junk) Municipal Bond Funds

Unrated municipal bonds, and those with low credit ratings are forced to offer higher yields to compensate for the greater risk. Financial institutions buy these bonds and package them as high-yield municipal bond funds. High-yield municipal bond funds include bonds issued to fund nursing homes, **CCRCs**, and projects that partner with private industry, such as corporations and industrial parks. (See *Chapter 7: Municipal Bonds* for greater detail.) Though municipal bonds have a reputation for being "safe" investments, high-yield municipal bonds funds are just as risky as high-yield corporate bond funds and should be carefully watched. High yield municipal bond funds are available as closed-end and open-end mutual funds.

Money Market Mutual Funds

These funds resemble traditional money-market funds except that their income is tax-exempt and, as a consequence, they offer a smaller pre-tax yield. They contain short-term notes with an average maturity of 90 days and a maximum maturity of 13 months. Tax-exempt money market funds buy municipal bonds, tax-free **commercial paper** issued by municipalities, **variable-rate debt, auctionable rate securities,** and long-term bonds sold with short **puts** (options to require the issuer to redeem the bonds within seven days, 30 days, quarterly, or annually depending on the issue). The name of the fund indicates the nature of its holdings.

These funds are both national and state-specific, and may contain bonds subject to AMT unless otherwise specified. State-specific municipal bond money market funds are appropriate for investors in high income brackets who live in states that charge a high income tax.

U.S. Government Bond Funds

Government bond funds invest a minimum of 80 percent of their total assets in a variety of U.S. Treasury securities and U.S. agency bonds, which have almost no credit risk. They may also include mortgages, some which are backed by government agencies and some which are not. Some funds allow the trading of **futures** and **options** to increase returns, or follow strategies to optimize **total return**. Some include the separate trading of **STRIPS**. Read the prospectus of a government bond fund carefully and be sure you understand what you are buying.

You can set up an account and purchase individual treasury bonds directly from the U.S. Treasury at **www.treasurydirect. gov** in increments of as little as $100. Buying shares of a government bond mutual fund, in contrast to buying individual bonds, gives you instant access to a large and diversified portfolio of bonds of varying maturities. The yields and total returns of government bond funds tend to be slightly lower than those of other bond funds because of their lower **credit risk**. Bond funds have management fees and expenses associated with them.

Short-Term Government Bond Funds

The maturities of the investments in a short-term government bond fund are under five years in most cases. The most common investment mix includes short-term U.S. Treasuries or agency issues along with cash. The short maturities minimize **interest rate risk** and keep the prices of these funds relatively stable.

Immediate Government Bond Funds

The maturities of the bonds in intermediate government bond funds typically range from five to ten years. Some intermediate funds include international as well as domestic government bonds. The prices of intermediate government bond funds can fluctuate as much as five percent in response to interest rate changes.

Long-Term Government Bond Funds

Long-term government bond funds are created with a variety of investment objectives and holdings. Long-term bonds are considered to have the highest risk, to be associated with inflation, and change in interest rates over time. Prices of long-term government bond funds can fluctuate as much as 10 percent.

GNMA Bond Funds

GNMA funds invest in mortgage-backed securities guaranteed by Ginnie Mae. These funds are popular and therefore highly liquid. The large funds are diverse enough to provide protection from principal prepayment. When interest rates go down and large numbers of mortgages are refinanced, this type of fund does not perform as well as funds with noncallable bonds. GNMA funds are sold as open-end mutual funds.

Inflation-Protected Securities Funds

Inflation-protected securities funds consist primarily of TIPS issued by the U.S. Treasury. They are regarded as conservative investments for people who are worried about inflation risk, but when inflation is rising and TIPS are in demand, fund share prices rise and produce a higher total return. These funds do not do as well when the rate of inflation is low.

It is advantageous to own TIPS through a fund instead of individually. Each year the principal of a TIPS is increased by an inflation adjustment. This amount is taxable annually as income, even though you will not receive the money until the increased principal is paid out at maturity. A TIPS fund pays out the annual inflation adjustment to investors along with the interest, by selling a portion of their bond holdings corresponding to the amount of the adjustment for that year.

CASE STUDY: MUTUAL FUND PROSPECTUS, TIPS FOR READING ONE

Excerpt from the Web site of the Securities and Exchange Commission (**www.sec.gov/answers/ mfprospectustips.htm**)

"When you purchase shares of a mutual fund, the fund must provide you with a prospectus. But you can — and should — request and read a fund's prospectus before you invest.

The prospectus is the fund's primary selling document and contains valuable information, such as the fund's investment objectives or goals, principal strategies for achieving those goals, principal risks of investing in the fund, fees and expenses, and past performance.

The prospectus also identifies the fund's managers and advisers and describes its organization and how to purchase and redeem shares. The prospectus also acts as an "owner's manual" after you've invested in a fund.

CASE STUDY: MUTUAL FUND PROSPECTUS, TIPS FOR READING ONE

While they may seem daunting at first, mutual fund prospectuses contain a treasure trove of valuable information. The SEC requires funds to include specific categories of information in their prospectuses and to present key data (such as fees and past performance) in a standard format so that investors can more easily compare different funds..

Here's some of what you'll find in mutual fund prospectuses:

Date of Issue-The date of the prospectus should appear on the front cover. Mutual funds must update their prospectuses at least once a year, so always check to make sure you're looking at the most recent version.

Risk/Return Bar Chart and Table-Near the front of the prospectus, right after the fund's narrative description of its investment objectives or goals, strategies, and risks, you'll find a bar chart showing the fund's annual total returns for each of the last 10 years (or for the life of the fund if it is less than 10 years old). All funds that have had annual returns for at least one calendar year must include this chart.

Except in limited circumstances, funds also must include a table that sets forth returns — both before and after taxes — for the past 1-, 5-, and 10-year periods. The table will also include the returns of an appropriate broad-based index for comparison purposes. Here's what the table will look like:

	1-year	5-year (or life refund)	10-year (or life refund)
Return before taxes	___%	___%	___%
Return after taxes on distributions	___%	___%	___%
Return after taxes on distributions and sale of fund shares	___%	___%	___%
Index (reflects no deductions for [fees, expenses, or expenses])	___%	___%	___%

Note: Be sure to read any footnotes or accompanying explanations to make sure that you fully understand the data the fund provides in the bar chart and table. Also, bear in mind that the bar chart and table for

CASE STUDY: MUTUAL FUND PROSPECTUS, TIPS FOR READING ONE

a multiple-class fund (that offers more than one class of fund shares in the prospectus) will typically show performance data and returns for only one class.

Fee Table-Following the performance bar chart and annual returns table, you'll find a table that describes the fund's anticipated annual fees and expenses. hese include the shareholder fees and annual fund operating expenses described in greater detail in our publication on Mutual Fund Fees and Expenses. The fee table includes an example that will help you compare costs among different funds by showing you the costs associated with investing a hypothetical $10,000 over a 1-, 3-, 5-, and 10-year period.

Financial Highlights-This section, which generally appears toward the back of the prospectus, contains audited data concerning the fund's financial performance for each of the past 5 years. Here you'll find net asset values (for both the beginning and end of each period), total returns, and various ratios, including the ratio of expenses to average net assets, the ratio of net income to average net assets, and the portfolio turnover rate.

Shareholder Information -The prospectus contains information on how to purchase and redeem shares of a fund. This section contains information on whether the fund requires shareholders to maintain a minimum account balance, and discloses the fund's minimum initial or subsequent purchase amounts, if any. In addition, it contains important information on the tax consequences of buying, holding, selling or exchanging the fund's shares.

File Number - Each fund is required to provide a file number on the back page of its prospectus. This file number, which begins with 811-, is used to catalog all of the fund's filings in the SEC's EDGAR database, and can be used to find documents the fund has filed with the SEC. To search for information using a fund's file number, visit our EDGAR database (**www.sec.gov/edgar/searchedgar/companysearch.html**)."

CHAPTER 11

Exchange Traded Bond Funds

What is an Exchange Traded Fund?

An Exchange Traded Fund (**ETF**) is a fund containing assets that track the performance of a particular index or commodity. Shares of an ETF can be bought and sold throughout the day on the stock market, just like shares of stock. Each share of an ETF represents a share of the underlying assets held by the fund. As the prices of those underlying assets rise and fall, the value of the ETF shares rise and fall with them.

ETFs are **open-ended**, meaning that as the demand for shares of the fund increases, new shares are created and the holdings of the fund are enlarged. When the price of ETF shares rise above the value of their underlying securities, a process called **arbitrage** is used to bring the price back into line with the **net asset value** (NAV) of the ETF shares. If demand for an ETF should decline, outstanding shares are redeemed and the underlying securities sold.

An ETF involves three entities: a **sponsor**, **authorized participants**, and a **trust company**. The sponsor is normally a bank or other large financial institution. Major sponsors of ETFs include Vanguard, Barclays Global Investors^{SM}, and State Street Global Advisors®. Authorized participants are large institutional investors, specialists, or market-makers who are given the authority to create and redeem ETF shares. The trust company, commonly a bank, physically holds the securities underlying an ETF in trust. The authorized participants act as third parties, buying up baskets of assets that reflect the composition of the index tracked by the fund and exchanging them with the fund sponsor for a large block of newly created ETF shares, known as a creation unit. Creation units vary in size, but are characteristically made up of between 20,000 and 50,000 shares of the ETF. This third-party arrangement reduces tax liability for investors.

Bond ETFs are structured as **regulated investment companies (RICs)**. The manager of an RIC is not required to hold all the bonds in an index, but can select sample bonds from the index and then optimize the portfolio so that it follows the performance of the index it is tracking as closely as possible. The manager of an RIC may also add bonds that are not included in the index to the portfolio. A RIC can hold illiquid assets that could not ordinarily be included in a fund and compensate by selecting other tradable bonds to track the performance of an index.

Advantages of Bond ETFs

Diversity

ETFs represent an assortment of securities selected from a particular index or benchmark. Their objective is to follow the market performance of the index as a whole. Like mutual funds, ETFs make it possible for an individual investor to own a share of hundreds of bonds, rather than investing in just one or two individual bonds. Private investors can enjoy the same advantages as large institutional investors: exposure to a variety of bond issues and the protection offered by a diverse portfolio of holdings. If one or two individual bonds drop in value, large institutional investors have the resources to offset the loss with gains in the value of other bonds. A private investor, on the other hand, runs the risk of losing a large part of his or her investment capital if a bond defaults or is sold at a loss and may never recover from lost opportunity and the resulting loss of income. Investing in an ETF offers individual investors the same kind of safety cushion that is available to large investors with expansive portfolios.

Transparency

By definition, an ETF is required to make available at all times information about its underlying assets. At any time, the investor can look at a prospectus online or request a printed copy of a prospectus, which shows exactly which bonds are included in the ETF and what fees and expenses are incurred by the fund. ETF shares are traded on the stock market throughout the day, and an investor can watch prices and track the intraday value of the fund. The exchange on which an ETF is trading is responsible for calculating its estimated NAV — the actual value of its underlying securities — throughout the day. The estimated NAV of all ETFs is calculated every 15 seconds and is posted on stock exchanges and a number of investment Web sites, including those of the ETF sponsors. The NAV of an ETF is not necessarily its market price, but it indicates the estimated price at which the ETF should be selling. Investors can easily detect when an ETF is **selling at a premium** (the market price is higher than the actual value of the ETF) or **selling at a discount** (the market price is lower than the actual value of the ETF), and make investment decisions accordingly.

The Complete Guide to Investing in Bonds and Bond Funds

Lower Fees and Commissions

Management costs are normally lower than mutual funds because most ETFs are **passively managed**. Bonds are bought and sold only when necessary to maintain integrity with the fund index, thereby reducing expenses. The portfolios of actively managed mutual funds experience a high turnover, as their managers strive to execute investment strategies and maximize returns. Managers of actively managed mutual funds must maintain some cash in the portfolio for redemptions; the **opportunity cost** of maintaining this cash reserve instead of investing it is estimated to be around .04 percent.

Many bond mutual funds have **load** or **exit** fees, amounts that an investor pays to enter or exit the fund, in addition to commissions, which must be subtracted when calculating returns from an investment. Shares of an ETF are not sold directly by the company sponsoring it, but on the open market through a brokerage. To purchase or sell shares in an ETF, an investor pays a commission, just like a regular equity security.

Because an ETF is linked to an index and not actively managed, it is not paying the salaries of market analysts and active fund managers, only a licensing fee to the provider of the index.

> **TIP: Look at Expenses Carefully**
>
> ETFs normally have lower expense ratios than comparable mutual funds, but there are situations in which a mutual fund is a better option. A mutual fund charges a one-time load fee, while each purchase of an ETF incurs a trading fee. If you are investing small amounts at regular intervals, the accumulated trading fees will eat into your returns and ultimately cost you more than the fees and management costs of the mutual fund.

Tax Efficiency

ETFs are tax-efficient because they are structured to minimize capital gains tax. If a mutual fund sells some of its assets for a profit, the individual investors in that fund are required to pay capital gains tax (about 15 percent in most cases), even if the fund as a whole loses value during the year. An individual investor who owns shares of an ETF is not liable for capital gains tax if the underlying assets are sold at a profit by the fund because those securities are effectively owned by a third party. When an authorized provider (AP) creates or redeems shares of an ETF, it performs an in-kind exchange, not a cash transaction, with the ETF sponsor.

ETFs are not tax-free. Interest paid by an ETF is taxable as income. An investor pays capital gains tax when he or she sells shares of an ETF at a higher price than he or she paid for them, unless the ETFs are held in a tax-free or tax-deferred account such as an IRA or an ESA.

Ease of Purchase

ETF shares can be bought and sold anywhere, and shares of ETFs from different providers can be managed in a single brokerage account. Comparable low-cost index mutual funds are often available only from a single provider, so that an investor who wishes to hold more than one index mutual fund in his or her portfolio has to maintain several separate accounts. It takes only minutes to set up an online brokerage account and begin purchasing ETFs. International ETFs allow U.S. investors to buy into foreign bond markets using U.S. dollars by making simple transactions through a U.S. brokerage.

Bond ETFs are more liquid than bonds themselves and can be bought and sold at any time on the stock exchanges. ETFs also provide a means of quickly putting excess cash to productive use, and of immediately adding a new bond category to a portfolio. With one or two transactions, investors are able to move large amounts of capital from one bond category to another.

> **TIP: Liquidity is Related to Market Demand**
>
> Purchase of a bond ETF does not necessarily guarantee liquidity. If the market demand for shares of a particular ETF is low, it may be difficult to find a buyer. If you want to invest in bonds with the option of being able to sell them quickly when cash is needed, you should select more popular, broad-market bond ETFs. You can evaluate the liquidity of a bond ETF by looking at its total assets, trading volume, and age. This information is available in the ETF prospectus and on brokerage Web sites. A bond ETF with a high trading volume and a large amount of assets relative to other ETFs will be easier to sell.

No Maturity Date

Unlike bonds, bond ETFs do not have a maturity date. When the bonds held in an ETF mature, the money from the principal repayment is reinvested in new bonds rather than the principal being returned to investors. Therefore, the investor does not have to periodically look around for new bond investments.

> **TIP: Bond ETFs Do Not Guarantee the Return of Capital**
>
> Owning shares of a bond ETF is not the same as owning a bond. When a bond matures, the investor receives his or her capital investment back. If shares of a bond ETF are sold at a time when the bonds held by that ETF are selling at a discount in the secondary market, the investor may not be able to retrieve the original investment.

Steady Stream of Income

Most individual bonds pay interest semiannually. Bond ETFs characteristically distribute monthly dividends, which can include both interest income on the underlying bonds and capital gains.

ETFs Behave Like Stocks

Shares of ETFs are sold on the stock exchanges throughout the day and can be employed in all the investment strategies that are used with stocks: **options**, buying on **margin**, **market timing**, **hedging**, and **leveraging**. The market price of ETF shares is updated regularly throughout the day, and they can be bought and sold quickly. Although a risky strategy, active traders can attempt to increase their returns by buying and selling bond ETFs, using the same strategies as with equity ETFs and individual stocks. During the stock market decline of 2008, when the demand for bonds suddenly increased, active traders were able to buy and sell bond ETFs just as they would shares of a stock whose price was rapidly accelerating.

Because bond ETFs can be purchased on margin and sold short, they can act as a vehicle for hedging against interest-rate fluctuations.

TIP: You are Responsible

All of the advantages offered by ETFs are only beneficial if you, as an investor, use them in the right way. It is your responsibility to read the prospectus of each fund and determine whether it fits your investment goals. Some ETFs have a relatively high expense ratio, which should be taken into consideration. Easy access to detailed information about ETFs and their estimated intraday values may tempt an investor to trade too frequently and run up trading fees, which eat into returns.

Bond ETFs

Though the public U.S. fixed-income market is much larger than the public U.S. equity market, less than 60 of the approximately 700 ETFs on the market in early 2008 were bond ETFs. In response to the declining stock market and the corresponding interest in bonds and bond funds, ETF providers had created more than 40 new offerings by mid-2008. Both bond issuers and bond providers have recognized the potential for selling bonds through ETFs, and are now creating new financial products that will be easier to market.

TIP: Costs are Especially Important

Because bonds offer a lower rate of return than stock investments, it is important to look at the expense ratio of a bond ETF in relation to its rate of return. The real return on bonds, adjusted for inflation, has historically been only 2.5 percent. Even a moderate expense ratio can seriously diminish your returns.

Treasury Bond ETFs

The U.S. Treasury bond market is the most liquid fixed income market in the world; trillions of dollars in U.S. Treasury bonds are traded every year. The Lehman Brothers Treasury indexes are most popular as benchmarks for bond ETFs. **Barclays iShares**℠ offers six Treasury bond ETFs, benchmarked to Lehman indexes.

Five **Ameristock®** ETFs track Ryan ALM Treasury indexes. The **PowerShares® 1-30 Laddered Treasury (PLW)** is based on the Ryan/Mergent 1-30 Year Treasury Laddered Index, which measures the potential return of U.S. Treasury securities with a yield curve based on 30 U.S. Treasury bonds with fixed interest rates, scheduled to mature in an annual sequential (laddered) structure.

State Street Global Advisors offers three U.S. Treasury ETFs, including the short-term **SPDR Lehman 1-3 Month T-bill ETF,** based on Lehman Brothers 1-3 Month U.S. Treasury Bill Index.

Treasury Inflation Protection Securities (TIPS) are securities issued by the U.S. government which are protected against inflation by making adjustments to their principal amount based on changes in the Consumer Price Index-U (CPI-U). TIPS have a fixed interest rate, which naturally increases returns as the capital is increased to counter inflation. To compensate for the guaranteed protection against inflation, the interest rate on these bonds is lower. **SPDR® Barclays TIPS ETF (IPE)** aims to track the Barclays U.S. Government Inflation-linked Bond Index. **iShares Lehman TIPS Bond ETF (TIP)** follows the performance of the inflation-protected sector of the U.S. Treasury market as defined by the Lehman Brothers U.S. TIPS index.

Sovereign bonds are issued by national governments. The **SPDR Lehman International Treasury Bond ETF** tracks the performance of the Lehman Brothers Global Treasury ex-US Index, which includes Treasury bonds of investment-grade countries outside the United States, such as Austria, Italy, Germany, Belgium, Canada, Denmark, and France.

Treasury Bond ETFs				
Ticker	Symbol	Expense Ratio	Exchange	Inception Date
Ameristock/Ryan 1 Year Treasury ETF	GKA	0.15	Amex	6/28/2007
Ameristock/Ryan 10 Year Treasury ETF	GKD	0.15	Amex	6/28/2007

Treasury Bond ETFs				
Ticker	Symbol	Expense Ratio	Exchange	Inception Date
Ameristock/Ryan 2 Year Treasury ETF	GKB	0.15	Amex	6/28/2007
Ameristock/Ryan 20 Year Treasury ETF	GKE	0.15	Amex	6/28/2007
Ameristock/Ryan 5 Year Treasury ETF	GKC	0.15	AMEX	6/28/2007
BARCLAYS ISHARES US TREASURY BOND ETFS				
iShares Lehman Short Treasury Bond	SHV	0.15	NYSE	1/5/2007
iShares Lehman 1-3 YR Treasury Bond	SHY	0.15	NYSE	7/22/2002
iShares Lehman 3-7 YR Treasury Bond	IEI	0.15	Amex	1/5/2007
iShares Lehman 7-10 YR Treasury Bond	IEF	0.15	NYSE	7/22/2002
iShares Lehman 10-20 YR Treasury Bond	TLH	0.15	NYSE	1/5/2007
iShares Lehman 20+ YR Treasury Bond	TLT	0.15	NYSE	7/22/2002
STATE STREET SPDR US TREASURY BOND ETFS				
SPDR Lehman 1-3 Month T-Bill ETF	BIL	0.14	Amex	5/25/2007
SPDR Lehman Intermediate Term Treasury ETF	ITE	0.14	Amex	5/23/2007
SPDR Lehman Long Term Treasury ETF	TLO	0.14	Amex	5/23/2007

Treasury Bond ETFs				
Ticker	Symbol	Expense Ratio	Exchange	Inception Date
SPDR Lehman International Treasury Bond ETF	BWX	0.5	Amex	10/2/2007
POWERSHARES US TREASURY BOND ETFS				
PowerShares 1-30 Laddered Treasury	PLW	0.25	Amex	10/11/2007
STATE STREET INTERNATIONAL TREASURY BOND ETFS				
SPDR DB Intl Govt Inflation-Protected Bond	WIP	0.5	Amex	3/19/2008
SPDR Lehman International Treasury Bond ETF	BWX	0.5	Amex	10/2/2007
TIPS ETFS				
iShares Lehman TIPS Bond ETF	TIP	0.2	NYSE	12/4/2003
SPDR Barclays TIPS ETF	IPE	0.19	Amex	5/25/2007

TIP: Interest on U.S. Treasury Bond ETFs is Taxable

Interest paid on U.S. Treasury Notes is taxed as income by the federal government, but not by state or local governments.

TIP: U.S. Treasury Bonds are Easy to Buy

An individual investor can easily buy U.S. government bonds directly from the official Treasury Web site (**www.savings-bonds.gov**) without paying any transaction fees. The extra effort involved in managing a portfolio of individual bonds may be worthwhile, if it avoids transaction fees and fund management expenses. Also, you will have direct control over your investment, and can be sure that all of your capital will be returned if you hold the bonds to maturity.

> ## TIP: Other Bond Funds Have High Credit Ratings
>
> There are bond ETFs that do not consist exclusively of government bonds, but hold other bonds with high credit ratings, and may offer higher rates of return.

Municipal bond ETFs

State Street Global Advisors offers four SPDR Municipal Bond ETFs. **PowerShares** offers **PowerShares Insured National Municipal Bond Portfolio, PowerShares Insured California Municipal Bond Portfolio,** and **PowerShares Insured New York Municipal Bond Portfolio,** which track the performance of top-rated, insured municipal bonds.

Corporate Bonds

Barclays launched the first corporate bond ETF, iShares iBoxx Investment Grade Corporate Bond ETF, in July 2002. It measures the performance of approximately 100 investment-grade, highly liquid corporate bonds. Several of them are Yankee bonds, issued by foreign companies, but are denominated in U.S. Dollars. Several ETFs provided by Vanguard and Barclays are benchmarked to the Lehman Brothers Short-term Credit Index, Intermediate-term Credit Index, and Credit Index, which holds investment-grade corporate bonds along with some asset-backed securities.

The **iShares iBoxx $ High Yield Corporate Bond ETF (HYG), PowerShares High Yield Corporate Bond Portfolio (PHB), and SPDR Lehman High Yield Bond ETF (JNK)** track the performance of less-than-investment-grade corporate bonds, or junk bonds. Junk bonds offer higher interest payments because of the increased risk of default. High-yield corporate bond ETFs offer higher returns than other bond ETFs, but lower returns than the stock market on the whole.

TIP: ETFs Can Overlap

If you purchase bond ETFs from different fund families such as Barclays and State Street, it is possible that their holdings may overlap because the methods used by each fund to track its indexes differ. You can avoid overlap by buying all of your bond ETFs from one fund family or carefully reviewing the holdings of each fund to make sure you maintain the diversity of your portfolio.

Composite Fixed-Income ETFs

Composite fixed-income indexes combine different types of bonds and fixed-income securities into one index. Lehman Brothers has several investment-grade Government/Credit Indexes, classified according to the average maturity of the bonds. These indexes do not contain mortgages. Several Barclays and Vanguard ETFs track these indexes by sampling ranges of securities that approximate key risk factors and other characteristics of the indexes as a whole.

The Lehman Aggregate Bond Index tracks more than 7,000 U.S. fixed-income securities and measures the performance of the U.S. investment-grade bond market. The **Vanguard Total Bond Market ETF (BND), SPDR Lehman Aggregate Bond ETF (LAG),** and the **iShares Lehman Aggregate Bond ETF (AGG)** all use sampling methodologies to follow the Lehman Aggregate Bond Index.

The Claymore **U.S. Capital Markets Bond ETF (UBD)** follows Dorchester Capital Management Company's Capital Markets Index (CPMKTS), a market-weighted index including 9,673 equity, fixed-income, and money-market instruments.

TIP: Higher Yields Mean Higher Risk and Higher Expenses

Bear in mind that the higher yields of the junk bond ETFs come along with higher risk and expense ratios. While most bond ETFs have expense ratios ranging from 0.15 to 0.25 percent, the expense ratio for high-yield bond ETFs is between 0.4 and 0.5 percent.

SECTION 2: CREATING YOUR BOND INVESTMENT STRATEGY

CHAPTER 12

Choosing a Strategy

Define Your Financial Goals and Requirements

Bonds are used in a number of investment strategies. Traditionally, investing in the equity (stock) market is considered the best means of substantially increasing your savings because the return on bonds is lower than the return on stocks. When the economy is weak and the stock market is in a decline, though, there is a risk that some or all of the capital invested in stocks will be lost. Most private investors maintain a certain percentage of their portfolio in bonds to preserve capital and provide a safety net.

Large institutional investors, such as charitable foundations and pension funds, use bonds to earn a steady rate of return, which is compounded as interest payments on the bond portfolio and is reinvested.

Individuals use bonds to provide themselves with a steady, predictable stream of income while preserving their capital. Bond mutual funds, UITs, and bond ETFs also offer periodic payments, though the amount may vary as bonds in the funds mature and are replaced with new investments.

Individual investors may choose bonds as a means of setting aside savings for some future expense, such as a child's education or the down payment for a home, while earning regular interest income, which can either be spent or added to the savings.

The first step in executing a successful bond strategy is to determine your financial goals and requirements. Take a few minutes to ask yourself some questions:

- Why am I investing? What do I hope to accomplish?

- How much money do I have to invest?

- Will I be investing all of it at one time, or at regular intervals?

- Do I need a regular stream of income now? How much do I need? How much will I need in the future?

- Will I need a large amount of money for some purpose at a specific date? How much money will I need? (See Chapter 18: Bonds as Savings for help.)

- What is my income tax bracket? Do I pay state or local taxes?

- Is there a possibility that I will need to withdraw funds in the near future?

- Do I want to leave an estate for my children or a legacy for some public purpose?

  Write down the answers to these questions; they will determine your investment strategy. The more specific your answers are, the greater the likelihood your strategy will succeed. Review these questions once every year or so. If your answers change, you will be able to adjust your investment strategy accordingly to make sure you stay on track.

Take a look at your answers.

- **Why am I investing? What do I hope to accomplish?**

  Be honest and pragmatic. When your goals are clearly defined, it is much easier to respond to shifts in the economy or changes in your own personal circumstances. If your objectives are redefined a few years from now, you will be able to assess your investment strategy and reallocate your assets effectively.

  Are you investing because you want to attempt to make extra money by buying and selling bonds on a regular basis? In that case, your approach will require much more effort to keep yourself informed, and you will be looking at many indicators of a bond's value besides its price and coupon rate.

- **How much money do I have to invest?**

  With your financial goals in mind, look at the amount of money available for investment. This includes not only your current savings, but future earnings and funds received from the sale of an asset such as a house or business or an inheritance. What kind of return will you need to realize on that amount to accomplish your goals?

  Although savings bonds and Treasuries are available in smaller denominations, a typical bond issue is sold in increments of $1,000, $5,000, or $10,000. If your initial investment is less than $5,000, a bond mutual fund or an ETF may be a better choice because it spreads your investment over a range of bonds instead of concentrating it all in one place.

- **Will I be investing all of it at one time or at regular intervals?**

  Most bond purchases involve a transaction, or broker's, fee. If you plan to invest a smaller amount, such as a monthly payroll deduction, at regular intervals, a bond mutual fund is your best option because your money goes to work immediately and interest can be reinvested. If you have an account with a brokerage, your money can accumulate in a money market account at a lower rate of interest until there is enough available for a bond purchase.

- **Do I need a regular stream of income now? How much do I need? How much will I need in the future?**

  If you are buying bonds because you need the income from regular interest payments, your greatest concern will be a bond's coupon rate and maturity date. Buy bonds with interest payments scheduled in different months and bonds with different maturities so that all of your capital does not have to be reinvested at the same time. Be careful when purchasing callable bonds.

  Some bond mutual funds and ETFs also offer regular payouts, but the exact amount is unpredictable.

- **Will I need a large amount of money for some purpose at a specific date? How much money will I need?**

  Are you buying bonds to save for a future expense, such as a home purchase or a college education? Buy bonds that mature around the time when you will need your capital returned. If you will be reinvesting the interest payments, look at the YTM of a bond to see how much you can expect to realize, but remember that, as we said in Chapter 3, YTM assumes that all reinvestments are made at the current interest rates, so actual returns may differ depending on the direction of rates.

- **What is my income tax bracket? Do I pay state or local taxes?**

  Interest from U.S. Treasury bonds is exempt from federal income tax, and income from many municipal bonds is exempt from state or local taxes. If you are in a high tax bracket, avoid corporate bonds or hold them in a tax-deferred account such as an IRA.

- **Is there a possibility that I will need to withdraw funds in the near future?**

  If you anticipate that you may need to sell your bonds before they reach maturity, choose bonds with a shorter maturity or low duration since their price will fluctuate less with moves in interest rates. A bond fund or an ETF is also a good choice, because your shares can be cashed out or sold at any time.

- **Do I want to leave an estate for my children or a legacy for some public purpose?**

  Some bonds have estate clauses allowing them to be redeemed at face value upon the death of the bondholder. Otherwise, allow for the possibility that the bonds may be sold before they reach maturity.

CASE STUDY: GETTING STARTED WITH BONDS

William Nonte, *Financial Advisor*
CERTIFIED FINANCIAL PLANNER ™
GunnAllen Financial
2295 S. Hiawassee RdSuite #304
Orlando, FL 32835
(321) 293-0287
bnonte@gunnallen.com
www.billnonte.com

Bill Nonte is originally from Indiana but has lived in Orlando since 1992. He was a Certified Public Accountant prior to becoming a financial advisor and Certified Financial Planner. He enjoys all sports, especially golf.

"A financial advisor can remove most of the "noise" in the financial marketplace for his or her clients. There are so many investment choices available to the investor these days. It is the financial advisor's job to find the best investments in the marketplace and match them to each client's unique financial objectives and risk levels. In the end, it saves the investor a lot of time and money."

"If you want to begin investing in bonds, do some research on bond in vesting. Obviously, you can find tons of material on the Internet or in your local library. Then, interview a couple of financial advisors who are familiar with the nuances of bond investing. Pick the one you feel most comfortable talking to and the one whom you think has your best interests in mind."

"The minimum amount of investment capital that a beginning investor should have available for a bond investment varies. The better question is, 'what type of income stream is an investor looking for?' Once you know that answer, you can look at current bond yields and back into the investment amount necessary."

If an investor has a limited amount of capital, are mutual funds a better choice?

"Absolutely. Mutual funds allow investors to diversify their holdings over a broad range of bonds with a small initial investment. This would not be possible if they were buying individual bonds; more of their eggs would be in one basket and that could be risky. Also, due to volume purchases, mutual funds typically have access to lower purchase prices when compared to the individual investor."

"The biggest mistake made by inexperienced investors is that they do not

CASE STUDY: GETTING STARTED WITH BONDS

match their unique investment objective and risk level to the appropriate investment idea. This usually spells trouble in the short run."

Is there a danger that the increased the demand for bond mutual funds and ETFs brought about by the downturn in the stock market will artificially raise the prices of these funds?

"It is a possibility. That is why it is important to purchase bonds in a mutual fund / ETF or to "ladder" your bond holdings by maturity date if you are purchasing individual bonds. Diversification is very important."

How has the greater availability of information on the Internet affected the bond market?

"More information always leads to fairer prices for any product you are considering purchasing. Bonds are no exception to this rule. More information is a good thing."

Will state budget deficits due to reduced income from real estate and sales taxes due to the mortgage crisis affect the ability of issuers of municipal bonds to meet their obligations?

"There could be isolated instances of defaults on municipal bonds due to the poor economy but it is very rare. Muni bonds are typically very safe. If you are concerned about default, you can purchase only muni bonds that are insured against default. Your return will be lower but you will be able to sleep better at night knowing you have another layer of safety with the bond insurance."

Do you think enough is being done to educate investors? Is the government doing enough to encourage savings?

"I do think the government is doing what they need to do to encourage retirement savings. Many tax-deferred savings programs are available to investors now. Obviously, the government can't "force" people to save; they must take on that responsibility for themselves.

But the vehicles are there if investors are willing to take advantage of them (such as IRAs, 401(k) programs, and so on). As far as education goes, that is somewhat up to the investor. The information is there if they will take the time to find it and read it.

Understanding the Risks of Bond Investing

When an investor purchases shares of a company's stock in the stock market, it is with the expectation that as the company grows and expands its business, the value of those shares will increase. There is always the risk that the company's shares will decline in value or that the company may operate at a loss or go bankrupt, resulting in the loss of the investor's capital. Different types of risk are associated with investing in bonds. When an investor purchases a bond, he or she is loaning money to the bond issuer. A bond is essentially a promise to pay a fixed interest rate over a specified period and to return the capital at a certain date. There is always a risk that the issuer of a bond may fail to fulfill this promise. In the section on credit ratings, we explained that the likelihood of this happening is very remote for some bonds and a real danger for others. Loaning money for periods of time at fixed interest rates also exposes an investor to a number of other, less obvious types of risk. The greater the risk associated with a bond issue, the greater the incentive that must be offered to induce an investor to loan money. Risk is an important factor in deciding the interest rate to be offered by a new bond issue, the price of the bond on the secondary market, and the willingness of the investor to purchase the bond.

Large institutional investors, seeking the highest possible return on their investment capital, carefully analyze historical trends as well as the financial stability of a bond issuer before making a decision to buy. They look at the big picture, the performance of the bond indexes and the outcome of certain types of investment over time. Their conclusions are reflected in the daily fluctuations of the bond market and in the U.S. Treasury auctions. Many institutions implement rules to limit the types of risk they are allowed to undertake. As an individual investor, you have only a limited amount of capital to invest and a few decades in which to achieve your investment objectives. Even a small mistake might result in substantial losses. It is important to have a good understanding of the types of risk recognized by large investors, and the effect they might have on you.

Some of these risks affect only investors who expect to sell bonds on the secondary market before they reach maturity; others also affect buy-and-hold investors who buy bonds because they need a steady stream of income, or because they know they will need a large amount of money for a future event such as the purchase of a house, higher education, or retirement.

The risks involved in bond investing include:

Default Risk

Default risk is the risk that the agency or company issuing the bonds will not be able to pay you back. Bond credit ratings, designed to assess default risk, are reliable, but there is always a possibility that something unforeseen may occur, and the bond issuer will be forced to default on the loan.

Inflation Risk

Prices on almost all consumer goods and services increase over time, as inflation erodes the buying power. The Federal

Reserve Board of the United States by law has to meet four times a year, but more recently meets eight times per year to set interest rates, in an attempt to manage both inflation as well as economic growth. While the rate of inflation tends to remain fairly steady under normal circumstances, the times when the inflation rate becomes much higher or lower than average can seriously impact the rate of return on bonds.

Just like inflation erodes the buying power of your salary as prices of good increase, it also erodes the value of your bond investment. If you invest $1,000 in a 30-year bond today, any inflation experienced by the economy resulting in higher process for good and services, will result in that $1,000 having less purchasing power in 30 years when the bond matures. The interest rate on the bond or what is called the nominal rate has to be adjusted to what is called the **real interest rate**, which takes into account the effects of inflation.

Inflation-protected bonds are immune to this risk, but they offer a much lower interest rate. If **deflation** occurs, the protection they offer becomes meaningless and you are left holding low-interest bonds. Remember, the inflation adjustment on these bonds is subject to taxation.

Interest Rate Risk

If the prevailing interest rate jumps to 10 percent and you purchased a bond at an earlier prevailing interest rate of 5 percent, you will be stuck with an investment that returns only 5 percent when you could be getting much better returns somewhere else. If you try to sell the bond on the **secondary market**, you will have to accept a discounted price and take a loss. If you hold the bond to maturity, you will suffer a **loss of opportunity** — the chance to earn much higher returns by investing your money elsewhere. The longer the maturity of a bond, the greater the likelihood that interest rates will rise before it matures (**interest-rate risk**). A three-year bond will have a far lower interest-rate risk than a 20-year bond.

Interest rates are in constant fluctuation in most markets and economies. Changes in interest rates have a tremendous impact on the bond market, particularly on intermediate- and longer-term bonds. Short-term bonds characteristically do not react strongly to changes in interest rate due to their shorter duration.

Timing Risk

The longer an investor holds a bond, the greater the possibility of exposure to interest rate risk, inflation risk, and default risk. Most investors are willing to take risks if the potential rewards are good enough, so bond issuers compensate for the additional risk, known as timing risk, by offering higher interest rates for long-term bonds.

Bonds are also subject to **timing risk** in the secondary bond market. When an investor decides to sell a bond before it reaches its scheduled maturity, the value of the bond will be determined by the supply and demand balance at the time of sale.

Market Risk

Market risk is associated with all types of bonds, but it particularly affects bond mutual funds. The price at which an investor is able to buy and sell a bond fund depends upon supply and demand in the bond market. Unlike a bond itself, which promises to return the investor's capital at maturity, a bond mutual fund constantly rolls capital over into new bond purchases as old bonds reach maturity. If an investor sells his shares of a bond mutual fund at a time when demand and prices are lower than when the fund was bought, there is a risk that some of the original capital will be lost.

Market risk also affects investors who wish to sell an individual bond prior to its scheduled maturity date. When demand is low, it may be difficult to find a buyer who is willing to pay what the bond was originally worth.

Liquidity Risk

Liquidity risk is the risk that an investor may not be able to find a buyer for bonds when he or she needs cash. Once bonds have been purchased for a portfolio, it may be difficult to sell them. Although the bond market is larger than the stock market, much of the activity within the bond market is generated by institutional investors rather than individual investors. The most active bond issues are found within the Treasury market, both in the primary and secondary markets.

If an investor intends to hold his or her bond until its maturity, liquidity risk is not of particular concern. Investors who prefer more liquid investments can purchase or invest in bond mutual funds or ETFs rather than in individual bonds.

Investors concerned with liquidity should seek out more well-known bond issues that historically have a strong trading volume in the secondary markets. If the secondary market for a bond issue is active, investors are more likely to get a better price for their bond than if the issue is thinly traded.

Call Risk and Reinvestment Risk

Some corporate and municipal bonds include **call provisions**, giving the issuer the right to redeem the bond prior to its scheduled maturity date. Falling interest rates are the most common reason for calling in a bond, but a bond might be called early if, for example, a municipal project finds another, less costly form of financing. The risk to the investor is that the bond will be called prematurely, obliging him or her to look for reinvestment options that will almost certainly have lower coupon rates than the bond that was called, and also diminishing expected annual income. Most callable bonds offer investors a higher coupon rate than non-callable bonds to compensate for this investment risk.

Tax Risk

The interest received on bonds, depending on the type of issue, can be subject to federal, state, or local income taxes, and also to capital gains taxes. Because rates of return on bonds are already relatively low compared to say equities, these taxes can significantly reduce the investment return realized from a bond investment. Tax laws can change over the period of bond ownership, making a bond investment less profitable or increasing the returns to the investor depending on if the tax rates are increased or decreased. It is best to consult a tax advisor to determine the best investment strategy for your personal situation prior to making investment decisions.

Investors in bond mutual funds are required to pay capital gains taxes on any profits realized by the selling activities of the fund's portfolio manager during the year, even though those profits have be reinvested by the fund. For this reason, bond mutual funds are often held in a tax-deferred investment account. (See *Chapter 14: Evaluating a Bond Investment: Your Taxes.*)

Credit Rate Risk

Bonds are loans to bondholders, and with any loan, there is a risk of default. Bonds are given **credit ratings**, just like any borrower. It is possible for the credit rating of a bond issuer to be upgraded or downgraded during the life of a bond. If a bond's credit rating is upgraded, the value of that bond on the secondary market will increase correspondingly. Likewise, if the bond's credit rating is downgraded, the bond's value on the secondary market will often decline. A change in credit rating will not affect an investor who intends to hold bonds until maturity unless they become a forced seller because of minimum credit rating requirements or concerns about potential default.

How Much Risk Can You Afford?

Many investment questionnaires ask you to determine how much risk you can "tolerate." A better question is, how much risk can you afford? How much money do you have? How much money can you afford to lose? The answer to this question determines the makeup of your portfolio and the types of bonds or bond funds you should select. Is your mortgage paid off? Are you about to retire, or are you in mid-career, with time to recover from a possible loss? Do you have other sources of income? Are you investing your life savings, or do you have a little windfall that you want to set aside for the future? Are you relying on this investment to pay for your child's college education? Is someone in your family disabled? Are you in good health?

One of the great appeals of a bond investment is that you can sleep peacefully at night, confident that your savings are secure. Taking on a risk that you cannot afford can cause anxiety and stress and take an unwanted emotional toll on your life.

TIP: High Returns are Associated with Greater Risk

Perhaps you have heard a friend or colleague bragging about achieving great financial success with a particular strategy or investment, and been tempted to adopt the same strategy yourself. Remember that your friend achieved this success because he or she took risks that you might not be willing to take. You might not be as lucky. People rarely brag about their mistakes and losses; your friend may not be telling you about other ventures that did not turn out so well.

The recent trend away from pension benefits and toward individual retirement accounts (IRAs) and 401(k) plans places much more responsibility on individuals to prepare for their financial security when they are no longer able to work. Not having enough savings for retirement can also be considered a risk. Today, only 25 percent of employers in the United States offer retirement pensions, and the average U.S. household has only $40,000 set aside for retirement. If you are earning a regular salary and need to dramatically increase your retirement savings, you are taking a risk by not investing a portion of your portfolio in stocks or in bonds with higher returns. A consultation with a financial advisor can help you determine the best way to allocate your investments for both growth and preservation of capital. Advice is also available on Web sites such as **www.morningstar.com**, **www.kiplinger. com/yourretirement**, and **www.smartmoney.com**.

CHAPTER 14

Evaluating a Bond Investment

Predicting the Future

Understanding Interest

At least four, but typically eight, times a year, the Federal Open Market Committee (FOMC) of the Federal Reserve meets to set a target federal funds rate, the interest rate at which private depository institutions (mostly banks) lend cash to each other from their balances at the Federal Reserve to other depository institutions, usually overnight. Members of the FOMC include the Board of Governors of the Federal Reserve System, the president of the Federal Reserve Bank of New York and a rotating selection of presidents of the other 11 reserve banks. The federal funds rate controls the supply of available cash and affects short-term interest rates. A change in the **federal funds rate**, or even a change in expectations about the future level of the federal funds rate, can set off a chain of events that will affect other **short-term** interest rates, longer-term interest rates, the foreign exchange value of the dollar, and stock prices. Even experts cannot predict whether the FOMC will decide to change the federal fund rates, and there is no accurate model to predict exactly how interest rates will respond if a change is made because many other economic factors come into play.

Interest rates have a direct effect on the return you can expect to realize on a bond investment. To sell a new bond, the issuer must offer a coupon rate, adjusted to compensate for risk, which is comparable with the prevailing interest rate. When interest rates fall, callable bonds will be redeemed at the earliest call date, cutting off interest income and forcing you to reinvest at the lower rate.

Interest rates, more than anything else, determine the price of bonds on the secondary market. If you sell a bond before it matures, its price will be affected by current interest rates. When current interest rates are lower than the bond's coupon rate, buyers are willing to buy the bond at a price higher than its face value (**premium**) so that they can receive a higher annual income than is offered by new bond issues. If the current interest rate is higher than a bond's coupon rate, it would be priced at a **discount** to compensate for the fact that it will provide less income from interest then comparable new issues. The price paid for a bond is factored into the calculation of its **yield**, the total return that can be realized from a bond investment. The bond's price must be lowered until its yield is comparable with similar, newly issued bonds.

The interest rate on the 30-year U.S. Treasury note serves as a benchmark for long-term bonds. Bond traders keep a close watch on interest rates, trying to anticipate when they are about to rise or fall, buying bonds when their prices are low, and selling them when the prices go up. Investors who rely on bonds for a fixed income must be aware of the effect that interest rate changes may have on their portfolio, particularly if they hold short-term or callable bonds. Buy-and-hold investors in non-callable bonds will receive scheduled interest payments on their principal, as planned, but because interest rates are closely associated with other economic factors such as inflation, the strength of the dollar, the stock market, and the cost of borrowing money for a mortgage or car loan, they may affect the overall value of the investment at maturity.

Bond traders use **duration**, a measure of how much a bond price will respond to changes in interest rate, to compare the relative **interest rate** of two or more bonds with different issue and **maturity** dates, **coupon rates,** and **yields to maturity**. (See *Duration* in *Chapter 3: The Fundamentals of Bond Investing*.)

Yield Curve

Interest rates on bonds of different maturities do not rise and fall together. Short-term rates and long-term rates often move in opposite directions. The overall pattern of this interest rate movement is an indication of the direction the economy is about to take. Economists capture the overall movement of interest rates by plotting the interest rates for various maturities of U.S. Treasury bills and bonds on a graph called a **yield curve**. The interest rates on short-term three-month T-bills closely follow the current federal funds rate. Interest rates on the long-term 10- and 30-year Treasuries, which are set at auction by the bids of large institutional investors, are a reflection of how these large investors believe the economy will behave in the next decades.

You can find current and historical yield curves on the Internet at Stockcharts.com (**http://stockcharts.com/charts/YieldCurve. html**) or SmartMoney.com (**www.smartmoney.com/onebond/ index.cfm?story=yieldcurve**).

In **normal** circumstances, when there is little economic disruption, the yield curve slopes gently upward as maturities lengthen and interest rates increase. Investors naturally expect to be compensated with higher interest rates for the increased risk of holding long-term bonds to maturity. The interest rate on 30-year Treasuries is typically 3 percent higher than the interest rate on short-term securities. Abnormal shapes, such as steep, inverted, or flat (humped) yield curves, signal turning points in the economy. When the interest rates for long-term Treasuries become more than 3 percent higher than those of short-term Treasury note, the yield curve becomes **steep**, an indication that investors expect the economy to strengthen in the next few years. They fear that they will be locked into low interest rates and demand greater compensation. When long-term interest rates drop below the rates offered by short-term notes, the yield curve is **inverted**. Investors anticipate that the economy is entering a rapid decline and want to lock in whatever interest rate they can before the rates drop even further. A **flat**, or **humped**, yield curve in which the difference between short-term and long-term interest rates is small, indicates that the economy may be on the verge of sliding into a recession.

Bond investors look at yield curves to identify the point at which the yield curve **peaks**: the bond maturity at which interest rates stop rising and begin to level off. All other considerations aside, the greatest yield can be realized by buying bonds of that maturity. For example, if interest rates level off after a 5-year maturity, the additional interest offered for a 10-year or 30-year bond is not enough to compensate for the additional risk associated with it.

Bond traders attempt to profit by buying bonds just before interest rates go down, and then selling them at a higher price. They cut their losses by selling before bond prices drop, or by selling short. In periods of economic stability, the yield curve may remain almost unchanged for long periods of time, and bond prices fluctuate very little.

Your Taxes

Before making any kind of bond investment, it is important to understand how, and when, the interest income from that bond will affect your income tax return. Your income tax status determines what types of bonds you should buy, and what kinds of accounts you should keep them in. The income from a taxable bond may be reduced if it bumps you into a higher income tax bracket. By choosing your bonds wisely, you can minimize tax liabilities and get the most out of your investment. Tax laws change every year. If your portfolio is complex, you have a very large income, or you have recently experienced a major lifestyle change such as retirement, job loss, or a career change, you may want to consult a tax advisor before purchasing bonds. Look for an enrolled agent (EA), a CPA with tax expertise, or a financial planner. The National Association of Tax Professionals (NATP) Web site (**www. natptax.com**) offers an online search, or you can ask friends for referrals.

Tax-exempt Municipal Bonds
(See *Chapter 7: Municipal Bonds.*)

Interest received from municipal bonds is exempt from Federal income tax and, in many cases, from state and local taxes. Because tax liability is one of the factors that determines the market yield of a bond, municipal bonds can offer a lower rate, given its lower tax liability, allowing governments to borrow money more cheaply to fund public projects.

If you are in a high-income tax bracket, tax-exempt municipal bonds or municipal bond funds are a good choice. They are especially popular with retirees who typically have few tax deductions such as dependants and mortgage interest. If you are in a low-income bracket, you are not likely to benefit as much from the tax exemption and should instead choose stable taxable bonds such as Treasuries or high-grade corporate bonds that offer a higher rate of return. Tax-exempt municipal bonds should not be held in tax-deferred accounts because the tax benefits do not apply and other investments offer better returns.

If you live in a state such as New York or California that has a high state or local income tax, purchase municipal bonds from within that state. Some states, like Florida, do not tax income from out-of-state municipal bonds. However, Florida does tax the market value of financial instruments issued by non Florida issuers making it desirable for Florida residents to invest in state issuers.

A number of Web sites offer taxable **equivalent yield calculators** that allow you to compare the yield from a tax-exempt municipal bond with the yield from a taxable bond:

- Morgan Stanley (**www.morganstanleyindividual. com/markets/bondcenter/TEYCalculator/**)

- Franklin Templeton (**www.franklintempleton.com/ retail/jsp_cm/education/fund_basic/types/tf_calc.jsp**)

- SIFMA Foundation for Investor Education

(**www.pathtoinvesting.org/calcs/taxyields/calculator_ taxyields.htm**)

Not all interest income from municipal bonds is tax-exempt. Income from some municipal bonds is subject to the AMT. Municipal bonds or bond funds that are subject to the AMT must indicate this in their prospectuses. Certain bond funds are specifically designed to avoid the AMT. Owners of shares in a municipal bond mutual fund or ETF must pay capital gains tax on profits realized from the fund's sale of bonds, even when that money has been reinvested in the fund. Tax losses are not passed through to the investor.

Municipal Bonds and Capital Gains Tax

If you purchase a tax-exempt municipal bond at a discount to its face value and hold it to maturity, the difference between the face value and the price you paid is subject to a 15 percent capital gains tax in the year the bond matures. When purchasing a municipal bond at a discount, capital gains tax must be factored into the expected return. When taxes are taken into account, a bond selling at a discount may not be as good an investment as it appears to be.

Effect of Capital Gains Tax on the Return from a Discounted Municipal Bond						
Bond (2-year maturity)	Coupon Rate	Face value	Current Market Price	Principal plus Interest after 2 Years	Return	Return after Taxes
Par (not taxed)	4%	$1,000	$1,000	$1,080	$80.00	$80.00
Premium (not taxed)	6%	$1,000	$1,037.70	$1,120	$82.30	$82.30

Effect of Capital Gains Tax on the Return from a Discounted Municipal Bond						
Discount (Capital Gains Tax of 15% on difference between price and face value)	2%	$1,000	$960.22	$1,040	$79.78	$73.81

The "De Minimus" rule

The "De Minimis" tax rule states that if you purchase a bond at a discount and the discount is equal to or greater than a quarter point (.0025 percent) of the face value per year until maturity, the difference between the face value and the discounted purchase price will be taxed as ordinary income, not as capital gains. If you are in the top tax bracket this could mean the difference between paying 15 percent and 35 percent on the gain.

Taking the discounted bond from the example above, which matures in 2 years, if you purchase the $1,000 bond for less than $995, the difference between the face value and the discounted price will be taxed at the higher income tax rate, and the return will be significantly lower.

Bond	Coupon Rate	Face value	Current Market Price	Principal plus Interest after 2 Years	Gain	Gain after Taxes
Par (not taxed)	4%	$1,000	$1,000	$1,080	$80.00	$80.00

Bond	Coupon Rate	Face value	Current Market Price	Principal plus Interest after 2 Years	Gain	Gain after Taxes
Premium (not taxed)	6%	$1,000	$1,037.70	$1,120	$82.30	$82.30
Discount (Capital Gains Tax of 15% on difference between price and face value)	2%	$1,000	$960.22	$1,040	$79.78	$73.81
Discount (Income Tax of 35% on difference between price and face value)	2%	$1,000	$960.22	$1,040	$79.78	$65.86

Alternative Minimum Tax (AMT)

The **alternative minimum tax (AMT)** was introduced by the Tax Reform Act of 1969 to prevent wealthy taxpayers from claiming tax exemptions to avoid paying income tax. Initially, it targeted 155 high-income households in the United States, but the Tax Reform Act of 1986, signed by Ronald Reagan, expanded the AMT to target tax deductions, such as exemptions for dependants and personal tax exemptions, that most Americans receive. Though regular federal income tax brackets, exemptions and deductions are adjusted every year for inflation, the rules for the alternative minimum tax have not been changed. As salaries and annual incomes have gradually increased with inflation, more and more people have become subject to the AMT every year. In 1970, only 19,000 people owed the AMT; millions owed it in 2007. A brief issued by the Congressional Budget Office (CBO) (No. 4, April 15, 2004), concluded that "by 2010, if nothing is changed, one in five taxpayers will have AMT liability and nearly every married taxpayer with income between $100,000 and $500,000 will owe the alternative tax." Reform of the AMT is under discussion in Congress, but it is uncertain what changes will be made and when.

The AMT is like a separate tax system with its own set of rules and deductions. It is so complex that the only way to know whether you owe the tax is to fill out IRS Form 6251. If the AMT calculated on Form 6251 is higher than your regular income taxes, you must pay the AMT instead. Tax preparation software can run the AMT calculation for you, and the IRS Web site offers an online "AMT Assistant" (**www.irs.gov/ businesses/small/article/0,,id=150703,00.html**) to help you determine if you will be subject to the AMT. You can also consult a professional tax advisor or an accountant. Knowing whether you are subject to the AMT will help you determine what type of bond investments to buy, and what kind of account they should be held in.

IRS Form 6251 strips away most of the standard deductions and exemptions allowed under regular income tax rules, and substitutes its own. You lose exemptions for yourself and your dependents, and write-offs for state, local, and foreign income taxes as well as your home-equity loan interest, if the loan proceeds are not used for home improvements. Itemized medical expenses must amount to 10 percent of your income before they can be deducted. The AMT exemption ($66,250 for 2007 joint filers; $44,350 for unmarried persons; $33,125 for those married filing separately) is then deducted from your income. This exemption is reduced by 25 cents for each dollar of AMT taxable income above $150,000 for couples ($112,500 for singles and $75,000 for married filing separate status). AMT is 26 percent for the first $175,000 ($87,500 for married couples filing separately) and 28 percent on anything over that. Regular income tax rates for 2008 were 25 percent on incomes from $32,550 to $ 78,850 and 28 percent on incomes from $78,850 to $164,550.

Anyone with an annual income over $75,000 and some large deductions might be subject to the AMT. Taxpayers with several children, interest deductions from second mortgages, capital gains, high state and local taxes, and incentive stock options are the most vulnerable. If your annual income is over $100,000 you should definitely run the calculation. Approximately 15 percent of people earning $75,000 to $100,000 a year must pay the AMT.

Tax- Exempt Municipal Bonds and the AMT

Interest income from most municipal bonds is exempt from federal income tax and from most state or local income taxes. Interest from **private-activity bonds** that finance "nonessential" projects such as sports stadiums and convention centers, or projects backed by private companies, such as a bond issued to upgrade airport facilities backed by an airline, is subject to the AMT. Because the ATM tax liability eats into the interest earned on the bond, these bonds typically offer a higher interest rate as compensation. Municipal bond funds and ETFs that offer tax-exempt income often include some of these bonds in their portfolios because of their higher yields. Interest income from private-activity bonds held by a fund is also subject to the AMT. Prospectuses and listings of municipal bonds indicate whether they are subject to the AMT, and their annual statements tell you how much of the interest income is taxable.

Very rarely, if it is determined that the funds raised by a bond issue are not being used for their intended purpose, the IRS changes the tax exempt status of a municipal bond and makes it taxable. In these cases, unhappy investors are left holding a taxable, low-interest bond which is very difficult to sell.

Many investors do not learn that they are subject to the AMT until they do their annual tax returns or are contacted by the IRS. Suddenly, they must pay interest on income from a bond or fund that they previously believed to be tax-exempt. Some bond funds aim to be AMT-free and indicate this on their prospectuses.

AMT and Capital Gains

If you purchase a bond at a discount and redeem it at face value, or if you sell it on the market at a higher price than you paid for it, you realize a profit that is taxed as a long-term capital gain. Both federal income tax and the AMT tax long-term capital gains at 15 percent. If the gain is large enough, though, it may cause you to lose your personal AMT tax exemption ($44,350 for unmarried persons). This exemption is reduced by 25 cents for each dollar of AMT taxable income above $112,500 for singles ($150,000 for couples). For every $1,000 of long-term capital gain your income tax goes up by $150 (15 percent). If your AMT taxable income is more than $112,500, that added

$1,000 also eliminates $250 of your exemption (25 percent), adding another $70 to your tax bill.

> ### TIP: Before Selling Your Bonds, Determine Whether You are Subject to the AMT that Year
>
> If you are just on the borderline between paying regular income tax or the AMT, a long-term capital gain realized from the sale of bonds might raise your income enough to push you into the "AMT zone." If you are already subject to the AMT that year, you might be able to protect your exemption by distributing the sale of your bonds over several years.

Tax-Deferred Accounts

Tax-deferred accounts are created to encourage and reward individuals who save money for education or retirement. (See *Chapter 18: Bonds as Savings.*) Eligible investors are allowed to make taxable or tax-deductible (depending on the type of account) contributions to a tax-deferred account, which is then invested in bonds, stocks, mutual funds, ETFs, and other financial products. Income from interest or dividends is reinvested in the account, and income tax on these earnings is deferred to allow a larger amount to be invested. When withdrawals are eventually made from a tax-deferred account, the accumulated earnings are taxed as income along with any previously untaxed principal. In some circumstances, withdrawals are tax-exempt.

These accounts are subject to strict rules and penalties, such as annual contribution limits, income restrictions, and minimum ages for withdrawals. Only earned income can be contributed to tax-deferred retirement accounts, so that once you leave the workforce, you can only hold existing investments in them.

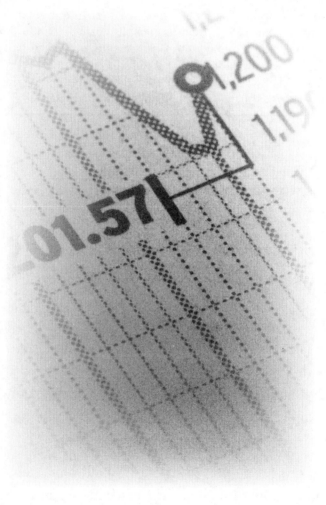

CHAPTER 15

Doing the Research

Acommon rule of thumb for investors is "do not buy what you do not understand." Ultimately, you are the one who will enjoy the benefits or suffer the consequences of your investment decisions. You owe it to yourself to spend some time reading and investigating. Financial information is sometimes couched in jargon and trade terminology, but there is nothing that cannot be explained if you keep asking until all your questions are answered. If, after reading all about a prospective investment, questions still linger in your mind, it is probably because something significant has been left unsaid. That missing information may be the key to your success or failure.

Bonds and other financial products are essentially merchandise, like televisions and automobiles, and brokers and financial institutions are salesmen. Just as you do not base your decision to buy an automobile on a car dealer's sales pitch, you should not base your decision to buy a bond only on the sales literature or your broker's enthusiastic endorsement. Make up your own list of questions on aspects of an investment which are important to you, and conduct your own research.

Where to Find Information

Over the last decade, the Internet has brought about a revolution in the investing world, making information that was previously the exclusive domain of professional financiers and brokers available to individual investors wherever they live and work, 24 hours a day. Business annuals, yearbooks, magazines, and information on financial institutions can be found in public libraries. Two monthly publications, the *Mergent Bond Guide* and *Standard & Poor's Bond Guide* are available in many libraries. The latest updates and real time information on market fluctuations are reported on the Internet. Many organizations provide educational materials online, and investment companies offer access to online calculators and research tools. Developments occur so rapidly in the financial markets that the information in books is often outdated just a few weeks after it has been printed.

General information about bonds and bond investments is available on the Web sites of numerous government agencies, professional organizations, financial publications, and investment companies.

Government Agencies

Government agencies not only post detailed rules and regulations, but speeches and reports prepared by their staffs, and commentary by various officials and professionals:

- **Federal Reserve (www.federalreserve.gov)**: Information on monetary policy, banks and interest rates, minutes of committee meetings.

- **Internal Revenue Service (IRS) (www.irs.gov)**: Tax code, instructions, and forms.

- **Securities and Exchange Commission (SEC) (www. sec.gov)**: Education for individual investors, laws and regulations governing the financial markets, compliance information, registration, and background checks for brokerages.

- **Financial Industry Regulatory Authority (FINRA) (www.finra.org)**: FINRA is a merger of NASD and the New York Stock Exchange's regulation committee, subject to oversight by the SEC. It oversees the operations of the stock exchanges and enforces federal securities laws and regulations. The FINRA Web site offers education for investors and numerous reports on individual companies and their compliance with the law.

- **Municipal Securities Rulemaking Board (MSRB) (www.msrb.org)**: The Municipal Securities Rulemaking Board was established in 1975 by Congress to develop rules regulating securities firms and banks involved in underwriting, trading, and selling municipal securities. It sets standards for all municipal securities dealers, and is subject to oversight by the SEC.

- **Treasury Direct (www.TreasuryDirect.gov)**: Offers product information and research across the entire line of Treasury Securities, from Series EE savings bonds to Treasury Notes. Individuals can open TreasuryDirect accounts and purchase Treasury Bills, Notes, Bonds, Inflation-Protected Securities (TIPS), and Series I and EE savings bonds in electronic form.

Professional Associations

Professional associations try to promote the business interests of their members by enforcing business standards and providing education for consumers:

- American Association of Individual Investors (AAII) (**www.aaii.com/bonds**): A non-profit, membership association that provides free education and advice for individual investors, including sample portfolios.

- American Enterprise Institute for Public Policy Research (AEI) (**www.aei.org**): A private, nonpartisan, not-for-profit institution dedicated to research and education on issues of government, politics, economics, and social welfare. Provides in-depth analysis of economic policy.

- Government Finance Officers Association (GFOA) (**www.gfoa.org**): Information on recommended financial practices for state and local governments.

- Investment Company Institute (**www.ici.org/**): The national association of U.S. investment companies, including mutual funds, closed-end funds, exchange-traded funds (ETFs), and unit investment trusts (UITs) seeks to encourage adherence to ethical standards and offers investor education about mutual funds.

- National Association of Tax Professionals (NATP) (**www.natptax.com**): Tax information and directory search for professional tax advisors.

- National Federation of Municipal Analysts (NFMA) (**www.nfma.org**): Established in 1983 to provide a forum for issues of interest to the municipal analyst community, its membership includes nearly 1,000 municipal professionals. It is a cosponsor of EMMA (**www.emma.msrb.org**), a site offering extensive information on municipal bonds.

- Securities Industry and Financial Markets Association (SIFMA) (**www.sifma.org**): Represents more than 650 member firms of all sizes, in all financial markets in the U.S. and around the world. Sponsors Path to Investment (**www.pathtoinvesting.org**), an educational site for investors and InvestinginBonds.com (**www. investinginbonds.com**).

Financial Journals and Publications

This is where you go to get an up-to-date picture of the financial markets and current economic trends. Financial journals, magazines and publications provide coverage of important issues by journalists, analysts, and commentators. You can find explanations of complex financial instruments, news of new bond issues and funds, predictions about the economy, reviews of brokerages and funds, personal recommendations, and daily commentary on the national and global financial markets. The writers are typically required to disclose their professional affiliations and whether they have a personal interest in the investments they are writing about. Always read several articles on a subject before reaching a conclusion, and be aware of the author's orientation. Visit some of these sites regularly to keep yourself abreast of the latest developments:

- Business Week (**www.businessweek.com**)

- CNN Money® (CNN®, Fortune®, Money Magazine) (**www.money.cnn.com**)

- Forbes.com® (**www.forbes.com**)

- Investment News (**www.investmentnews.com**)

- Investopedia® (**www.investopedia.com**): Sponsored by Forbes, this Web site provides tutorials, educational materials, and a glossary of investment terms.

- Kiplinger.com℠ (**www.kiplinger.com**)

- SmartMoney® (**www.smartmoney.com**)

- The Motley Fool℠ (**www.fool.com**)

- *The Wall Street Journal* (**www.online.wsj.com/public/us**)

- Yahoo! Finance (**www.finance.yahoo.com**)

Brokerage and Financial Sites

Brokerage and financial Web sites provide detailed information about individual stocks, bonds and funds, prices, market movements, investing tools, access to prospectuses, and often professional blogs and commentary.

- EMMA (**www.emma.msrb.org**): EMMA makes available official statements for most new offerings of municipal bonds, notes, 529 college savings plans, and other municipal securities since 1990 and provides real-time access to prices at which bonds and notes are sold to or bought.

- Incapital, LLC℠ (**www.incapital.com**): Incapital underwrites and distributes fixed-income securities and structured notes through over 900 broker-dealers and banks in the US, Europe, and Asia. Their Web site offers investment tools and an educational program for bond investors (**www.bondschool.com**).

- Morningstar, Inc. (**www.morningstar.com**): Morningstar, Inc., a leading provider of information on investment products, has its own ranking system for hundreds of bond funds. Its bond calculator allows you to compare two or more bonds. Its subsidiaries include Morningstar Associates, LLC and Ibbotson Associates, Morningstar® Managed Portfolios, and Investment Services, Inc., a registered investment advisor and broker-dealer.

- MuniNetGuide (**www.muninetguide.com**): Online guide and directory to municipal-related content on the Internet with a unique emphasis on municipal bonds, state and local government, and public finance.

- New York Stock Exchange (NYSE) (**www.nyse.com**): The NYSE provides a trading platform for bond traders and an online dictionary of bond terms.

- Trade Reporting and Compliance Engine^{SM} (TRACE) (**www.investinginbonds.com**) (**www.cxa. marketwatch.com/finra/BondCenter/Default.aspx**): Created under the auspices of the SEC, TRACE offers price information on bond sales within 15 minutes of a trade. You can use TRACE to find the last price at which a particular bond traded. TRACE information is also displayed on other brokerage and financial sites.

Many financial advisors and brokerages offer education and investment tools on their Web sites. These are the sites where you will look for specific corporate or municipal bond offerings (See *Chapter 19: Buying and Selling Bonds: Choosing a Brokerage*.), and they often provide access to prospectuses, sales literature, and other information about each bond. Remember that these sites are created as sales vehicles, and double-check the recommendations they make by comparing them with comparable offerings on other sites.

Prospectuses and Sales Literature

Every bond issuer and fund company is legally required to provide potential investors with a prospectus detailing the structure of the bond offering, its special features, liabilities, and the strengths and weaknesses of the bond issuer. Electronic Municipal Statistics (**www.emuni.com**) provides free access to all municipal bond official statements submitted to it for publication by bond issuers and underwriters. If the terminology is abbreviated or unfamiliar, use an investment glossary or simply type the term into a search engine until you find a definition you can understand.

Sales literature emphasizes the major characteristics of a bond offering, but may gloss over important details such as risk or a call provision. Be wary of over-simplified promises and exaggerated adjectives, and be sure to examine the prospectus carefully, as well as looking at overall market conditions, before making a decision.

A final source of information is a customer service representative from the bond issuer itself.

TIP: Take it with a Grain of Salt

Always check the source of information when doing your research, and be conscious of any bias that might affect its accuracy. A financial advisor may be selling his own investment program, a journalist may be seeking notoriety by over-reacting, or an organization may be protecting the interests of its members at your expense. Get information from several sources before reaching a conclusion. If you come across a contradiction, try entering the bond name in a search engine and look for additional articles or commentary.

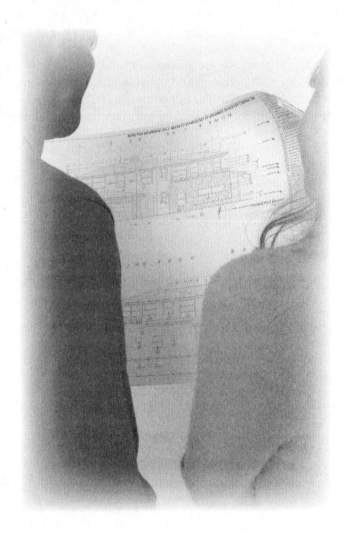

CHAPTER 16

Building Your Bond Portfolio

Planning Your Strategy

Now that you have clearly defined your financial needs and goals, determined your tax status, and done some research on bonds, it is time to plan your investment strategy.

How much of your portfolio should be invested in bonds?

The answer to this question depends on how you intend to use your money: for growth, income, or savings. A comparison of returns on the S&P's 500 stock market index and 5-Year Treasury bonds from 1946 to 2007 shows that the inflation-adjusted annual return on stocks during that period was much higher than that of bonds, but bonds provided a higher annual income than stocks.

Average Returns, Growth, and Income for 1946 - 2007			
	Stocks	Bonds	Cash
Average Annual Return	11.4%	5.9%	4.6%
Average Annual Return After Inflation	7.4%	1.9%	0.6%
Average Annual Growth	7.4%	0%	0%

Average Returns, Growth, and Income for 1946 - 2007			
Average Annual Income	4.0%	5.9%	4.6%

**Figures from "Stocks, Bonds, Bills and Inflation—2008 Yearbook,"
Ibbotson Associates, Chicago.**

Stocks also exhibit much greater volatility than bonds. Volatility translates directly into the possibility that on the day you need your money, it will not be there. Bonds are regarded as a stable investment; invest in good-quality bonds and you can expect to receive regular interest payments and your capital at maturity. Stocks offer a greater opportunity for growth, coupled with the added risk of losing some of your investment capital if you have to withdraw from the market at the wrong time. If your priority is growth, a portion of your portfolio should be invested in equity. Most growth investors allocate between 20 percent and 60 percent of their portfolios to less volatile bonds and other fixed-income investments, and the remainder to stocks. The following chart shows typical stock/bond allocations for different types of buy-and-hold portfolios:

Allocation of Stocks and Bonds in a Portfolio			
	Global Equity (Stocks)	Fixed Income (Bonds)	Expected Long-Term Return
Income Oriented	20%	80%	5.8%
Conservative	40%	60%	6.4%
Moderate	50%	50%	6.7%
Moderate Growth	60%	40%	7.0%
Aggressive	80%	20%	7.7%

Historically, bonds have manifested a low correlation to stocks. When the stock market is in a decline, as it was in

2008, bonds tend to hold their own very well. When the stock market is doing well, equity investments bring in substantially higher rates of return than bonds. Conventional wisdom dictates that as you approach the point when you will begin to withdraw money from a growth portfolio, you should move an increasingly larger segment of your portfolio into bonds and fixed-income investments to avoid sudden losses just before you need your money. **Life-cycle investment strategies** place a large percentage of stocks in the portfolio of a young person in the workforce and gradually move the allocation into bonds as the person ages and approaches retirement.

Because you are not a statistic or an average, you should design your portfolio around your particular circumstances, as defined by your answers to the questions in the previous exercise. Your need for financial growth should be balanced with your other needs, such as access to funds in an emergency, money to pay for a college education, or a down payment on a house or business in a specific year, or the responsibility of providing for a disabled family member. Bonds are the vehicle for successfully meeting these needs.

The Power of Compounding

Bond investments are also a vehicle for stable growth if the regular interest payments they provide are reinvested. The Rule of 72 estimates how many years it will take you to double your money at a particular annual rate of return: simply divide 72 by the rate of return. For example, if you invest $10,000 at an annual rate of return of 6 percent, and regularly reinvest the interest at the same rate, you will have doubled your investment in 12 years. The challenge is finding a way to reinvest your money at the same rate of return.

Allocating your bond portfolio

Divide the bond portion of your portfolio into three segments:

Funds for Emergencies

How well-equipped are you to deal with emergencies such as a serious illness, sudden job loss, car accident, or death in the family? Your first priority is to place a certain amount of your portfolio into short-term bonds, Treasury bills, EE or I savings bonds (if you can hold them more than one year), CDs, or money market accounts which give you quick access to cash when it is needed. These investments bring in lower rates of return, but your returns may be much lower if you are forced to sell a long-term bond before it reaches maturity. If you have insurance, a good line of credit, or other sources of cash for emergencies, you do not need to keep as much in short-term securities. Most accountants recommend placing enough cash for 6 months' living expenses in reserve before beginning a large-scale investment program.

Capital Preservation

The major portion of your bond portfolio should be placed in good-quality, **plain vanilla** bonds that can be held to maturity. These include:

- Treasury bonds, both coupon and zero coupon

- TIPS bonds and I savings bonds if you are worried about inflation

- EE savings bonds

- Agency bonds, both coupon and zero-coupon, but not mortgage-backed bonds

- Highly rated and insured municipal bonds

- Highly-rated corporate bonds

- Highly-rated Yankee bonds

- FDIC-insured CDs issued through a bank or broker

This portion of your portfolio can be designed to contribute to a fixed-income stream, or the interest payments can be reinvested for growth. The specific selection of bonds, and the type of account (taxable or tax-deferred) in which they are held should be based on your tax status.

Longer-term bonds have a higher yield, but there is an increased market risk if you have to sell the bonds before they come due. No-load funds and ETFs containing similar high-quality bonds are also appropriate.

Speculation and Growth

A small portion of your portfolio can be invested in bonds and bond funds that involve more risk, but offer higher returns. While these investments promise rapid growth, they can also result in big losses and should not be undertaken until you have enough stable, good-quality investments to take care of your basic needs. If you are just starting out as an investor, you may want to "gamble" with a small percentage of your portfolio, but always keep the proportion small in relation to more stable investments.

Speculative bond investments include:

- Non-rated or poorly rated corporate and municipal bonds (junk bonds)

- Emerging market bonds

- Foreign bonds sold in foreign currencies

- CMOs (collateralized mortgage obligations) and individual market securities

- High-yield municipal and corporate bond funds, leveraged funds

- Longer maturity bonds, due to their longer duration and high sensitivity to interest rate moves.

High-yield bonds may be tempting for income-oriented investors, but default, or in the case of mortgage bonds, the gradual depletion of capital, may result in a lower income than anticipated.

Diversification is important in a speculative bond portfolio to protect from default risk, market risk and interest rate risk (in the case of mortgage bonds). If all your bonds are of a similar type or belong to the same market sector, they will all be affected by the same economic ups and downs. Diversification is not as important for a portfolio of Treasuries or high-quality corporate and insured municipal bonds, since default risk is minimal.

TIP: Do Not Buy What You Do Not Understand

Remember that a high yield is typically associated with high risk. Before buying a high-yield bond or bond fund, be sure you understand its structure, the risks involved and the tax consequences.

Rebalance Your Portfolio Regularly

Review your bond portfolio at regular intervals for shifts in its allocations of cash, stable and speculative investments. If the speculative portion has grown out of proportion, shift some of it into more stable bonds, or begin reinvesting the interest payments in more conservative investments to preserve your gains.

Protecting Yourself from Risk

No one can accurately predict when interest rates will go up or down, or exactly what the economy will be like in five or ten years when a bond matures, but you can use several strategies to "immunize" your portfolio against some types of risk.

Buy new issues and hold them to maturity

Avoid **market risk** (the risk that the value of your bond on the secondary market will go down) by buying new issues and holding them to maturity. You will receive your principal and the promised interest, no matter how much market prices have fluctuated during the life of the bond.

Buy bonds with a high credit rating

Avoid **default**, or **credit risk**, by buying only good quality municipal or corporate bonds with high credit ratings, insured bonds, or Treasuries and agency bonds.

Build a bond ladder

You can protect your portfolio from interest rate risk by creating a **bond ladder**. Rather than buying one $100,000 ten-year bond, buy ten $10,000 bonds with varying maturities beginning with one year and going up to ten years. Each time a bond matures, use the proceeds to buy another bond that matures one year later than the top bond on your ladder.

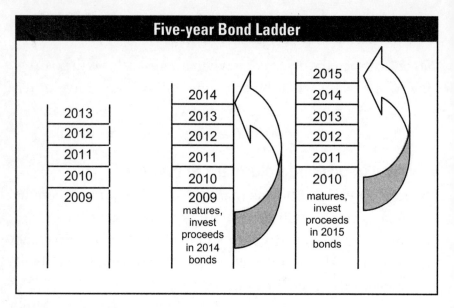

Build your ladder with non-callable bonds that meet your need for a cash income. A bond ladder gives you a diverse portfolio of short, mid, and long term bonds, with a relatively stable current yield. If interest rates go up, you have a bond maturing every year that you can reinvest at a higher interest rate to increase your yield. If interest rates drop, only a small portion of your portfolio (the maturing one-year bond) must be reinvested at the low rate. When you need to withdraw extra cash, you know you will have a bond maturing soon. Your ladder can be made up of bonds that mature at intervals longer than one year apart, but it will be less responsive to changes in interest rate. Five years is the minimum length of time for which a bond ladder strategy is effective. The longer the maturities of the bonds in your ladder, the higher the yield as well as the greater the duration risk.

A relatively short ladder can be constructed of CDs, which can be purchased without fee at many banking institutions with maturities ranging from six months to five years. You can also build a ladder using Treasury bills that mature in three-, six-, or 12-month intervals, or Treasury notes that mature in two, three, five, or ten years, purchased directly from **www. treasurydirect.gov**.

You can customize your bond ladder to match your specific financial needs, for example, targeting maturities in certain years to cover education costs. You can also diversify by adding different types of bonds or other debt obligations. U.S. Treasury notes and bonds, or high-quality municipal bonds, are best for ladders because the supply is plentiful and there is little risk of default. A broker or bank can construct a bond ladder for you of any length, using government and corporate securities purchased at original issue or in the secondary market, but it will cost you more because of brokerage fees and trading commissions. Most discount brokerages will let you create your own bond ladder with corporate bonds. Some also offer ready-made bond ladders with specific investment goals.

Your bond ladder should coordinate with your entire investment portfolio to provide maximum protection against interest rate risk. For example, if you are investing a large amount of money from another source, such as a severance package, royalties, a contract, an insurance settlement, inheritance, or IRA distribution in a certain year, you do not want bonds in your ladder maturing in the same year.

Bond Strategies

High Income Tax Bracket

Tax-exempt municipal bonds are the best choice if you are in a high income tax bracket. (See *Chapter 14: Evaluating a Bond Investment: Your Taxes.*) Avoid bonds subject to the AMT and taxable municipal bonds. Look for bonds that are exempt from state and local taxes. Select bonds with high credit ratings. Do not buy all your bonds from one issuer, geographic area or industry sector; diversify your portfolio across industries and maturity dates. Create a laddered portfolio to protect yourself from reinvestment risk.

You can benefit from tax-free municipal bonds even if you are in the 25 percent tax bracket. In 2007, individuals whose taxable income exceeded $31,850 and married couples whose combined taxable income exceeded $63,700 were in the 25 percent tax bracket. During the credit crunch in 2008, municipals actually yielded in excess of treasuries due to the temporary dislocation in the market, so tax analysis was irrelevant in deciding to buy them.

Low Income Tax Bracket

If you are in a lower income tax bracket, buy STRIPS, TIPS, Treasuries, agency bonds, taxable municipal bonds, and corporate bonds with high credit ratings. They bring in higher returns than tax-free municipal bonds. You can use a tax-equivalent yield calculator such as those mentioned in Chapter 13 to compare the returns of taxable and tax-free bonds for someone of your income level.

Because you are unlikely to be subject to the AMT, consider purchasing AMT municipal bonds, which typically offer yields 20 to 30 basis points higher than those of other municipal bonds of the same credit quality. Remember that these bonds are more difficult to sell. You may become subject to AMT in the future if your annual income increases, or you lose tax exemptions as dependants leave home.

Saving for a Specific Financial Goal

Select bonds that will mature around the date that you will need the money. If current interest rates are low, put a portion of your portfolio (but not all of it) into bonds with short-term maturities and reinvest as they come due. That will give you a chance to take advantage of rising interest rates when they occur; there is no guarantee, though, that interest rates will move one way or the other.

Reinvest the interest if possible; keep it in a money market account until you have enough to buy a bond or CD.

Starting Out With $25,000 or Less

If you are starting your bond portfolio with $25,000 or less, purchase short-term or intermediate-term bonds. Avoid long-term bonds, because you will be exposing yourself to **market risk** if you need money and have to sell the bonds before they mature. Buy TIPS bonds, agency bonds, CDs, EE, and I savings bonds. You do not need to worry about name diversity because you are buying bonds with good credit ratings. TIPS bonds and savings bonds can be bought directly from **treasurydirect.gov**. If possible, keep the interest income in a money market account until you have enough to purchase another bond.

Create a five-year bond ladder and extend it to ten years when you have more capital to invest or if you do not need an emergency reserve. If you are in a high-income tax bracket, consider a tax-exempt municipal bond fund or ETF instead.

CASE STUDY: BOND INCOME IN RETIREMENT

Wilford Fraser

Wilford Fraser, a former petroleum geologist, lives in Florida and receives a steady income from his bond investments.

"The main factors I look at in assessing a bond fund are the interest rate and whether the bonds are insured. I need to be able to calculate what my income will be, and I cannot afford to lose my capital if an issuer defaults.

Also, tax free bonds are attractive in that not only is your taxable income lower but you might also benefit from a lower tax bracket.

I have resisted the temptation to load my portfolio with riskier investments to make up for my lost income due to the lower interest rates. It's akin to someone taking a pay cut to retain the job."

CHAPTER 17

Bonds as a Source of Steady Income

Bonds are attractive investments because of their safety, predictability, and regular interest payments. Once you have accumulated enough capital, you can create a bond portfolio that will provide you with a steady income while preserving your assets.

Retirement

A year before you plan to retire, review your financial circumstances and identify the changes you will need to make to your portfolio. Will you need to withdraw funds to carry out retirement plans, such as purchasing a motor home or traveling around the world? Will you sell your home and add to your investment capital? When you are no longer under your employer's health plan, how will you pay for health insurance? When will you start receiving social security or medicare benefits?

Your tax status may change now that you are no longer receiving an income from your job. If you are now in a lower tax bracket, consider selling your tax-free municipal bonds and investing in safe taxable bonds that bring in a higher rate of return. If you are still in a high-income tax bracket, tax-free municipal bonds or bond funds are still the best option.

If you continue to work after retirement, you can contribute up to a certain amount of earned income (either wages, self-employment income, or alimony) to a Roth IRA at any age as long as your AGI is under the threshold. You can start withdrawing funds without penalty from your IRA or Roth IRA when you reach the age of 59½ and will be required to make a minimum annual withdrawal from your IRA after the age of 70½. Withdrawals from your IRA will be taxed as income in the year they are distributed; only the earnings portion of withdrawals from a Roth IRA are taxed, because the contributions were not tax-deductible.

Building a Fixed-Income Portfolio

When you are ready to replace a monthly paycheck with a regular income from your retirement savings, it is time to convert your portfolio from a savings vehicle to an income generator. Selling your shares of stock will incur capital gains taxes on any profits you have made, and a withdrawal from your tax-deferred retirement account will be taxable as income. You can also redeem your EE and I savings bonds and purchase Treasuries offering a regular interest payment instead. (The interest income on savings bonds will be taxed in the year that they are redeemed.)

Bonds pay interest semiannually. Purchase bonds that pay interest in different months, and time the payments to coincide with your financial requirements. The types of bonds you buy should be determined by your tax status. Buy non-callable (bullet) bonds to be sure of receiving the expected income. If you purchase callable bonds for their higher yield, be aware of their call dates and have an alternative plan ready. Choose high-quality or insured bonds. Remember that high-yield bonds generally carry more risk and that you could lose your capital if you invest in junk bonds. Protect yourself from interest rate risk by laddering your bonds so that they mature in different years.

SCHEDULED REGULAR INCOME PAYMENTS			
Monthly	Payment Schedule	Quarterly	Payment Schedule
Bond A	January and July	Bond A	January and July
Bond B	February and August	Bond B	January and July
Bond C	March and September	Bond C	January and July
Bond D	April and October	Bond D	April and October
Bond E	May and November	Bond E	April and October
Bond F	June and December	Bond F	April and October

Mortgage-backed bonds, stock dividend funds, bond mutual funds and ETFs also provide monthly income, but the amount varies from month to month and may include capital gains income or repayment of principal. Preferred stocks promise an annual dividend. All of these options are subject to loss of capital if the market price of shares drops, or the underlying loans default.

CASE STUDY: MUNICIPAL BONDS AS A SOURCE OF RETIREMENT INCOME

Vivian Nostrand

Vivian Nostrand retired in Florida after a long career working in New York City. A widow for 17 years, she relies on the regular income from her investments in bonds for her living expenses.

"I have been investing bonds for about sixteen years now. I first began buying bonds because most of my portfolio was invested in stocks and certificates of deposit, and I thought it prudent to diversify. At the time, corporate bonds and notes were yielding relatively high interest rates (roughly 7 to 9 percent), so I invested in a number of corporate bonds, including some General Electric Company and utility company offerings. When interest rates fell, though, most of the bonds were called and I sought another safe source for investing my money at a good rate of return. In addition, I had several two-year Treasury notes, which paid good interest for several years, but then became unattractive when the interest rates declined.

At that time, I became conscious of the tax liabilities generated by the interest from bonds and other investments, so I opted to buy tax-exempt municipal bonds. Since Florida had an Intangible Property Tax which taxed the interest on out-of-state municipal bonds, I chose to buy Florida "munis." The Intangible Property Tax was repealed after 2006, and since then, I have bought out-of-state municipal bonds, though I still own some of the Florida bonds. Also, I once invested in a municipal bond mutual fund, but sold my shares in that because of the service charges involved. Now I own only individual bonds. (For some of these, there has been a minimal transaction fee of less than five dollars.) So I have accumulated enough bonds to have my own "municipal bond fund." The bonds represent financing for a variety of projects such as highways, airports, ports, water and sewer systems, health and education facilities, cultural facilities, state university student housing, and so on.

The yield on the tax-exempt munis that I now hold ranges from 4.25 to 5.375 percent, providing me an equivalent or better income than the net income from taxable bonds that pay higher interest rates. I am invested in long-term bonds, with maturity dates from 20 to as long

CASE STUDY: MUNICIPAL BONDS AS A SOURCE OF RETIREMENT INCOME

as 30 years after date of purchase. The maturity date doesn't matter to me because I am more interested in the income they pay twice a year. Different bond issues pay interest in different months, and the income is staggered so that I have money being deposited into my brokerage money market account each month. I do also own one tax-exempt municipal bond ETF, that pays monthly dividends and trades on the NYSE just like a stock.

I buy my bonds through a brokerage firm. When my broker notices that I have accumulated a substantial amount of cash in my account, he calls me and says, "Hey, I have a good deal you may be interested in!" He seems to apportion these offerings among his clients and might, for instance, offer an individual client the opportunity to invest from $10,000 to $25,000 in a particular bond. Also, he looks for reliable, high-grade, insured bonds, often at a discount.

I have had only one "bad" experience with a municipal bond from an Arizona health facility. Several years ago, my broker called and advised me to sell at least half of my holdings in that bond because it looked as though the issuer might be going to default on the interest payments. I followed his advice, but the issuer did not default. The remaining half that I held onto is still yielding the same income today, so I lost the opportunity to make twice that much!

One pitfall of investing in bonds is to be holding long-term bonds when interest rates keep rising. If your financial circumstances should force you to sell a bond before it reaches maturity, you will take a loss if the bond has depreciated in market value. Further, if you hold the bonds during a rising rate cycle, you miss the chance to invest your money at the higher rates. Of course, when the interest rate falls below what you are receiving, you do well.

I feel that bonds are a good vehicle for retirement savings because they are a relatively stable investment over the long term. When one is older, as I am, one cannot afford to be frivolous. Some of my bonds have call features, but they guarantee to pay at least the face value of the bond, or, in some cases, 1 percent more. Most also feature an "estate clause" that allows the bonds to be redeemed at face value in case of one's death."

CHAPTER 18

Bonds as Savings

Bonds are ideal instruments for saving for retirement, or for specific financial objectives such as the purchase of a business or a home, a college education, or a once-in-a-lifetime vacation. If you purchase good-quality bonds, you can expect the principal to be returned in full on a specific date, and the regular interest payments can be reinvested or used for living expenses. At minimum, you will receive the capital plus interest, and by reinvesting the interest, you can increase your savings. If the right opportunity arises, you may be able to realize even more by selling the bonds before they mature. Purchase Treasury bonds, EE savings bonds, agency (but not mortgage) bonds, corporate bonds with high credit ratings, Yankee bonds with high credit ratings, or FDIC-insured CDs with maturities that target the date when you will need the money. If you are concerned about inflation, buy TIPS and I savings bonds. If you are in a high-income tax bracket, invest in highly-rated tax-exempt municipal bonds. U.S. Treasuries can be bought in $100 increments, allowing you to add to your savings at regular intervals. Bond mutual funds often provide a higher rate of return than CDs or individual bonds if you reinvest the interest. Select a no-load, good-quality fund with low expenses, and set up an automatic investment plan with regular transfers from your checking account.

Saving for Education

Bonds and bond funds are well-suited for education savings because they offer a stated interest rate and the return of your principal at maturity. Purchase bonds that will mature in the years when your child is 18, 19, 20, and 21 and in time to pay for graduate school. Reinvest the interest by keeping it in a money market account until you have accumulated enough to buy another bond or by purchasing U.S. Treasuries. A bond mutual fund allows you to make regular contributions and automatically reinvests the interest. Since bond fund prices can be volatile, consider moving the funds to a CD, savings account, or to a money market account with the same company that sponsors the mutual fund two years before the cash is needed.

How Much Will an Education Cost?

The total cost of a college education is increasing at twice the rate of inflation. According to the *2007 Annual Survey of Colleges* (College Board®, New York, N.Y.), the average cost of tuition and fees for a four-year private college in 2007 -2008 was $23,712, the average in-state tuition with fees for a four-year public college was $6,186, and the average out-of-state tuition with fees for a four-year public college was $16,640. In one year, the cost of tuition had increased 6.3 percent for private colleges and 6.6 percent for public colleges. Room and board averaged $7,404 per year at public colleges and $8,595 at private colleges. These figures do not include other expenses such as medical insurance, the cost of travel, books, supplies, clothing, and other needs. The total cost of an education will be higher if the student does not complete a degree in four years.

You can find helpful college cost calculators and worksheets online at:

- PrincetonReview.com **(www.princetonreview.com/ college/finance/tcc)**

- Savingforcollege.com **(www.savingforcollege.com)**

- Finaid.org **(www.finaid.org)**

- Collegeboard.com **(www.collegeboard.com/parents)**.

Understanding Financial Aid

Not all education expenses come out of a parent's pocket. Approximately two-thirds of all full-time undergraduate students receive grant aid. In 2008, more than $130 billion dollars in financial aid was available to students in the United States. A diligent student, or one who excels in athletics, music, art, or another specialized field, may qualify for a merit-based scholarship. When you are designing your college savings plan, it is important to optimize your student's eligibility for financial aid. According to **Finaid.org**, your **Expected Family Contribution (EFC)**, the amount of tuition that you are expected to pay, is calculated according to this formula:

- Parental Income (22-47 percent of adjusted gross income from federal income tax return)

plus

- Parental Assets (3-5.6 percent of non-retirement assets, including prepaid tuition plans, 529 Savings Plans, and brokerage/mutual fund accounts)

plus

- Student Income (50 percent of any student income over $3,000)

plus

- Student Assets (20 percent of all assets, including UGMA/UTMA accounts and other savings)

Assets, such as savings accounts, held in the student's name will be assessed at a much higher percentage than parental assets.

Tax-Deferred or Tax-Free Education Accounts

The U.S. government allows two types of tax-deferred accounts for education savings, **Coverdell Education Savings Accounts (CESAs)** and **529 Plans**.

Coverdell Education Savings Account (ESA)

An ESA, like a Roth IRA, allows you to make an annual non-deductible contribution to a specially designated investment trust account. Anyone can open an ESA account and the beneficiary does not have to be a relative or family member. The beneficiary can withdraw funds in any year and use them tax-free for qualified higher education expenses (QHEE) and even for some elementary and secondary school expenses such as tuition and computers. If the beneficiary withdraws more than the amount of qualified expenses, the earnings portion of that excess is subject to income tax and an additional 10 percent penalty tax.

You can open an ESA account with any bank, mutual fund company, or financial institution that can serve as custodian of traditional IRAs. A parent or guardian of the beneficiary will be made responsible for the account. Your cash contribution can be invested in any qualifying investments, including bonds, available through the sponsoring institution.

Several rules limit the effectiveness of ESAs:

- You cannot make any further contributions to an ESA after the beneficiary's eighteenth birthday.

- A beneficiary can receive only $2,000 in total contributions per year.

- Joint tax return filers with **adjusted gross incomes (AGIs)** above $220,000 and single filers with AGIs above $110,000 cannot contribute to an ESA. This requirement can be circumvented by gifting the $2,000 to a child or another relative and having them contribute to the ESA account.

- The ESA must be fully withdrawn by the time the beneficiary reaches age 30. If it is not, the remaining amount will be paid out within 30 days, subject to tax on the earnings and the additional 10% penalty tax. The ESA can be rolled over to a younger relative.

- Unless Congress changes the legislation governing ESAs, certain benefits expire after 2010. K-12 expenses will no longer qualify, and the annual contribution limit will be reduced to $500. It is likely that the benefits will be extended.

529 Plans

Under Section 529 of the federal tax code, there are two types of state-sponsored education savings accounts which offer tax benefits: prepaid tuition plans and 529 plans. A prepaid tuition plan locks in the current tuition rates at public state colleges for a future education. A prepaid plan guarantees payment upon maturity, so it can be considered a safe investment. Prepaid tuition plans are offered by a number of states. You do not have to be a resident of that state to contribute, but the plans have drawbacks. Most of them cover tuition at a public university in their home state; even if they allow you to use the funds at a private or out-of-state school, you will have to make up the difference. Tuition is only part of the cost of a higher education; you will still need a substantial amount of money to cover the student's living expenses.

A 529 plan is a state-sponsored college savings plan. Withdrawals are exempt from federal income tax when used for qualified higher-education expenses. In most states, withdrawals are also state-tax-free, and some states offer their residents a state-tax deduction or credit on contributions. Over 80 of these state-sponsored 529 plans exist today, each with its own rules, fees, and investment choices. In 2006, Congress passed the Pension Protection Act, making the tax advantages associated with 529 withdrawals permanent.

You can find detailed information about all the 529 plans on **savingforcollege.com**. **Morningstar.com** compiles an annual list of the best and worst 529s. You do not have to be a resident of a particular state to invest in its 529 plans. Most 529 plans are administered by a financial company that offers a selection of investment choices.

The 529 plans offer several advantages which make them attractive:

- Investments are selected and portfolio allocations are decided by experienced fund managers with clear financial objectives.

- Contributions can be made in small increments such as payroll deductions without incurring additional trading fees.

- Many 529 plans offer the capability of reallocating assets in the fund free of charge.

- There is no deadline for use of the funds; a beneficiary can use the money from a 529 throughout his or her lifetime.

- Most state plans cap contributions at between $230,000 and $300,000. Any contribution over $12,000 annually may be subject to the gift tax, but a one-time five-year contribution of $60,000 is allowed, with the gift tax exemption distributed over the ensuing five years. This allows a parent or grandparent to set aside $60,000 in one year to grow, tax-free, in a 529 account.

- The contributor retains control of the 529, and can change the beneficiary to any family member of the original beneficiary, including spouses, children, and cousins.

- Withdrawals for the amount of a student's qualified education expenses are tax-free. The earnings on non-qualified withdrawals are taxable at the student's income tax rate, plus a 10 percent penalty. If a student receives a scholarship, the 10 percent penalty may be waived for a withdrawal equaling the amount of the student's tuition.

- Grandparents can set up a 529 to support the education of a grandchild without affecting that child's eligibility for financial aid. If the child wins a scholarship, any funds left over in the 529 can be transferred to another beneficiary in the family. Some 529 plans allow grandparents to contribute to a parent's account.

529 plans offer several advantages over ESAs: anyone can contribute to a 529 plan regardless of income; contributions are not limited to $2,000 per year; and control of the 529 account remains in the hands of the contributor. Most 529 plans allow the contributor to decide when withdrawals are made and for what purpose. A contributor can reclaim the funds in a 529 plan at any time; the earnings portion not devoted to qualified higher education expenses will be subject to income tax and an additional 10 percent penalty tax.

TIP: Research Your 529 Plan Carefully

Do your research carefully before investing in a 529 plan. Look closely at the investment options offered by the plan, and at the fund's historical returns and volatility. Keep expenses at a minimum; look at the expense ratios of the underlying investments, the plan's management costs, enrollment fees, and any brokerage commissions you may be paying. Some providers, like T. Rowe Price (Alaska) and Fidelity (Delaware, New Hampshire, and Massachusetts), offer no-commission plans. If you enroll through a broker or financial advisor, you may be able to negotiate. Make sure you understand all the details of the plan and what education expenses it will cover.

TIP: Not All Education Expenses Qualify

Distributions from 529s and ESAs are tax-free only when they are used for "qualified education expenses" such as tuition, fees (such as activity and lab fees), books, supplies, and equipment (if specifically required in a course syllabus). The amount allowed for "living expenses" is the cost for room and board as determined by the educational institution for federal financial aid purposes. Any tax-free scholarship money is subtracted from the total amount of qualified expenses. Many education expenses such as transportation costs, computers, telephone bills, the cost of furnishing a dorm room or apartment, stationery and art supplies, and other incidentals are not qualified expenses.

Education Savings Bond Program

The Education Savings Bond Program, introduced by the Treasury Department in 1990, allows an investor to exclude the interest income from the redemption of I bonds or series EE savings bonds from taxable income if it is used to pay tuition for the bond holder, spouse, or dependent child at a qualified institution of higher education.

All I bonds are eligible for this program; EE bonds must have been purchased after December 31, 1989. You must have been at least 24 years old on the first day of the month in which you purchased the savings bonds. If you are using the income for yourself, the bonds must be registered in your name; if for a spouse, you must file a joint tax return. In order to claim the exemption for a child's tuition, the child must be listed as a dependent on your tax return. The bonds must be registered in your name or your spouse's name; the child can be listed as a beneficiary, but not as a co-owner. The funds can only be used for tuition and fees at a post-secondary institution that is eligible to participate in a student aid program that is administered by the U.S. Department of Education. In addition, your annual income must be below a certain level in the year that you use EE or I bonds for educational purposes. (You can find all the details in IRS Publication 970 and the instructions for IRS Form 8815.) Married couples must file jointly to be eligible for the exclusion.

Funding Higher Education with IRAs and 401(k)s

Some parents and grandparents use IRAs as vehicles for college savings. You can withdraw funds from a traditional or Roth IRA (See *Chapter 18: Bonds as Savings: Tax Free and Tax-Deferred Retirement Savings Accounts.*) for qualified education expenses, without paying the 10 percent withdrawal penalty. Qualified higher education expenses include tuition, fees, books, supplies and equipment, as well as certain room and board expenses if the student is enrolled at least half time in a degree program. The entire amount of a withdrawal from a traditional IRA is subject to income tax, as is the earnings portion of the withdrawal from a Roth IRA. The entire distribution from a Roth IRA is tax-free if you have reached age 59½ and have held the Roth IRA for at least five years.

You can borrow up to half your vested balance in your 401(k) plan or $50,000, whichever is less, to pay for higher education for yourself, your child, or your spouse. Such loans typically charge a percentage point or two above the prime lending rate, and are not taxed as income. The loan must be repaid within five years, and if you leave your employment for any reason, you may be required to make immediate repayment or pay income tax and a 10 percent early withdrawal penalty on the balance. In cases of extreme hardship, you can also withdraw funds from your 401(k) to pay for qualified education expenses, subject to income tax and the early withdrawal penalty if you are younger than 59½ .

TIP: Your Individual Retirement Account (IRA) is a Last Resort

Unless you already have a retirement income, 401(k)s and IRAs should be used to fund education only as a last resort. The withdrawal will count as untaxed income on next year's FAFSA, and reduce the student's eligibility for need-based financial aid. Money taken from an IRA cannot be replaced, except through limited annual contributions. You will lose not only the amount you withdraw, but all the earnings it might have brought you, and you will lose many of the benefits of an IRA as a tax shelter. You will be funding your children's education at the risk of becoming a burden to them in your

> **TIP: Your Individual Retirement Account (IRA) is a Last Resort**
>
> later years. Low-cost federal education loan programs, such as the Stafford loan for students and the PLUS loan for parents, offer flexible repayment terms, partial tax deductibility, deferments, and forbearance. There are no federal grants or low-cost loans to fund your retirement. Private student loans can be paid off in the future with any funds left over from your retirement.

Tax-Free and Tax-Deferred Retirement Savings Accounts

It is never too early to begin saving for retirement. The sooner you put your money to work, the more you will have in your retirement account when you reach 65. Determine how much money you will need in retirement and where that money will come from. (See *Chapter 12: Choosing a Strategy: Define Your Financial Goals and Requirements*.) Many experts say that you will need about 75 to 85 percent of your current income to maintain your standard of living in retirement. According to life expectancy charts, you can expect to live for 15 to 20 years past retirement, assuming you retire at age 65. Subtract other sources of income, such as social security payments, pensions, and inheritances, and you will have an approximate idea of how much you need to save to be financially independent during your retirement. Consider how inflation will affect your retirement savings; in 10, 20, or 30 years the cost of living will be higher and you will need more dollars to maintain the same lifestyle.

The U.S. government allows two types of tax-advantaged accounts for retirement savings: 401(k) plans and IRAs. These plans defer income tax on earnings in retirement savings accounts, and in some cases on contributions, giving you more money to invest during your working life. According to the Investment Company Institute (**www.ici.org**), 71 percent of all U.S. households have retirement plans through work or IRAs. These plans offer a variety of investment opportunities and often leave it up to you to decide how your portfolio is allocated. If retirement is a long way off and you can handle some risk, you might choose to invest in stock or equity mutual funds that, though more volatile, offer a higher potential for long-term return than do more conservative investments. As retirement approaches, it is advisable to move your assets into more stable bonds or bond funds so that they will be available for you when you need them.

401(k)s, Solo 401(k)s, and Roth 401(k)s

Company **401(k)s**, Solo **401(k)s,** and **403(b)** plans (available only to certain employees of public schools and tax-exempt organizations) are tax-deferred plans that allow workers to make pre-tax contributions to an investment account. Income tax is deferred on the investment and earnings until they are withdrawn from the account. Strict restrictions are placed on withdrawals, and funds withdrawn from the account before its owner reaches the age of 59½ are subject to an excise tax equal to 10 percent of the amount distributed. Minimum withdrawals must begin by April 1st of the calendar year after the owner reaches age 70½. A self-employed individual can set up a Solo 401(k) plan. Contributions to a **Roth 401(k)** plan are made after-tax and qualified withdrawals are tax free.

The greatest benefit of 401(k) plans is that many employers match employees' contributions up to a certain percentage of their salaries to motivate employees to remain with the company longer. This is free money and you should take full advantage of it. Participants in a 401(k) plan must select from among the investment options offered by the plan provider, and cannot invest in individual bonds. Most 401(k) plans offer a selection of bond mutual funds, some of which are created specifically for the plan. Buy bond index funds, money market funds, short-term bond funds, GNMA funds, and high-dividend paying stock funds. These funds guarantee a flow of dividend and interest income that can be compounded, but the fund prices themselves are subject to the fluctuations of the market. Remember to look at the funds' expense ratios when allocating your 401(k) portfolio and avoid those that charge high management fees. When you leave the company or retire, you will be able to roll the 401(k) over into an IRA, which will give you more flexibility and control over your investment choices.

IRAs and Roth IRAs

IRAs were created by the Employee Retirement Income Security Act (ERISA) in 1974, to provide a tax-advantaged savings vehicle for individuals not covered by employer-sponsored retirement plans and to preserve rollover assets from employer-sponsored plans when individuals change jobs or retire. By the end of 2006, Americans were holding an estimated $4,232 billion dollars in IRAs. Contributions to a **traditional IRA** are tax-deductible, and taxes on the earnings are deferred until the money is withdrawn, allowing all earnings to be reinvested. Strict restrictions are placed on withdrawals, and funds withdrawn from the account before its owner reaches the age of 59½ are subject to an excise tax equal to 10 percent of the amount distributed. Minimum withdrawals must begin by April 1st of the calendar year after the owner reaches age 70½. Anyone can open an IRA, regardless of their income.

Roth IRAs were created by the Taxpayer Relief Act of 1997. Contributions to a Roth IRA are counted as taxable income on your tax return, but all your earnings and principal can be withdrawn tax-free if you follow the rules. Withdrawals of principal can be made at any time without penalty, but any withdrawals of earnings before the account holder reaches the age of 59½ are subject to a 10 percent penalty (there are exceptions if the money is withdrawn for certain purposes). There is no mandated withdrawal after the owner reaches a certain age. The tax benefits of a Roth IRA are not realized until the funds are withdrawn, and though a spouse can inherit the Roth IRA without penalty, other heirs will pay income tax on the funds in it. In most cases, the Roth IRA is more advantageous than the traditional IRA, because it allows withdrawals of principal and because taxation rates may rise considerably by the time you begin to make withdrawals. As of 2007, Roth IRAs were available only to single-filers making up to $101,000 or married couples making a combined maximum of $159,000 annually.

The maximum allowable contribution to either type of IRA for 2008 was $5000 for anyone 49 or younger, and $6000 for anyone 50 and older. This limit will be raised in $500 increments depending on the rate of inflation. Contributions must be made by April 15th of the following year. You can open an IRA or a Roth IRA with a bank or a brokerage, and select any of the investments they offer. A brokerage is likely to offer more investment options than a bank. Many brokerages and banks allow you to open an IRA account online. When deciding where to open your IRA, look for:

- A good selection of investment options including mutual funds and bond ETFs.

- Low commissions and account fees.

- The ability to make automated fund transfers from your bank account.

- The minimum balance required to open an account or purchase a fund.

If you are making small, regular contributions, a low-cost bond mutual fund may be a better choice. You can also put your money aside in a money market account and make one or two larger contributions to the IRA during the year.

Taxable and Tax-advantaged Accounts

Even after you reach the age of 70, you can let your savings continue to grow in an IRA account without penalties, as long as you withdraw the mandated **required minimum distribution (RMD)** every year. Unfortunately, limits on the size of contributions restrict the amount of money you can put into a retirement account. You will need to make the most of tax-advantaged accounts while maintaining the rest of your savings in a taxable account.

The asset allocations in your portfolio should be spread across both types of accounts, with those generating the most taxable income and those with the most potential for growth in an IRA and investments with possible tax benefits in the taxable account. If you are in the 25 percent tax bracket or higher, you should buy tax-exempt municipal bonds for your taxable account. If you are in a low-income bracket, buy taxable bonds and hold them in your taxable account, because the yield on taxable corporate bonds is higher than the tax-equivalent yield of municipal bonds.

All distributions from your IRA account (but not a Roth IRA account) or pension fund are taxable at your regular income tax rate in the year that they are paid out. For this reason, you should keep stocks and mutual funds that generate capital gains in your taxable account, where those gains will be taxed at the lower capital gains tax rate of 15 percent.

TIP: Don't Miss Your RMD

Minimum annual withdrawals from an IRA must begin by April 1st of the calendar year after the owner reaches age 70½. The IRS uses life expectancy statistics to calculate the minimum withdrawal amount, which is a percentage of your IRA based on your age. The withdrawal is taxed according to your regular income tax rate. Failure to withdraw triggers an excess accumulation tax amounting to 50 percent of the required distribution that wasn't taken. If you have a large amount in your IRA and are in a lower tax bracket (10 percent or 15 percent), you can begin withdrawing just enough every year from your IRA to stay within your tax bracket when you are 59½, pay income tax on it, and transfer it to a Roth IRA. That way you will reduce the amount in your IRA, making the future RMD smaller. Funds in a Roth IRA can stay there indefinitely. Assets held in an IRA are subject to income tax when they are inherited by a beneficiary.

Bonds and Estate Planning

U.S. Savings Bonds

U.S. savings bonds can be registered with a co-owner or a beneficiary to avoid probate if the bond owner dies before redeeming the bonds. A bond registered under co-ownership can be cashed in by either co-owner without the knowledge or approval of the other. Gift tax may apply if the co-owner does not provide half of the cash with which the bond is purchased. A savings bond registered with a beneficiary can only be cashed in by the owner until his or her death, after which it becomes the property of the beneficiary. Bonds which are not redeemed before the owner's death, and which are not registered with a co-owner or beneficiary will become part of the owner's estate and will go through probate.

Survivor's Option

Although not common today, some corporate and municipal bonds offer a **survivor's option** or **"death put"** provision that allows the beneficiary of the bond holder's estate to put (sell) the bond back to the issuer at par in the event of the bondholder's death or legal incapacitation. Bond issuers have differing rules on when and how the option can be exercised; for example, it might be invalid if the bondholder had a terminal illness when the bond was purchased, or a minimum period of time must have elapsed since the bond was purchased. These options are often included in smaller, less liquid bonds. Some limit the amount that an individual investor can redeem; AES will redeem no more than $25,000 per owner.

CHAPTER 19

Buying and Selling Bonds

You can create a simple, inexpensive bond portfolio yourself by opening an account with **www. TreasuryDirect.gov** and buying U.S. government bonds and savings bonds of varying maturities. All other bond transactions are carried out through brokerages, except for some mutual funds which are sold directly by financial institutions. Not all stock brokers are knowledgeable about bonds; it is important to find a bond broker who is experienced with the type of bonds in which you are interested.

Choosing a Brokerage

A bond broker is an individual licensed by the Financial Industry Regulatory Authority (FINRA) to buy and sell bonds for investors. A bond broker may work for a brokerage firm and sell bonds from the firm's inventory, or may work independently using a bond inventory from a network of bond dealers and traders that sell and resell bonds. A bond broker can work with you to determine your investment goals and appropriate investments. If you elect to buy bonds through a full-service broker or discount brokerage, you will probably work with an individual bond broker. Your relationship with your bond broker is important; the bond broker will notify you when bonds are due and when you have accumulated too much cash in your account from interest payments and need to seek an investment. If you feel intimidated by a bond broker, or have difficulty communicating, try someone else.

Some online bond brokers exclusively offer the sale and purchase of bonds, and many traditional full-service brokerages also offer online accounts and sell bonds through their Web sites. Competition for online customers has motivated these companies to offer increasingly sophisticated investment tools on their Web sites, including access to extensive research, online classes, newsletters and commentary, and various calculators for comparing returns on different investments. Online bond brokers typically do not offer consultation and advice; after you have found the bonds you want, they simply carry out the purchase order.

If you do not want to pay the commissions and fees of a full-service brokerage, but need professional assistance to define your financial objectives, determine your optimum portfolio asset allocations, and select bonds, consult a fee-only financial planner. A fee-only CFP (Certified Financial Planner) will charge only an hourly or one-time consultation fee and does not receive commissions from the sale of financial products. To check the accreditation and legal status of bond brokers or financial advisors, look them up on the SEC (www. sec.gov/investor/brokers.htm) or FINRA (www.finra.org/ Investors/ToolsCalculators/BrokerCheck/index.htm) Web sites. The SEC site also has information on the regulatory compliance of brokerages.

Look for a brokerage firm that trades the kind of bonds that you want to buy, and accommodates your investment style.

Some brokerages specialize in municipal bonds, and even in specific geographical regions, industry sectors, or bonds with low ratings.

Find a brokerage which offers the services you need, and a Web site that is easy for you to use. Reviews and charts comparing all the online brokerages can be found on financial Web sites such as SmartMoney **(www.smartmoney.com)**, The Motley Fool **(www.fool.com)**, and Stocks and Mutual Funds **(www. stocksandmutualfunds.com)**. Find out what the transaction and account fees will be, what type of commission will be charged, what minimum investment is required, and whether there are any inactivity charges, monthly activity fees, or account maintenance fees. Brokerages may charge a flat fee per trade, a percentage of the face value of the bond, or a fee for each bond traded.

Some larger brokerages offering online bond trading are:

- Ameriprise® **(www.ameriprise.com)**
- Charles Schwab® **(www.schwab.com)**
- E*Trade Financial® **(www.etrade.com)**
- Firstrade℠ **(www.firstrade.com)**
- Fidelity℠ **(www.fidelity.com)**
- OptionsXpress **(www.optionsxpress.com)**
- Scottrade® **(www.scottrade.com)**
- T. Rowe Price **(www.troweprice.com)** Bond funds
- TD Ameritrade **(www.tdameritrade.com)**
- Vanguard **(www.vanguard.com)**

- WallStreet*E (www.wallstreete.com)

Bond brokers:

- FMSBonds℠ (www.fmsbonds.com) Municipal bonds

- JBHanauer & Co. (www.bondsearch123.com)

- Anderson Wealth Management Group of Raymond James™ & Associates (www.raymondjames.com/searchforbonds)

TIP: Watch Out for Conflicts of Interest

Be wary of brokers who strongly promote specific products or try to steer you toward one investment when you have inquired about another. A brokerage may offer incentives to brokers to sell certain products, or they may be able to earn higher commissions than they would on the bonds you want to buy. Do some independent research to determine whether their advice is valid. A broker who strongly promotes mutual funds instead of individual bonds may not have enough knowledge or experience with the type of bond you wish to buy.

Buying Bonds

In addition to the brokerage fee, a mark-up or commission is often worked into the price of a bond. The price you see online, or the price you are initially quoted, may not be the price you pay for a bond. Brokerages employ bond traders who buy and sell bonds, and brokers who communicate with clients and arrange sales and purchases. A broker may be able to offer you a better price than what was initially quoted, if the bond trader agrees to it. When you find a bond you would like to buy online, it is a good idea to call and speak to the broker before placing an order. Small quantities of bonds left over after large sales to institutional traders are often sold off to individual investors at a discount. Sometimes a broker will offer you an incentive to purchase all of an odd lot. A small number of bonds may be sold all-or-nothing (AON), meaning that you must buy the entire lot.

> **TIP: Small Lots are Easy to Buy and Difficult to Sell**
>
> You can often get a good price on odd lots of bonds, but small quantities of bonds are harder to sell if you decide not to hold them to maturity. If you expect to sell bonds before they mature, purchase them in lots of $25,000.

When a trade is "done away," the broker has to purchase the bonds from another brokerage. Two mark-ups are then included in the price, one when the bond is sold to your brokerage, and one when it is sold to you. Discount brokerages that sell mostly outside inventory charge a flat fee instead of a second mark-up.

Transactions of Treasury bonds settle (are completed) the next day; corporate and municipal bonds typically settle three days after the trade unless you have made other arrangements with your broker.

Once you have purchased a bond, the broker will send you a confirmation in the mail including the amount purchased, the trade and settlement dates, unit price, total cost, accrued interest and whether the bond is callable.

Making the Most of Your Bond Portfolio

There are a few simple rules you can follow to keep your bond portfolio growing and to get the most out of your bond investments:

Save as much and as early as possible

Our materialistic culture offers many temptations and encourages spending on bigger houses, more luxurious cars, appliances, travel, and the latest electronic gadgets. There is a trade-off. Indulge yourself now, or curb your impulses and enjoy a comfortable, independent, worry-free lifestyle later. The sooner you make a habit of regular saving, the sooner you will achieve financial freedom. Reinvest interest payments whenever possible, instead of spending them.

Don't lose money

Stick with U.S. government bonds and stable, high-quality municipal bonds. Riskier bonds offer higher returns, but a single default can wipe out years of growth. Make sure you fully understand a bond investment before you put your money into it.

Keep expenses to a minimum

Buy U.S. Treasuries and savings bonds directly from **www. Treasurydirect.gov**. Always be conscious of brokerage commissions and trading fees when buying and selling bonds. Hold bonds until maturity whenever possible. If you are buying a bond mutual fund or ETF, compare expense ratios and choose no-load funds and those with low expense ratios. Choose a savings plan that minimizes trading costs.

Maximize tax benefits

Evaluate the tax consequences of a bond before purchasing it. Keep taxable bonds in tax-deferred accounts whenever possible. Do not allow income from taxable bonds to bump you into a higher income tax bracket. If you are in a high income tax bracket, invest in tax-exempt municipal bonds. Re-assess your tax status whenever your income or your family situation changes.

> ## TIP: Cheapest is Not Always Best
>
> You want to avoid unnecessary expenses, but there are times when higher costs are justified. A good broker may be able to find you a discounted price on the bonds you want, even though his commission is a little higher. A mutual fund or ETF may have better underlying investments than another fund with a lower expense ratio. Always compare similar funds to see if the higher expense ratio might be justified by less risk and higher returns.

When to Sell Your Bonds

There are times when it is appropriate for a buy-and-hold investor to sell bonds.

The price of a Bond In the Secondary Market Goes Up

If the price of a bond has appreciated in the secondary market, and you can use the cash or want to invest in another type of asset, sell the bonds and take the profit.

Your Tax Status Changes

If retirement or another life event puts you into a low income tax bracket, you may want to sell your municipal bonds and buy taxable bonds with higher returns. Conversely, you might find yourself in a higher tax bracket when you get a promotion or inheritance, dependents leave home, or your mortgage is paid off. In that case, it is time to switch to tax-exempt bonds.

Rules governing the government tax code change every year. If a major change is made to the rules for the AMT, for example, you may no longer be subject to it.

You Move to Another State

Municipal bonds that were exempt from state and local taxes in one state may not be exempt in another. Some states, like Texas, do not tax interest from any municipal bonds.

You Need to Rebalance Your Portfolio

If you want to change the target asset allocations in your portfolio, or if your portfolio has deviated from its original asset allocations, you may need to sell bonds of one type and purchase bonds of another. You may have been reinvesting the higher yields from junk bonds until they are out of proportion to your more stable bonds, or you may have redeemed bonds to pay for your child's college education. Check your portfolio allocations when the market fluctuates significantly or when you make significant withdrawals.

Tax Loss Strategy

If interest rates are rising and bond prices have fallen, you may want to sell a bond or bond fund at a loss to reduce the amount of taxable income in a given year. Proceeds from the sale can be used to purchase another bond of similar maturity or credit quality in a different market sector. The IRS 30-day wash-sale rule does not allow you to claim a capital loss on a security sale if you buy a "substantially identical" security within 31 days. Bond mutual funds, except for index funds, are different enough from each other to fulfill the requirements of this rule.

Bond Swaps

Bond swapping is a management technique used to tailor a portfolio to achieve particular investment goals. Bonds are sold and simultaneously replaced, often at the same price, with an equal number of bonds that have different characteristics. A maturity swap exchanges bonds of different maturities, such as long-term bonds for bonds of shorter maturities; a quality swap upgrades safety by purchasing high-grade bonds; a yield swap aims to maximize return on invested capital by purchasing deep discount bonds when rates are falling or lower-grade bonds with higher yields; and a tax swap creates a tax loss offsetting capital gains by selling a bond at a discount and substituting a similar bond to preserve the original investment.

You might execute a bond swap if you need a larger current income stream and are not concerned about future risk, or if you no longer need access to cash for emergencies and want to invest in long-term bonds with higher interest rates. A bond swap involves trading fees and commissions. If you are exchanging one type of bond for another, make sure you calculate the yields correctly and that the bond swap is worthwhile.

Active Trading with Bond Funds and Bond ETFs

The term "bond traders" is used in reference to institutional investors and brokerages that buy and sell large quantities of bonds and attempt to profit from price fluctuations in the secondary bond market. While individual investors can benefit by using bond traders' strategies to select bonds and to decide when to buy and sell them, it would be difficult for an individual to become an active bond trader. Institutional investors and brokerages have exclusive access to some bond issues, and receive price discounts for buying in large quantities. Except for U.S. Treasuries and savings bonds, bonds are sold over-the-counter by brokerages and financial institutions who make money from the mark-up, or difference between the ask price and the bid price. Real-time price information is often not available for small issues of bonds or those that are sold infrequently. The amount that you receive or pay for a bond may vary considerably from the previously quoted price.

Because bond prices move with interest rate changes, they may remain relatively stable for long periods of time. Bond prices rise when interest rates go down, or when the stock market is in a decline. If you feel confident that these conditions are about to occur, you can profit by buying bonds and selling them on the secondary market when the prices go up. Some bonds are illiquid or difficult to sell in small quantities. Having said this, it is very difficult for individual investors to be profitable traders of bonds. This is because the commissions and bid/offer spreads are significantly higher than equities and these costs significantly eat into profits. Also, the small size an individual investor trades may affect liquidity. U.S. Treasuries are liquid in small sizes like $5,000, but municipals and corporates are less liquid in what are called odd-lot sizes which is then $500,000 or $1 million range. Some less liquid corporates won't trade in sizes less than $5 million. Remember that bond prices go up in difficult times because their predictable returns are more attractive to investors than the uncertainty of the stock market. Unless you plan to spend the money realized from a bond sale or know of a better investment, you may be better off holding on to those bonds yourself. Shares of bond ETFs, which trade on the stock exchanges, can be bought and sold using market timing and other active trading techniques that are used in trading stocks.

CHAPTER 20

What Is on the Horizon

An important attribute for a successful bond investor is the ability to envision the future. What will the economy be like in two, five, ten, or 30 years? How will the United States adapt to globalization? What countries and cities will become flourishing business and financial centers? Which political systems might pose a threat to the financial stability of the world? How will the Internet change the way we do business? What changes will occur in sectors such as health care, insurance and education? What kind of pressures will global warming and environmental destruction place on national and local governments? Which industries will experience the most growth and expansions, and which ones will become obsolete? How will the transportation sector react to oil shortages? The first decade of the twenty-first century has been a period of rapid, and sometimes unexpected, change. A responsible and informed investor can study the lessons of the past, look at the changes taking place, and find direction for the future.

New Investment Offerings

The corporations, governments, and government agencies that issue bonds are essentially purveyors of debt, subject to the whims of the market and obliged to listen to the demands of customers, both institutional and private investors, who are shopping for the best ways to invest their savings. In response, new and creative ways of packaging bond investments are constantly emerging. A recent example is STRIPS, which began as an initiative of the private sector and were officially endorsed by the U.S. Treasury in 1985. Cash-strapped governments will find creative new ways to collateralize debt, such as tobacco bonds, which came into wider use during 2007, when states began to experience budget shortfalls as the economy stalled and the subprime mortgage crisis played out.

New mutual funds and ETF offerings will appear to satisfy the increasing demand for fast and easy access to bond markets. Custom index funds designed to achieve particular investment objectives, and whole-portfolio funds will increase in number and size.

Globalization

As American corporations have taken their manufacturing and research overseas and entered into business arrangements with partners in other parts of the world, the U.S. economy has become increasingly linked to the economies of Europe and Asia. Industrial development in China, India, and Russia has created new investment possibilities. At the same time, burgeoning middle classes in many developing countries are purchasing cars, homes, travel, and consumer goods commensurate with their newly acquired wealth. Middle class families not only want cars and homes, they want to invest their money in global financial markets.

Foreign countries will make their financial products increasingly available to American investors, and foreign investors will continue to purchase American government and corporate debt. There will be a greater need for international regulatory bodies to provide oversight, implement fiscal standards, and fight fraud and organized crime. Legal and financial crises may occur as different cultural traditions come into contact. New products, such as ETFs and bonds structured to comply with the requirements of Sharia (Muslim or Islamic law), will be created to satisfy specific religious and cultural needs.

Another area of international activity will be to confront the poverty that still exists in many parts of the world, solving the present food crisis, equitably distributing precious resources such as water and oil, resolving political conflicts, providing health care, and producing enough energy for the world population — all of which will require financing.

Increased Transparency and Regulation

The subprime mortgage crisis of 2007 and 2008 is another example of how the irresponsibility of one financial sector can inflect serious harm on the national and even the world economy. Just as previous economic catastrophes — such as the Wall Street stock market crash on October 29, 1929, which resulted in the creation of the **SEC** and the Black Monday crash on October 19, 1987, which prompted the introduction of a trading curb on the NYSE — brought about reform and increased financial oversight, future threats to economic stability will increase fiscal regulation. The U.S. government is still formulating regulations to prevent the excesses that led to the collapse of several major financial institutions in 2008. Government or professional bodies will implement more rules and standards to protect investors and prevent the issuers of bonds from incurring more debt than they are able to carry.

In July 2002, in response to a request from SEC Chairman Arthur Levitt, the National Association of Securities Dealers (NASD, which merged with the NYSE's regulation committee to form FINRA in July 2007) launched TRACE (Trade Reporting and Compliance Engine) to facilitate the mandatory reporting of over-the-counter secondary market transactions in eligible fixed-income securities. All broker/dealers who are FINRA member firms have an obligation to report transactions in corporate bonds within 15 minutes of a trade. Studies have shown that the availability of real-time price data to the public resulted in lower transaction costs for both institutional and private investors. The data has also allowed academics, regulators, and market participants to achieve new market insights and has facilitated the creation of ETFs, which rely on regular pricing information. The SEC is able to use automated surveillance from the TRACE data to detect possible regulatory violations and provide better protection for investors.

Organizations such as the Securities Industry and Financial Markets Association (SIFMA), which represents 650 member firms and is "committed to enhancing the public's trust and confidence in the markets, delivering an efficient, enhanced member network of access and forward-looking services," will emerge as the forefront of a movement to create more transparency. SIFMA members have supported the creation of **Investinginbonds.com**, a Web site which makes real-time prices and market information for corporate and municipal bond trades available to the public.

More Participation by Individual Investors

Historically, the bond market has been dominated by institutional investors such as pension funds and insurance companies that bought and sold large quantities of bonds. Data collected after the launch of TRACE in 2002 revealed that though institutional investors account for most of the volume of bonds traded, small retail-sized bond trades between dealers and private customers far outnumber institutional trades. The median trade size for 2003 to 2004 was only 32 bonds.

The recent movement in the United States away from company pension funds and towards individual retirement savings accounts has made American workers responsible for their own financial futures. Increasing numbers of investors are using online resources to create their own portfolios, and major brokerages offer a full line of financial products over the Internet. The Internet gives private investors easy and instant access to detailed information and allows them to conduct research that was done in the past only by financial analysts. Brokers and bond issuers are participating in this trend by streamlining the opening of accounts and allowing private investors to submit **expressions of interest** online. They are also creating products such as mutual funds and ETFs that make successful investing in bonds feasible for an investor with a relatively small amount of capital and designing systems so that investors can invest in bonds through regular monthly contributions to a retirement or education savings account.

U.S. government agencies have taken the lead in making information publicly available, providing educational materials, and encouraging the participation of individual investors. Not only will the government have to foot the bill if Americans fail to prepare adequately for their old age, but private individuals collectively represent a substantial source of investment capital, as demonstrated early in the twentieth century by the sale of Liberty Bonds.

On April 7, 2008, the U.S. Treasury introduced its new Treasury Automated Auction Processing System (TAAPS), an enhanced auction system that allowed the reduction of minimum bid amounts from $1000 to $100. Anthony Ryan, assistant Treasury secretary for financial markets, said, "U.S. Treasury securities, the world's safest, most liquid investments, should be accessible to the broadest universe of investors — large and small. Being able to buy securities in $100 increments adds a new degree of flexibility for all market participants." The reduction was the first since 1998, when the purchase amount was lowered to $1,000. Before that, the minimum purchase amount had been $10,000 for Treasury bills, and $5,000 for Treasury notes. The U.S. Treasury now makes it easy for an individual to purchase bonds directly from their Web site, at minimal expense.

New Methods of Bond Trading

Computer technology and the Internet have already transformed the stock market and made stocks accessible to the general public. Until now, the bond market has been much more difficult to organize, because bonds are not sold on central exchanges or electronic markets like stocks are, and because there are such large numbers of bonds. In

April 2008, the NYSE launched NYSE Bonds®, an automated bond trading system that will match orders by price and time and report quotations and trade prices in real time. The system will charge a transaction fee of 10 cents per $1,000 face value traded. NYSE Bonds allows trading in 6,000 debt securities, including the bonds of all NYSE-listed companies and their subsidiaries. Orders are routed to brokerages that have the bonds in inventory. NYSE Bonds currently attracts about 1 percent of total bond trades reported and is seeking to increase its market share by getting regulatory approval for broker/dealers to trade the bonds of its listed companies without those bonds being registered with the SEC.

Large brokerages, faced with this type of competition, will eventually either join forces to create a bond exchange of their own, or develop their own Internet-based trading engines. Some already offer their bond inventories to "affiliate" online brokerages. Institutional investors can transact on two Internet-based systems, Tradeweb® and MarketAxess, but these are not electronic markets — they are communications systems that allow institutional investors to ask for bids or offers from multiple dealers simultaneously.

Demographic Changes

For the first time in history, in 2007, more of the world's citizens were living in cities and urban areas than in rural areas. Migrations of people affect the demand for public services, create new tax revenue bases, and destroy old ones. Governments are turning to new technologies to provide education and health care to their rural residents. Major industries are closing down their factories or moving them overseas, resulting in economic slumps and undermining tax revenues in once-prosperous areas. Other areas are thriving as new high-technology businesses and services become established. These types of changes affect the credit quality of both municipal bonds and corporate bonds.

Highly developed economies such as Japan, China, and the United States are experiencing declining birth rates, while in Africa, more than half of the population is less than 15 years old. Fewer young people in the workforce must support social security programs and medical care for increasing numbers of elderly people. Fewer children in a family means there will be more old people without a caretaker. Factors such as these may result in a future demand for increased government spending and a growing need for assisted-living facilities and nursing homes. A few decades after that, the population of elderly will suddenly decrease.

An estimated 40 million Americans were without health insurance in 2007, indicating a need for more government involvement in health care or for reforms that would allow individuals to purchase their own insurance at affordable prices. Either possibility will generate the need for financing and the development of new industries or agencies.

Americans drove an estimated one billion fewer miles in July 2008 than they had in July 2007. Awareness of the energy crisis will lead to a rising demand for fuel-efficient transportation and cause people to live in areas closer to their jobs. Municipalities will be forced to find new sources of energy, and to seek funding to make up budget shortfalls.

Climatic change is creating water shortages in areas that formerly attracted large numbers of residents, such as Las Vegas, Phoenix, Dallas, and Atlanta. Governments will need to restrict water usage or find new sources of water, and eventually, a significant number of residents might move away. Restrictions on water use means lower revenue. Water shortages also mandate restrictions on new development and may impact projects to build or expand road and sewage systems. On a global scale, climatic change is making some areas uninhabitable and altering agricultural cycles, creating a shortage of food and a long-term opportunity for new agricultural industries.

New Technologies

The changes brought about by the Internet in the stock and bond markets are only one example of the rapid transformations that took place during the last two decades of the twentieth century and the first decade of the twenty-first century. Some technologies are so compelling that they simply eclipse existing business models and create an economy of their own. One example is the use of cell phones in under-developed countries, where the installment of traditional telephone lines seemed almost an economic impossibility. Small businesses in Africa or Latin America are able to communicate instantly with their suppliers by cell phone, and transactions that used to take days now take place in a few minutes. Cell phone cards are even used as a form of currency. Another example is online banking, which allows clients 24-hour access to their accounts and performs electronically many of the tasks that previously required hundreds of clerks. Debit and credit cards streamline business transactions. Online gamers have created a cyber-world with its own economy generating millions of dollars. Investors are easily able to cross international lines through the Internet, and banks have created international products to accommodate them.

New technologies are impacting the entertainment and education sectors. Universities are competing to expand their enrollment by offering long-distance degrees online. Long-distance learning brings in revenues from tuition and related fees and cuts costs by allowing a single professor to serve students in several areas. Students attending online classes do not require classroom buildings; some universities today do not even have a campus. The same technology is used by school districts to cut down on the number of teachers needed for special classes and to serve students who are disabled or live in remote areas. Conventions and business meetings are being replaced by Web-conferencing and online presentations that do not require the participants to travel to one location and use a convention facility.

The rapid rise of oil prices in 2007 and 2008 suddenly changed American consumers' taste in cars. Sales of the most popular pick-up trucks dropped by 28 percent while sales of fuel-efficient cars surged ahead. The production of hybrid cars and those using new energy sources will require the creation of new types of facilities and the retirement of others from use. Governments and municipalities will need financing to reduce their dependence on oil. If the population turns to electricity as a primary source of energy, more electrical plants will be required to generate it.

Passage of Time

The simple passage of time creates circumstances that may bring about changes in the bond market. The advent of automobiles in the first half of the twentieth century resulted in the massive construction of highways, bridges, and interchanges during the second half of the twentieth century, not just in the United States, but all over the world. Over time, this infrastructure has begun to deteriorate and large expenditures will be necessary to maintain or reconstruct it. The newness of the twentieth century has also worn off of school buildings, hospitals, government office buildings, and public parks.

The passage of time also allows the collection and analysis of historical market data. Some bond investment products are so new that reliable data, such as default rates and yield fluctuations, is not yet available for analysts to evaluate and compare. Only time will tell whether some of the indexed bond ETFs, STRIPS, or tobacco bonds will deliver promised results or serve the financing needs of the issuers. Some aspects of the modern economy, such as globalization, are also so new that it is difficult to predict how they will evolve.

Keeping Informed

None of these changes will immediately impact your current bond investments; nevertheless, you should be aware of developing trends as you reinvest and plan for the future. Buy-and-hold investors who bought 30-year Treasuries with 14 percent coupons in the 1970s were unpleasantly surprised when their bonds were called in 2001 when prevailing interest rates were around 4.5 percent. You should always have an alternate strategy in mind, and a plan in case one of your bond investments should be called or go into default.

Even a buy-and-hold investor should stay informed on the latest developments in the bond market and the economy. Do not just assume, for example, that inflation is going to increase at a steady 2 percent or that interest rates will remain stable. Be aware of how newsworthy events such as election results or natural disasters, might affect your investments. If the stock market takes a sudden tumble, think about the implications for your portfolio. There may be circumstances in which you will need to sell some of your buy-and-hold portfolio to stay on track.

Financial Web sites and the financial sections of the newspapers always have articles on significant events and economic indicators. FINRA's TRACE bond center (**http://cxa. marketwatch.com/finra/BondCenter/Default.aspx**) includes links to relevant news articles for each bond. Subscribe to a finance magazine such as K*iplinger's, Smart Money,* or *Forbes.* Instead of watching repetitive local news broadcasts on TV, switch to some in-depth news programs or take a few minutes to log on to the Internet and read the financial news. These articles discuss immediate events, but they can give you an insight into future trends.

Bond investing, just like any other enterprise, requires creativity, perseverance, and intelligence. Develop a good working relationship with your broker, find answers to all of your questions, and keep going until you are comfortable that you have a thorough understanding of your portfolio. You will experience the most success when you invest something of yourself along with your money.

Appendix A: Glossary

12b-1 fees - Fees charged by mutual funds to cover expenses such as marketing costs and customer service call centers.

Above par - Market value of a bond priced above its face value.

Accrued interest - Unlike equity dividends, which are only earned after a record date right before the dividend payout, the bondholder earns interest each day; it accumulates and then is paid on the period interest payment date. The amount that is earned but not paid.

Agency bonds - Bonds issued by agencies associated with the federal government.

Agencies - Bond issuing agencies of the U.S. government that may be explicitly guaranteed by the U.S. government like GNMA or implicitly guaranteed like FNMA.

Agency securities - Agency bonds.

All-bond portfolio - A portfolio composed entirely of bonds.

Alternative Minimum Tax (AMT) - A separate tax calculation intended to prevent wealthy taxpayers from avoiding income tax by claiming excessive tax exemptions.

Amex - American Stock Exchange.

Arbitrage - The creation or redemption of shares of an ETF by an authorized provider, to bring ETF prices into line with the value of the underlying securities.

Ask price - The price for which a seller offers a bond on the bond market. Sometimes called the offered price.

Auction rate security - A security whose interest rate is regularly re-set through a Dutch auction.

Authorities - Governmental conglomerates that issue bonds for transportation, housing, water and sewage, and other purposes.

Average life - The estimated time that it takes to return half of a mortgage pool's principal to the investor.

Baby bond - A bond with a face value of less than $1,000.

Back-end sales load - A fee paid when shares of a mutual fund are redeemed.

Bank loan fund - A fund that invests in loans made to companies with low credit ratings.

Basis point - One-hundredth of 1 percent. A measurement used to compare yield differences among bonds.

Bearer bond - A bond for which ownership is not registered with the issuer and which is not inscribed with the owner's name.

Below par - The market value of a bond sold at a price lower than its face value.

Bid price - The price which a buyer pays for a bond on the bond market.

Bond anticipation notes (BANs) - Short-term notes issued by a government or municipality to obtain interim funding for a project while a bond issue is being organized.

Bond banks - State financial entities the help smaller municipalities within a state lower their financing costs by selling bonds and using the proceeds to buy the small municipalities' bonds.

Bond equivalent yield - A calculation that allows the comparison of the yield of a money market or discount security, like a T-bill, with the yield of other types of bonds.

Bond fund - An investment pool that holds a portfolio of bonds.

Bond indenture - A legal contract detailing the conditions under which a bond is issued.

Bond index - A measure of performance of the bond market, created by selecting specific bonds and tracking their historical performance.

Bond mutual fund - An investment pool that invests in bonds.

Bond swap - A strategy in which one bond in a portfolio is sold and simultaneously replaced with another to benefit from a higher yield or different maturity.

Book-entry security - An investment which is recorded in account books only; no certificate is sent to the owner.

Bp (bps) - Basis points.

Breakpoints - The investment levels at which mutual funds offer a reduced sales load fee.

Bullet bonds - Non-callable bonds that will not be redeemed until their maturity date.

Calendar - A listing of upcoming bond issues.

Call option - A contract that allows the holder to purchase an investment at a fixed price within a specified time range.

Call premium - The amount above a bond's face value that the issuer must pay to the bondholder if the bond is called before it reaches maturity. (Call price)

Call price - The amount above a bond's face value

that the issuer must pay to the bondholder if the bond is called before it reaches maturity.

Call provision - An option allowing the issuer of a bond to call it in and return the investor's capital before the bond reaches maturity.

Capital gain - The amount by which the current value of an investment exceeds the price that was paid for it.

Capital loss - The amount by which the current value of an investment is exceeded by the price that was paid for it.

Certificate - Physical evidence of bond ownership.

Certificate of Participation (COP) - A lease purchase agreement that is divided and sold to multiple investors in a fraction form.

Change-of-control provision - A provision in a bond contract that allows the buyer of a corporate bond to return the bond at 101 percent of par

if ownership of the company changes hands.

Closed-end fund - A mutual fund with a fixed number of shares that are sold on the secondary market after the initial offering.

Collateral - Assets used to secure a loan.

Collateral trust bonds - Corporate bonds secured by financial assets.

Collateralized mortgage obligation (CMO) - A pool of mortgage pass-throughs which are sold as different classes of shares.

Commercial paper - Short-term debt with maturity of less than 270 days, issued by large corporations or banks to manage their working capital.

Companion bond - A share class of a CMO that absorbs excess prepayments and makes up for shortfalls in other classes.

Competitive bid - A bid at auction for U.S. Treasury

bonds specifying the interest rate that the bidder wants to receive.

Consumer Price Index for Urban Consumers (CPI-U) - An index representative of the buying habits of consumers living in households in Metropolitan Statistical Areas (MSA's) and in urban places of 2,500 inhabitants or more, approximately 80 percent of the non-institutional population of the United States

Continuing-care retirement communities (CCRCs) - Facilities or communities for the elderly that provide a range of services from assisted living to full-time nursing care.

Conversion price - The price at which common stock will be exchanged for a convertible bond.

Corporate bond - A bond issued by a corporation to raise capital.

Correlation - The degree to which two investments move together in the market.

Coupon rate - A bond's stated interest rate.

Credit rating - An assessment of a bond issuer's ability to meet its debt obligations.

Credit risk - The risk that a bond issuer will not be able to meet debt obligations.

Current yield - A calculation of the percentage yield of a bond incorporating its current market price and its interest rate.

Debenture - An unsecured corporate bond.

Deferred sales load - A fee paid when shares of a mutual fund are redeemed.

Denomination - A bond's face value.

Discos - Zero coupon discount notes with maturities of less than one year.

Discount - A bond is trading at a discount when it is selling for lower than its face value.

Diversification - The distribution of investment capital among investments of different types and different market sectors.

Dollar-cost averaging - An investment strategy in which a specific amount of capital is invested at regular intervals, instead of as a one-time lump-sum investment.

Dominion Bond Rating Service (DBRS) - The largest Canadian credit rating agency.

Downgrade - A reduction in a bond's credit rating.

Duration - A calculation of the number of years required to recover the true cost of a bond, expressed as a number of years from its purchase date.

Dutch auction - A process in which bidders submit the interest rate they wish to receive and buy orders are filled at the lowest interest rate first.

Enrolled Agent (EA) - A tax professional who has passed an IRS test covering all aspects of taxation, plus passed an IRS background check.

Equipment trust certificates - Corporate bonds secured by transportation equipment.

Equity - Ownership, or a share in ownership, of an asset or company.

Equivalent taxable yield - The yield of a municipal bond adjusted for an investor's income tax rate to compare the municipal (tax-exempt) bond to a U.S. Treasury.

Escrow bond - A bond whose issuer has already set aside assets in an escrow account to pay the interest and premium when the issue matures or reaches its call date.

Escrowed to maturity- A non-callable bond collateralized by U.S. Treasury securities in an escrow account that makes interest payments until the bond reaches maturity.

ETF - Exchange traded fund.

Exchange traded fund - An open-ended fund whose shares are traded on the stock market like stocks.

Exit fee - An amount paid by an investor to exit a mutual fund.

Face value - The amount that an investor will receive at a bond's maturity.

Fannie Mae - Federal National Mortgage Association.

Federal funds rate - The interest rate at which private depository institutions (mostly banks) lend cash from their balances at the Federal Reserve to other depository institutions.

Financial advisor - A professional who provides advice on financial management and can assist in creating and maintaining an investment portfolio.

FINRA - Financial Industry Regulatory Authority, the largest non-governmental regulator for all securities firms doing business in the United States.

First mortgage bonds - Corporate bonds secured by real estate or equipment, usually issued by electric utilities.

Fixed call option - An option to call in a bond on a specified date or after a specified time period.

Fixed rate - An interest rate that is fixed at a bond's issuance and remains the same throughout the life of the bond.

Flat - Description of a bond that trades without accrued interest, usually indicating that the issuer is financial difficulty and may not be able to pay its coupon.

Flat yield curve - A yield curve in which the difference between short-term and long-term interest rates is small.

Floating rate - An interest rate that is adjusted at regular intervals, either in conjunction with changes in the prime interest rate, or through auctions.

Floating-rate fund - A fund that invests in companies with low credit ratings.

Floating-rate note - A securities whose coupon is periodically adjusted based on a benchmark interest rate or a market clearing level if the bond was to be sold at par. Sometimes market participants call them floaters.

Floaters - Variable-rate bonds.

Freddie Mac - Federal Home Loan Mortgage Corporation.

Fund manager - A professional or a company who manages a fund's assets and makes strategic investment decisions.

Front-end sales load - A fee paid when you purchase shares of a mutual fund.

GAAP - Generally accepted accounting principles.

General obligation bond (GO) - A bond guaranteed by the taxing authority issuing the bond.

Ginnie Mae - The Government National Mortgage Association (GNMA), is a U.S. government-owned corporation within the Department of Housing and Urban Development (HUD) that provides guarantees on mortgage-backed securities backed by federally insured or guaranteed loans.

Global bond fund - A mutual fund that invests in bonds issued both outside the United States and domestically.

Government National Mortgage Association (GNMA) - See Ginnie Mae.

Government-sponsored enterprises (GSE)s - Private sector companies affiliated with, but separate from, the U.S. government.

High-yield bond - A bond which has some speculative characteristics.

Humped yield curve - A yield curve in which the difference between short-term and long-term interest rates is small.

HUD - Department of Housing and Urban Development.

Indenture - The legal agreement between bond holders and bond issuers.

Inflation-protected bond (inflation-protected security) - A bond whose face value is adjusted up or down according to the Consumer Price Index to account for inflation.

Institutional investor - A financial entity such as a bank, insurance company, investment manager, or hedge fund that manages money on behalf of others.

Interest rate - Amount that a borrower pays a lender to borrow money, expressed as a percentage of the amount being borrowed.

Interest rate risk - The risk that a rise in interest rates will cause a bond to drop in value.

Intermediate bonds - Bonds with maturities between five and ten years.

International bonds - Bonds issued by entities outside the United States.

International bond fund - A mutual fund that invests in bonds issued by entities outside the United States.

Interest risk - The risk that interest rates will rise after you purchase a bond.

Investment company - A company that pools investors' money in a professionally-managed portfolio.

Investment Company Act of 1940 - An act of Congress which separated investment companies (including mutual funds) from banks and set standards for their regulation.

Investment-grade bond - A bond with a credit rating of BBB or higher from Standard & Poor's or Baa3 or higher from Moody's.

Issuer - An organization, government entity, or corporation issuing bonds to raise capital.

Junior lien - A debt obligation which, in case of default, is given less priority than other, more senior debt obligations.

Junk bonds - Bonds with the lowest credit ratings that offer a higher interest rate to compensate for increased risk of default.

Last-trade price - The price at which a security last traded.

Lien - A legal security interest in real estate or property, created and publicly recorded for and until the satisfaction of a debt or mortgage.

Lien position - The lien position determines the order in which capital will be repaid to investors in the event of a default. First lien has priority.

Limited tax GO bonds (LTGO bonds) - General obligation municipal bonds that have a limited authority to raise taxes to repay the bond.

Liquidity - The degree to which an investment can be quickly and easily bought, sold, or redeemed for cash.

Load fee - An amount paid by an investor to enter a mutual fund.

Lockout - The period before a sequential mortgage-backed bond's first principal payment.

Long-term bonds - Bonds with maturities longer than ten years.

Low-load funds - Funds that charge smaller load fees of 1.5 percent to 3.5 percent.

Management fee - An annual charge assessed by the managers of a mutual fund.

Mark-up - The difference between the price at which a broker buys a bond and the price at which the broker sells it; a broker's commission on a bond sale.

Market price - Price at which a bond is sold on the secondary market.

Marketable security - A financial instrument that is not restricted from being resold to another individual or entity.

Maturity - The date on which an investor's capital will be returned, or the length of time for which a bond is issued.

Money market mutual fund - A mutual fund that holds very short-term debt instruments.

Mortgage-backed bonds - Bonds backed by pools of mortgages and sold on the secondary market.

Mortgage bond - A bond secured by a lien on real estate.

Mortgage pool - A block of individual mortgages, usually of similar maturities and interest rates.

Municipal bonds - Bonds issued by counties, townships, cities, or tax districts to finance projects such as roads, bridges, or other large construction projects.

Mutual fund - An investment pool with an undefined number of shares that continually redeems outstanding shares at net asset value.

Negative convexity - A pattern exhibited by mortgage-backed or other callable bonds, in which their prices fall lower and rise less than prices of U.S. Treasuries when interest rates fluctuate.

Net asset value (NAV) - A calculation of the value of a share in a mutual fund or an ETF, calculated by dividing the value of the underlying assets by the number of shares.

NYSE - New York Stock Exchange

Nominal yield - A bond's stated interest rate, or coupon, based on the face value of the bond.

No-coupon discount notes - Notes with maturities of less than one year that pay no interest, but are sold at a discount and redeemed at maturity for their face value; the difference between the two prices being the interest earned on holding the bonds.

No-load fund - A mutual fund that does not charge a fee to become a shareholder.

Non-callable bonds - Bonds that have no call provision and will not be redeemed until they reach maturity.

Non-competitive bid - A bid placed for U.S. Treasury bonds at auction that implies acceptance of the interest rate set by the auction.

Nongovernmental purpose bonds - Bonds issued by state or local government to fund projects that are associated with the private sector, such as hospitals or university dormitories.

Not-rated (NR) - Designation for a bond that has not been rated by one of the credit rating agencies.

NRSRO - Nationally Recognized Statistical Rating Organization, a designation given by the SEC to agencies qualified to provide objective, third-party assessments.

Open-ended fund - A mutual fund that increases its holdings as demand for the fund increases.

Opportunity loss - The potential to earn income that is lost when capital is tied up in a less lucrative investment, or is held in an inactive account.

Original issue discount (OID) - The amount below face value at which a bond is issued to investors.

Over-the-counter-market (OTC) - The buying and selling of bonds through a network of dealers and brokers.

PAC (Planned amortization class) bond- A mortgage pool divided into share classes that make regularly scheduled prepayments.

Par - A bond purchased at par is purchased for a price equal to its face value.

Portfolio theory - A method of reducing investment risk by creating a portfolio in which risky investments are balanced with secure ones.

Pass-through mortgage securities - Mortgage pools that pass both interest and principal repayments through to investors as they occur.

Peak (yield curve) - The bond maturity at which interest rates on a yield curve stop rising and begin to level off.

Plain vanilla - The most simple, conservative, traditional form of a financial instrument.

Pre-refunded bond - A bond whose issuer has already set aside assets in an escrow account to pay the interest and premium when the issue matures or reaches its call date.

Premium bond - A bond sold at a price higher than its face value.

Premium - The amount above its face value at which a bond is trading.

Prepayment - Early payment of principal on a bond prior to its maturity.

Prepayment speed assumption- PSA (Public Securities Association) standard.

Price transparency - The ability of investors to easily receive accurate price information.

Primary bond market - The first offering of new bonds to investors.

Principal - The amount that an investor will receive at a bond's maturity.

Principal prepayment - The early repayment of a loan before it is due, such as a mortgage which is paid off early, or a bond which is called before its maturity date.

Private activity bonds - Bonds issued by state and local governments to fund projects that benefit private entities.

Private placement - The sale of a bond issue to a single buyer or group of buyers.

PSA (Public Securities Association) standard - An estimate of the rate at which holders of home loans are likely to prepay their mortgages, used to calculate the average life of a mortgage-backed security.

Public power bond - Debt that is issued by a government owned electric utility such as the Municipal Electric Authority of Georgia.

Public purpose bonds - Bonds issued directly by state or local government entities to fund projects such as schools, sewage treatment plants and roads.

Purchasing power risk - Inflation risk.

PSA standard - An estimation of the prepayment speed of a mortgage bond, named for the Public Securities Association.

Put - A feature sometimes placed in a bond indenture that allows the bondholder to force a bond issuer to redeem a bond before maturity.

Put bond - A bond with a put option.

Put provision (put) - An option allowing a bond purchaser to force collection of the bond by the issuer prior to its scheduled maturity date.

Rate of return - The profit realized from an investment, including interest and capital gains, expressed as a percentage of the capital invested.

Real estate mortgage investment conduits (REIC, REMIC) - An investment vehicle that holds commercial and residential mortgages in trust and issues securities representing an undivided interest in these mortgages.

Real Estate Investment Trust (REIT) - A company that owns, and in most cases, operates income-producing real estate and distributes 90 percent of kits income to investors.

Real interest rate - The coupon rate of a bond adjusted for inflation.

Realized yield - The actual return on an investment over the period it is held, including returns on reinvested interest and dividends.

Redemption - Retirement of a debt security.

Refinancing - A process in which a mortgage holder takes out a new loan at a lower interest rate in order to repay the principal of an older, higher-rate loan.

Required minimum distribution (RMD) - The percentage of your IRA, based on your age, that you are required to withdraw and pay taxes on after your 70½ birthday.

Revenue anticipation notes (RANs) - Short-term notes issued by a government or municipality to obtain interim funding for operations until revenues such as state aid for school districts are received.

Revenue bond - A municipal bond issue that is backed by the revenue from a hospital, toll road or other public works project that charges user fees.

Risk - The uncertainty that an investment produce its promised return.

Sampling - A methodology used to track a bond index, in which a portfolio is constructed with representative bonds are selected from the index and other, similar investments to emulate the index performance.

Savings bond - A nonmarketable bond issued and guaranteed by the U.S. Treasury.

SEC - See Securities and Exchange Commission.

Secondary bond market - The sale of bonds held by investors who acquired them either from the bond issuer or from another investor.

Secured bonds - Debt which is secured with an asset such as real estate or industrial equipment.

Securities and Exchange Commission (SEC) - An independent agency of the U.S. government which holds primary responsibility for enforcing the federal securities laws and regulating the securities industry, the nation's stock and options exchanges, and other electronic securities markets.

Senior debt - A debt obligation which, in case of default, is given priority over other debt obligations with junior or subordinated liens.

Senior lien - A debt obligation which, in case of default, is given priority over other debt obligations.

Senior loan fund - A fund that invests in senior secured debt.

Senior secured debt - A loan that is backed by collateral and is repaid first in case of default.

Sequential bond- A bond that has class shares that absorb principal payments in a sequential order.

Serial bond - A single bond issue consisting of bonds with sequential maturities ranging from one to 30 years. This allows the issuer to avoid having all their debt coming due at one time.

Settlement date - The day on which cash or securities

are delivered to complete a transaction.

Short-term bonds - Bonds with maturities ranging from zero to five years.

Sinking fund - An escrow account created to set aside funds for the repayment of a bond issue.

Sovereign bonds - Bonds issued by national governments.

Sovereign risk - Risk associated with investing in a country whose political situation or fiscal policies may affect returns or cause losses.

Special tax districts - Sub-governmental entities created to provide specific services such as sewage, water, libraries, garbage collection, and fire protection to residents of a particular community or area.

Split rating - A discrepancy in the credit ratings assigned to the same bond by different credit agencies.

Spread - The difference between a bond's bid price and ask price.

State-specific bond funds - Mutual funds that purchase only municipal bonds from a specific state so that they are tax-exempt for investors living in that state.

Steep yield curve - A yield curve that rises steeply, indicating that investors expect interest rates to rise.

Subordinated debenture - Unsecured debt with a weak claim to payment (junior debt).

Subprime mortgage - A mortgage loan to a creditor with a low credit rating, usually at a much higher interest rate.

Super sinkers - Housing bonds with maturities of 20 to 30 years that are likely to be called in much sooner.

Support bond - A share class of a CMO that absorbs excess prepayments and makes up for shortfalls in other classes.

Syndicate-A group of banking firms that collaborates in selling an issue of bonds.

T-note - See Treasury note.

Tax and revenue anticipation notes (TRANs) - Short-term notes issued by a government or municipality to obtain interim funding until tax and revenues are received.

Tax anticipation notes (TANs) - Short-term notes issued by a government or municipality to obtain interim funding until taxes are collected.

Tax-exempt - A bond with interest income that is exempt from federal, state, or local income taxes.

Tennessee Valley Authority (TVA) - A federally-owned corporation created by congressional charter in 1933 to develop the Tennessee Valley region.

Term bond - A bond issue with a fixed, long-term maturity date and not subject to calls.

Timing risk - The risk that your bond investment will decrease in value over time.

TIPS - See Treasury Inflation -Protected Securities.

Total return - The total return, including interest income and capital appreciation, realized on a bond fund or a bond sold before it reaches maturity.

TRACE - Trade Reporting and Compliance Engine, an online reporting system operated by FINRA that mandates immediate reporting of bond trade prices and data.

Tranche - A share class of a CMO (collateralized mortgage obligation).

Transferable security - A debt instrument that can be resold to another individual or entity.

Treasuries - Bonds or notes issued by the U.S. Department of the Treasury.

Treasury bills - U.S. Treasury bills with short maturities of 4, 13, 26, and 52 weeks, that though technically not bonds, offer similar opportunities to investors.

Treasury bonds - Bonds issued by the U.S. Treasury with maturities of 10 to 30 years.

Treasury Direct program - A book-entry system operated by the U.S. Bureau of the Public Debt to record purchases of U.S. Treasury securities.

Treasury Inflation-Protected Securities - Securities issued by the U.S. Treasury which are protected against inflation by making adjustments to their face value in accordance with fluctuations in the Consumer Price Index.

Treasury notes - Notes issued by the U.S. Treasury with maturities of two, five, and ten years.

Turnover rate - The rate at which investments in a portfolio are liquidated and replaced with new investments.

Underwriter - An investment bank or brokerage house that purchases bonds from the issuer and re-sells them to investors.

Underwriting syndicate - A group of investment banks or brokerages houses that collaborate in underwriting a large bond issue.

Unit Investment Trust (UIT) - A passively managed fund holding a portfolio of specific bonds until maturity.

United States Treasury - The government executive agency responsible for promoting economic prosperity and ensuring the financial security of the United States.

Unlimited Tax GO bonds (UTGO bonds) - General obligation municipal bonds backed by a state or municipality's full taxation authority.

Variable-rate bonds - Bonds with interest rates that are periodically reset, commonly in line with the market insurance rates on specified dates.

Variable-rate debt - Debt with an interest rate that is reset at regular intervals to coincide with prevailing market rates.

Variable-rate demand note - A floating municipal note which allows the bondholder to put the bond at par back to the issuer on a periodic date which can be every 7, 30, 90, 180, or 360 days depending on the specific bond.

Yankee bonds - Foreign bonds that are denominated and sold in U.S. dollars.

Yield - Rate of interest on a bond investment.

Yield curve - A graphic depiction of the yields at different maturities of a specific investment.

Yield-to-average life - A yield calculation for bonds that are retired at regular intervals during the life of the bond issue, such as bonds with a sinking fund.

Yield to call - The income realized from the interest paid by a bond until it is redeemed (called) before it reaches maturity.

Yield to maturity - The income realized from the interest paid by a bond held until it reaches maturity.

Zero coupon bond - Bond which pays no interest but is sold at a substantial discount to face value; at maturity the investor receives the face value of the bond.

Bibliography

Brandes, Michael. *Naked guide to bonds: what you need to know, stripped down to the bare essentials*. New York: Wiley. 2003.

Little, Ken. *The pocket idiot's guide to investing in bonds*. Indianapolis, IN: Alpha Books. 2007.

Richelson, Hildy, and Stan Richelson. *Bonds: The Unbeaten Path to Secure Investment Growth*. New York: Bloomberg Press. 2007.

Scott, David Logan, and David Logan Scott. *David Scott's Guide to Investing in Bonds*. Boston: Houghton Mifflin. 2004.

Wild, Russell. *Bond investing for dummies. --For dummies*. Hoboken, N.J.: Wiley. 2007.

Web sites

Edwards, Amy K., *Corporate Bond Market Microstructure and Transparency - the US experience, US Securities and Exchange Commission* (**www.bis.org/publ/bppdf/bispap26g.pdf**)

Financial Industry Regulatory Authority, *FINRA Mutual Fund Expense Analyzer* (**http://apps.finra.org/investor_Information/ea/1/mfetf.aspx**)

Investment Companies Institute, *Statistics and Research* (**www.ici.org/**)

Lehmann , Richard, *The Great Tobacco Bond Scam, Forbes/ Lehmann Income Securities Investor*, November 19, 2007. (**www.forbes.com/personalfinance/2007/11/19/tobacco-bonds-cigarettes-pf-ii-in_rl_1119soapbox_inl.html**)

Linehan, Edmund J., *A History of the United States Savings Bonds Program. Washington D.C.: US Savings Bond Divison, Department of the Treasury. 1991.* (**www.treasurydirect.gov/indiv/research/history/history_sb.pdf**)

Litvack, David *Tobacco Bonds Provide Financing Options*, Financial Management, American City and County, May 1, 2001. (**http://americancityandcounty.com/mag/government_financial_managementtobacco_bonds/**)

Lockhart, James B., III (2008-09-07). *Statement of FHFA Director James B. Lockhart, Federal Housing Finance Agency.* (**www.ofheo.gov/newsroom.aspx?ID=456&q1=0&q2=0**)

Moyer, Liz, *NYSE Plunges into Bonds*, Forbes, March 23, 2007 (**www.forbes.com/home/business/2007/03/23/nyse-bonds-trading-biz-cx_lm_0323nyse.html**)

National Association of Counties, Certificates of Participation: An Innovative Financing Alternative For Counties, Jim Culotta, February, 1999. (**www.countyengineers.org/Template.cfm?Section=Publications&template=/ContentManagement/ContentDisplay.cfm&ContentID=5457**)

National Federation of Municipal Analysts (**www.nfma.org/ disclosure.php**)

Paulson, Henry M., Jr.; (Press release statement) (2008-09-07). *Statement by Secretary Henry M. Paulson, Jr. on Treasury and Federal Housing Finance Agency Action to Protect Financial Markets and Taxpayers*, United States Department of the Treasury. (**www.treas.gov/press/ releases/hp1129.htm**)

Publicbonds.org (**www.publicbonds.org/public_fin/default.htm**)

Rather, John, *A Skeptical New Look at Special Tax Districts, New York Times*, March 23, 2008. (**www.nytimes.com/2008/03/23/nyregion/ nyregionspecial2/23districtsli.html**)

Reuters, Moody's Methodology for Rating Public Power Bonds, April 8, 2008. (**http://uk.reuters.com/article/oilRpt/ idUKWNA200620080408**)

Securities and Exchange Commission, *Mutual Fund Fees and Expenses*. (**www.sec.gov/answers/mffees. htm#distribution**)

Seeking Alpha, *US Government Bond ETFs*, May 30, 2007 (**http://seekingalpha.com/article/30353-us-government-bond-etfs**)

Smith, Dawn . *Interesting, Indeed, Smart Money*, May 21, 2004 (**www.smartmoney.com/fund-screen/index. cfm?story=20040521**)

Steven , Paul Schott, *Keep Stable Value Funds Out of Auto Enroll*, (as published in Forbes, July 2, 2007) Investment Company Institute Statements and Publications, (**www. ici.org/statements/remarks/07_forbes_oped.html**)

Sullivan, Tom, 401(k) *Keys to Stable Value*, Barron's, March 10, 2008 (**http://webreprints.djreprints. com/1907060462084.html**)

Tax History Museum: The Civil War (**www.tax.org/ Museum/1861-1865.htm**)

Treasury Cuts Minimum Securities Purchase to $100, USA Today, March 22, 2008 (**www.usatoday.com/ money/perfi/bonds/2008-03-21-treasury-securities-minimum_N.htm**)

TreasuryDirect, *Treasury Inflation-Protected Securities (TIPS)*, (**www.treasurydirect.gov/instit/marketables/tips/tips.htm**)

U.S. Department of Housing and Urban Development, *Let FHA Loans Help You, Homes and Communities* (**www. hud.gov/buying/loans.cfm**)

U.S. Department of Transportation, Federal Highway Administration, *Garvee Bond Guidance*, (**www.fhwa.dot.gov/ innovativeFinance/garguid1.htm**)

U.S. Department of Veteran Affairs, *VA Reaching Out to Vets with Mortgage Problems*, June 12, 2008. (**www1.va.gov/ opa/pressrel/pressrelease.cfm?id=1514**)

Wayne, Leslie. *Wall Street; The Fuss Over Nonrated Bonds, New York Times*, January 24, 1993 (**http://query.nytimes. com/gst/fullpage.html?res=9F0CE2D71330F937A1575 2C0A965958260**)

Biography

Martha Maeda is an economic historian and writes on politics, ethics, and modern philosophy. After graduating from Northwestern University, she lived and worked in Australia, Japan, Latin America, and several African countries, before settling in the United States. She has a special interest in micro-economics and in the effects of globalization on the lives and businesses of people all over the world. Martha Maeda is also the author of *The Complete Guide to Investing in Exchange Traded Funds: How to Earn High Rates of Return – Safely.*

Index

A

Agency, 309, 314, 324, 327, 330-331, 189-190, 220, 254, 257, 260-261, 269, 33, 40-41, 47, 49, 81, 95-99, 109, 114, 116, 139-140, 147, 150, 19, 18, 6-7

B

Bond, 309-332, 23-29, 153-168, 173-185, 187-191, 195-208, 211-217, 219-225, 227-234, 236-238, 241-242, 245, 247-249, 251-259, 261-267, 269-270, 277, 280-281, 283-285, 287-296, 32-34, 297-298, 301-303, 305-308, 35-40, 42-59, 61-81, 83-84, 86, 88-95, 97, 99, 101-108, 110, 113-116, 118-123, 125-136, 141-152, 19-20, 15-18, 209

C

Corporate, 312-315, 329, 26, 28, 176-177, 180-182, 185, 187-188, 206, 215, 223, 232, 248, 255-257, 259-260, 266, 269, 284-285, 291, 299-301, 304, 41, 44, 47, 57, 63, 65, 67-70, 72, 76-80, 85, 102, 104-105, 109, 131, 137, 145

E

Education, 212, 214, 217, 220, 225, 232, 239, 243-244, 248, 253, 259, 266, 269-279, 294, 297, 301, 303, 306, 94, 110-111, 113, 9, 12

Exchange Traded, 315, 333, 153, 195, 43, 58, 12

I

Income, 309, 314, 320, 323, 326, 328, 330, 154, 156-161, 163-166, 175, 178-189, 191, 193, 197, 199, 201-202, 205, 207, 211-212, 214-217, 220, 224-225, 228, 231-239, 246, 251-252, 256, 258-267, 271-272, 274-284, 292-295, 31-33, 300, 38-39, 42-44, 52-55, 68-70, 73, 78, 80, 82-83, 85-86, 88-91, 93-94, 96, 98, 101-106, 108, 111-112, 116, 118, 126, 132-133, 135, 141, 143, 148-152, 19, 15-16, 5, 9, 12-14

International, 317, 160, 181, 190, 199, 203, 205, 299, 305-306, 42, 79, 99, 135, 7

Invest, 25, 155, 161, 172-173, 177-178, 182, 184-185, 187, 189-191, 200, 212-214, 220-221, 223, 232, 252-253, 261, 265, 267, 269, 274, 280-281, 292-293, 295, 31, 298-299, 301, 308, 76, 79-80, 98, 126, 148, 152, 19, 15

M

Mortgage, 310, 312, 315-316, 318-319, 321-323, 325-326, 332, 217, 225, 229, 232, 256, 269, 293, 298-299, 41, 68-69, 71, 95-96, 98, 100, 114, 125, 127, 140-152, 8

Municipal, 314, 318-319, 322-323, 325, 327-328, 331, 157, 159-160, 176, 187-189, 206, 215, 217, 223, 231-233, 237-238, 243-248, 254-257, 259-261, 263-264, 266-267, 269, 284-285, 289-293, 33, 301, 304

P

Portfolio, 309, 311, 315, 317, 321, 323, 327, 29, 153-157, 159-162, 164, 167, 172, 174, 176, 179-183, 186-187, 189, 193, 196-200, 205-207, 211, 223-226, 228, 231, 251-264, 266, 274, 280-281, 283, 287-288, 291, 294, 33, 298, 308, 42, 72, 75-80, 89, 111, 148, 151-152

R

Ratings, 310, 316, 318, 325, 28, 172, 175, 179-180, 185, 188, 206, 219-220, 224, 257, 260-261, 269, 289, 41, 46-49, 74-75, 77, 79-80, 106, 108, 122-123, 129-132, 139, 141, 6-7

S

Strategy, 311, 314, 155, 160, 165, 183, 201, 211-213, 224, 226, 251, 258, 279, 294, 307, 209

T

Treasury, 312, 314, 320, 324, 326-327, 330-332, 25-28, 155, 158, 189, 191, 202-205, 215, 220, 223, 228-230, 243, 251, 254, 258-259, 266, 269, 277, 291, 33, 298, 302, 40-41, 62-64, 68-70, 79, 81-93, 97-98, 103, 139, 151

Y

Yield, 310-311, 313-315, 317, 320-321, 323, 325, 328, 25, 28, 161-165, 174, 176-178, 181, 185-188, 202, 206, 228-232, 255-256, 258, 260, 265-266, 284, 294, 307, 36, 38-39, 41, 45, 48-59, 62-63, 77-78, 83, 85, 89, 92, 102-103, 115, 119, 122, 132-134, 137, 147, 149, 151, 17, 6, 8, 11